UNIVERSITY OF CENTRAL FLORIDA

TEXTS *and* TECHNOLOGY *Ph.D.*

ORLANDO, FL

UCF's Texts & Technology Ph.D. is part of a growing field combining scholarly study, creative production, and assessment of digital media texts. The future demands those who can analyze, synthesize, and produce new knowledge, and effectively communicate to a broad range of audiences.

Areas of Research Include:

- Digital archiving & editing
- Asset management
- Predictive modeling
- Information architecture
- Visualization
- Web design
- Distributed education
- Game design

This flexible, interdisciplinary curriculum encourages communicators and problem solvers who strive for leadership positions as educators, consultants, employees, and administrators.

Find out more online at
TANDT.CAH.UCF.EDU

composition STUDIES

Volume 42, Number 2
Fall 2014

Editor
Laura R. Micciche

Book Review Editor
Kelly Kinney

Editorial Assistants
Christina M. LaVecchia
Janine Morris

Former Editors
Gary Tate
Robert Mayberry
Christina Murphy
Peter Vandenberg
Ann George
Carrie Leverenz
Brad E. Lucas
Jennifer Clary-Lemon

Advisory Board

Linda Adler-Kassner
*University of California,
Santa Barbara*

Tom Amorose
Seattle Pacific University

Chris Anson
North Carolina State University

Valerie Balester
Texas A&M University

Robert Brooke
University of Nebraska, Lincoln

Sidney Dobrin
University of Florida

Lisa Ede
Oregon State University

Paul Heilker
*Virginia Polytechnic Institute
and State University*

Peggy O'Neill
Loyola College

Victor Villanueva
Washington State University

SUBSCRIPTIONS

Composition Studies is published twice each year (May and November). Annual subscription rates: Individuals $25 (Domestic), $30 (International), and $15 (Students). To subsccribe online, please visit http://www.uc.edu/journals/composition-studies/subscriptions.html

BACK ISSUES

Some back issues from volume 13.1 and forward are available at $8 per issue. Photocopies of earlier issues are available for $3. To order or inquire about availability, see http://www.uc.edu/journals/composition-studies/subscriptions.html. More recent back issues are now available through Amazon.com. To find issues, use the advanced search feature and search on "Composition Studies" (title) and "Parlor Press" (publisher).

BOOK REVIEWS

Assignments are made from a file of potential book reviewers. If you are interested in writing a review, please contact our Book Review editor at kkinney@binghamton.edu.

JOURNAL SCOPE

The oldest independent periodical in the field, *Composition Studies* publishes original articles relevant to rhetoric and composition, including those that address teaching college writing; theorizing rhetoric and composing; administering writing programs; and, among other topics, preparing the field's future teacher-scholars. All perspectives and topics of general interest to the profession are welcome. We also publish Course Designs, which contextualize, theorize, and reflect on the content and pedagogy of a course. Contributions to Composing With are invited by the editor, though queries are welcome (send to compstudies@uc.edu). Cfps, announcements, and letters to the editor are most welcome. Composition Studies does not consider previously published manuscripts, unrevised conference papers, or unrevised dissertation chapters.

SUBMISSIONS

For submission information and guidelines, see http://www.uc.edu/journals/composition-studies/submissions/overview.html.

Direct all correspondence to:

> Laura Micciche, Editor
> Department of English
> University of Cincinnati
> PO Box 210069
> Cincinnati, OH 45221–0069
> compstudies@uc.edu

Composition Studies is grateful for the support of the University of Cincinnati.

©2014 by Laura Micciche, Editor
Production and printing is managed by Parlor Press, www.parlorpress.com.
ISSN 1534–9322.
Cover art by Giovanni Weissman and design by Gary Weissman.

http://www.uc.edu/journals/composition-studies.html

composition STUDIES

Volume 42, Number 2
Fall 2014

From the Editor   9

Reprint of 1994 Interview with Winifred Bryan Horner   11
Lynée Lewis Gaillet and Shelley Aley
Updated Introduction by Lynée Lewis Gaillet

Composing With   28

Two Rooms   28
Jennifer Habel

Teaching with Love   30
Laura J. Davies

Articles   33

A Plea for Critical Race Theory Counterstory: Stock Story versus
Counterstory Dialogues Concerning Alejandra's "Fit" in the Academy   33
Aja Y. Martinez

Geneva Smitherman: Translingualist, Code-Mesher, Activist   56
Russel K. Durst

Immodest Witnesses: Reliability and Writing Assessment   73
Chris W. Gallagher

Disability Studies in the Composition Classroom   96
Ella R. Browning

Course Design   118

Engaging Writing about Writing Theory and Multimodal Praxis:
Remediating WaW for English 106: First Year Composition   118
Fernando Sánchez, Liz Lane, and Tyler Carter

Where We Are: Disability and Accessibility 147

Moving Beyond Disability 2.0 in Composition Studies 147
Tara Wood, Jay Dolmage, Margaret Price, and Cynthia Lewiecki-Wilson

Creating a Culture of Access in Composition Studies 151
Elizabeth Brewer, Cynthia L. Selfe, and Melanie Yergeau

Book Reviews 155

Reading Diverse Rhetors and Rhetorics: Rewriting History, Reimagining Scholarship 155
Reviewed by Virginia Crisco
Reviews of *Women and Rhetoric Between the Wars*, edited by Ann George, M. Elizabeth Weiser, and Janet Zepernick; *The Rhetoric of Rebel Women: Civil War Diaries and Confederate Persuasion*, by Kimberly Harrison; *Educating the New Southern Woman: Speech, Writing, and Race at the Public Women's Colleges, 1884-1945*, by David Gold and Catherine L. Hobbs

Vernacular Eloquence: What Speech Can Bring to Writing, by Peter Elbow. 163
Reviewed by Jacquelyn E. Hoermann and Richard Leo Enos

Reclaiming the Rural: Essays on Literacy, Rhetoric, and Pedagogy, edited by Kim Donehower, Charlotte Hogg, and Eileen E. Schell. 171
Reviewed by Jeffrey G. Howard

Writing as a Way of Being: Writing Instruction, Nonduality, and the Crisis of Sustainability, by Robert P. Yagelski. 175
Reviewed by Paula Mathieu

Literacy, Economy, and Power: Writing and Research After Literacy in American Lives, edited by John Duffy, Julie Nelson Christoph, Eli Goldblatt, Nelson Graff, Rebecca S. Nowack, and Bryan Trabold. 179
Reviewed by Kristina Fennelly

First Semester: Graduate Students, Teaching Writing, and the Challenge of Middle Ground, by Jessica Restaino. 182
Reviewed by Margaret Briggs-Dineen, Wendy Fall, Beth Godbee, Danielle Klein, Laura Linder-Scholer, Alyssa McGrath, Michael Stock, and Sarah Thompson

Contributors 186
Announcements 190

From the Editor

"I often feel like an incompetent." These are the first words spoken by Winifred Bryan Horner in an interview conducted by two of her former students, Lynée Lewis Gaillet and Shelley Aley, and published in this journal two decades ago. In honor of Horner's passing in February 2014, we are very pleased to reprint the 1994 interview in its entirety with a new introduction composed by Gaillet (to whom we are grateful for the suggestion to reprint the interview). The evidence in these pages of Horner's startling modesty—as encapsulated in the opening confession and, for example, when she notes that students mentor *her* as much as she does them—as well as her intellectual curiosity and advocacy of what she calls an "old-girl network" make this piece a moving tribute to Horner's person, career, and legacy.

Horner's interview ends with her noting that the "real reason for doing research" is "the ongoing conversation between students and teachers, and among scholars and researchers all over the world." Her words provide a lovely transition to our Composing With section. In the first selection, American poet Jennifer Habel locates us in domestic scenes of composing as she revisits Virginia Woolf's still prescient call for women to claim a room of their own, though Habel places us in *two* rooms—her writing room and her daughters' room. The second selection by Laura J. Davies immerses us in a very different composing environment: a classroom at the United States Air Force Academy where she is confronted by an empty seat, once occupied by a student who has committed suicide. Habel and Davies, in different ways, weave worlds of writing with some of life's greatest complexities: family, feeling, connection, loss, and resilience.

Filling out the rest of this issue are articles and a course design that circulate around access of one kind or another. Aja Y. Martinez challenges the inclusive ethos of composition studies through a critical, dialogic counterstory that foregrounds the difficulties Chican@s face in graduate programs. Martinez's article poses questions, and offers some answers, regarding how to change barriers to access. This question reverberates throughout Russel K. Durst's study of Geneva Smitherman, whose work has been central to debates about language access in postsecondary education. Chris W. Gallagher advocates a rhetorical theory of reliability that lines up with the ways in which we teach writing. I hear in this piece a commitment to making assessment an enterprise that values reader differences, dissensus, and inconsistency in an effort to construe reliability as multivalent—an access issue of another sort. Finally, Ella Browning's focus on disability studies in the composition classroom explicitly turns attention to the pedagogical and political importance of making access a priority for all of our students.

Browning's article can be read productively alongside contributions to the section Where We Are: Disability and Accessibility, which features two collaboratively written pieces: one by Tara Wood, Jay Dolmage, Margaret Price, and Cynthia Lewiecki-Wilson; the other by Elizabeth Brewer, Cynthia L. Selfe, and Melanie Yergeau. These contributors compel members of the field to develop proactive strategies that will lead to increased participation from a wider range of contributors in our field and classrooms. Both pieces argue that the field has made progress on these matters but needs to go further.

The Course Design by Fernando Sánchez, Elizabeth Lane, and Tyler Carter puts multimodality into generative conversation with writing about writing pedagogy. Though it didn't occur to me initially, in rereading this piece in the context of the issue, I find that the authors speak to access through inclusion of multimodality and expanded constructs of "writing."

We're pleased to present book reviews by Virginia Crisco, Jacquelyn E. Hoermann and Richard Leo Enos, Paula Mathieu, and Kristina Fennelly. We also include a graduate student group review by Margaret Briggs-Dineen, Wendy Fall, Beth Godbee, Danielle Klein, Laura Linder-Scholer, Alyssa McGrath, Michael Stock, and Sarah Thompson. Collectively, these reviewers cover a lot of ground, constructing a capacious and inspiring view of work in the field.

The broad representation of field interests in these reviews is a product of Asao Inoue's vision as Book Review Editor. We're grateful for his four years of service as we say farewell to him. With this issue, we're thrilled to welcome Kelly Kinney on board as our new Book Review Editor. Kelly brings a good deal of experience as a writer and teacher who, over the past five years, has instructed graduate students on how to write book reviews (an underappreciated service to the profession). Kelly is eager to work with authors and to sponsor a wide range of research emergent in and relevant to composition studies. Thanks to Kelly for accepting our invitation and seamlessly adapting to our workflow.

A few notes on what's upcoming:

- We are accepting submissions for our next Where We Are, focused on undergraduate writing majors and concentrations. For our cfp, please visit http://www.uc.edu/content/dam/uc/journals/composition-studies/docs/WWA%20CFP.pdf.
- Our spring 2015 issue is a special issue on Comics, Multimodality, and Composition, guest edited by Professor Dale Jacobs. Don't miss it!
- Spring 44.1 (2016) will be a special issue on Composition's Global Turn: Writing Instruction in Multilingual/Translingual and Transnational Contexts, guest edited by Brian Ray and Connie Kendall Theado. Proposals due **January 15, 2015**; cfp at http://www.uc.edu/content/dam/uc/journals/composition-studies/docs/CS%20Special%20Issue%20CFP.pdf.

For complete submission and subscription information, visit our website at http://www.uc.edu/journals/composition-studies.html. Also find us on Facebook and Twitter; we're always looking for new friends.

L.M.
Cincinnati, Ohio
September 2014

Reprint of 1994 Interview with Winifred Bryan Horner

2014 Introduction

Lynée Lewis Gaillet, Georgia State University

Winifred Bryan Horner—exemplary teacher, scholar, colleague, and mentor—passed away February 4th of this year. Many tributes to Dr. Horner are in press at this point[1]; however, revisiting an earlier interview with this great light provides a unique perspective on her accomplishments and opinions—delivered in her own voice.

Exactly twenty years ago, then editor of *Composition Studies*, Christina Murphy, commissioned Shelley Aley and me to interview Dr. Horner as part of an ongoing series of interviews with composition's preeminent figures. In March of 1994, at the annual Conference on College Composition and Communication meeting held in Nashville, the three of us delivered a panel presentation addressing Scottish rhetoric and afterwards shared lunch in Dr. Horner's hotel room to catch up. The conference theme that year was "Common Concerns, Uncommon Realities: Teaching, Research, and Scholarship in a Complex World." Dr. Horner's words and thoughts, reprinted below, certainly capture the theme of that year's conference as she reflects upon her career as a woman coming up through the ranks in a man's world and discusses the significance of her divergent work to date. In this interview, Dr. Horner reveals a unique model for blending the responsibilities of the academic triumvirate—teaching, service, and research—while striking a balance between a satisfying personal life and a fulfilling professional career.

Shelley and I had served as Dr. Horner's research assistants when she held the position as Radford Chair in Rhetoric at Texas Christian University (TCU); collectively, the assistants during her tenure at TCU were commonly known as the "Radford Rats." At the time of the interview, Shelley and I were brand-new assistant professors, and ironically, I had my first research assistant, David Hutto, whose task was to transcribe this interview. The scripted "interview" questions often gave way to personal discussions and sometimes irreverent comments. Laughing during the recording, Dr. Horner periodically would offer an aside imperative to the absent transcriber: "David, don't write that!"

Dr. Horner's sparkling wit and humanity lives on in her writings, and her generous spirit is evident in the work of her students and mentees who learned from her the value of paying it forward.

Notes

1. See the *Peitho* tribute (16.2 spring/summer 2014), which includes numerous pictures of Win's life, her obituary (that she penned), and remembrances from family members, colleagues and students; also, see two forthcoming pieces about Dr. Horner's contributions to the field in the *Peitho* 25th anniversary issue commemorating the founding of the Coalition of Women Scholars in the History of Rhetoric (by Hui Wu and Lynée Lewis Gaillet).

Interview with Winifred Bryan Horner

Original interview appeared in *Composition Studies/Freshman English News* 22.2 (1994): 15-29.

Lynée Lewis Gaillet and Shelley Aley

Win Horner is a master teacher. She is able to introduce her students into the realm of what Gary Tate, her colleague at Texas Christian University, calls "the discourse of ... the educated community" (McDonald 41). We noticed this quality as students in her literacy and orality seminar at Texas Christian University. We were nearly defeated by the dispersion and messiness evident in the course as she had designed it. Our educational experiences up to that point had been more traditional: lecture courses in literature that mainly disseminated information. This was not always the case, but literature courses at the time we were completing our M.A.s had traditionally privileged a particular canon. In Professor Horner's class, we were treading on entirely new ground—shifting ground, unstable ground—or so it seemed to us. And who was there to tell us what to think? Not Win Horner.

During our semester in her seminar, we discovered that a master teacher doesn't tell students what to think; she introduces students to the conversations taking place in an educated community, much in the way a host introduces new guests at a social gathering. A master teacher enables students to open their ears to the babble of discourse that is taking place around them and to make sense or non/sense of it as they will—according to their varied experiences, goals, and interests—eventually mingling their voices with those of the others. Win Horner is a master teacher in this wonderful way, and, as such, she has served as a model for what it is to be an outstanding teacher, scholar, mentor, colleague, and friend to both of us throughout our years at TCU and beyond.

Like many of her former students, we have remained good friends with Win Horner. Following our panel presentation on nineteenthcentury Scottish rhetoric at the Conference on College Composition and Communication this year, we lunched and visited with her, catching up on old times and planning future projects. Out of this conversation among friends comes the following interview, and we must admit that it is with deep regard for Win Horner that we sought and undertook this assignment.

Dr. Horner completed her A.B. in 1943 at Washington University and her M.A. in 1961 at the University of Missouri-Columbia. She began her career in 1960 as a part-time instructor at Missouri, eventually becoming a full-time tenured instructor in 1969. Describing Horner's struggle for recognition as a non-traditionalist in a male-dominated, traditional field, Theresa Enos states,

> Dr. Horner is both a role model for and mentor to many of us, especially the women who make up the majority of those working in rhetoric and composition. Without the many kinds of support she has given to us victims of professionalized gender bias, we might not be the staunch but weary survivors some of us have become. (9)

Horner served as the assistant to the Director of the Composition Program at MU from 1974-1980. She received her Ph.D. from the University of Michigan in 1975 and was promoted to full professor in 1984, a position for which she had to fight. In 1985, she accepted the Lillian Radford Chair of Rhetoric and Composition, the first twentieth-century chair of rhetoric and composition. She was the first person to hold the Chair (from 1985-1993) and the first woman to occupy an endowed chair at TCU. Presently in partial retirement, Horner serves as the TCU Cecil and Ida Green Distinguished Emerita Tutor and Lillian Radford Chair of Rhetoric Emerita.

Among her many publications, Dr. Horner has authored and edited landmark works in the profession, including *Composition and Literature: Bridging the Gap* (U of Chicago P, 1983), *The Present State of Scholarship in Historical Rhetoric* (revised edition, U of Missouri P, 1990), *Rhetoric in the Classical Tradition* (St. Martin's, 1988), and *Nineteenth-Century Rhetoric: The Scottish Connection* (Southern Illinois U P, 1993). Forthcoming works include *Three Nineteenth-Century Scottish Rhetoricians: Aytoun, Bain, and Jardine*, and *Essays on Rhetoric and Pedagogy in Honor of James J. Murphy*.

Dr. Horner holds numerous awards. In 1982, she won the University of Missouri Alumnae Anniversary Award for her Outstanding Contribution to the Education of Women and was made Fellow in the Institute for the Humanities at the University of Edinburgh in 1987. Also in 1987, she won a National Endowment for the Humanities Research Award. In 1990, she won the Award for Distinguished Alumna from the University Missouri, and in 1991 she was honored with a festschrift edited by Theresa Enos. For the support Horner has given women, *Rhetoric Review* honored her by naming the 1990-91 award for best essay "The Winifred Bryan Horner Award."

Dr. Horner lectures extensively both at home and abroad. She has presented papers in Amsterdam, Aberdeen, Gottengen, Edinburgh, Oxford, Tours, and Shanghai. She served as president for both the Rhetoric Society of America (1987-89) and The National Council of Writing Program Administrators (1985-87). Not having had a mentor of her own, Dr. Horner is aware of the importance of playing this role in the academic lives of her students. What is most notable about conversations with her is that she never neglects voicing interest in and listening to others. "And what are you working on?" she will always want to know. And then she will lend an educated ear and offer suggestions. Among her many achievements as a master teacher, exemplary scholar, mentor, colleague, and friend, this interest in others characterizes her as an outstanding role model.

LLG/SA First of all, you are well known for your teaching, your scholarship, and your service to the discipline, but how would you describe yourself?

WBH I often feel like an incompetent. I often feel as though maybe somebody, or lots of people, are going to find out that I really don't know so much, particularly in my classes, and then here (CCCC), when I give a paper. I have the sort of typical lack of self-confidence that I think many people have, and particularly women. But I *love* being reassured, over and over again.

LLG/SA Do you think that vulnerability in a sense is maybe a strength for you, or do you perceive it as a weakness?

WBH Oh, I don't know. It gets to my stomach sometimes. But it makes me realize that everybody feels vulnerable.

LLG/SA Do you see yourself more as a teacher or as a scholar?

WBH I really have trouble separating them, because, when I was negotiating this appointment at TCU, this new appointment, the vice president said to me you don't even have to teach, and I really didn't like that because I realized that most of my good ideas come in my teaching, from my students. Teaching is a two-way street. So I think if I gave up my teaching I would sort of dry up on the scholarship. I truly believe that.

LLG/SA Your students repeatedly cast you in the role of mentor. How do you feel about that responsibility?

WBH I'm going to write an article for Betsy Irvin on mentoring, and I think the thing about mentoring is that it's like being a parent. It's very important that you learn to let go. I really think that you mentor students until they don't need it anymore. And that can happen when they're firstyear graduate students or it may not happen until they're ten years out in the field. But I feel that then it becomes an equal relationship, and I almost think it gets to the place out in the world where your students are helping you, so that finally you are being mentored in a way by them. You'll find that in your relationships with your own children and graduate students. There comes a time when you've got to let go. And they're ready to be let go.

LLG/SA You've said that you were self-trained in rhetoric. How did you come into this field? What most influenced your theory and your practice?

WBH I came into the field because I was teaching writing as an adjunct, and I was even supervising the TAs who were teaching writing, and I didn't know anything about it. My first idea was to go into linguistics. I really knew nothing about rhetoric. Then I had a friend in the speech department, and she said I should study rhetoric. I classified myself at that point as in rhetoric and linguistics. Actually my degree was in English language and linguistics. I took most of my courses in the speech department.

LLG/SA What do you see as your contribution to composition and rhetoric and how do you feel about it?

WBH I'm glad you asked me that. I feel my contribution is to reexamine our history as teachers of composition, as people interested in teaching a communication skill to students. That's where I started and that's where I am now. I am in organizations where the history of rhetoric has been separated from the teaching of composition, and I feel so strongly that we are together in this and that the teaching of composition should never be isolated from rhetoric and the history of rhetoric.

LLG/SA Gary Tate says that several years ago if you tried to give a paper at CCCC that didn't include Aristotle, then the rhetoric police would come in and censure you. He thinks they divorced composition from everything but rhetoric. How do you see yourself fitting into Tate's description of the climate of rhetoric in the 70s?

WBH Well, I think I'm one of those, what do you call it?

LLG/SA The rhetoric police, the KGB of composition.

WBH I'm sorry, but I wanted to divorce literature from composition, but I had different ideas about that. Ed Corbett talks about it in his article in *Composition and Literature: Bridging the Gap* (1983). What I had experienced was training TAs; all of our teachers of composition were TAs in literature. All they studied was literature; we had no courses in composition. I wasn't capable of helping them. I used to conduct a threeday workshop, and I didn't know anything about composition theory or rhetoric theory. I just winged it. So I was eager to get literature out of the comp course, because the TAs spent the whole time teaching literature. They didn't know how to teach a composition course.

LLG/SA And they didn't *want* to teach it. That's lowly grunt work.

WBH Exactly. And when they'd been in the program a few years then they got to teach a sophomore English literature survey or a sophomore American literature survey, and they'd arrived. We used to recruit people—and I should make it clear this is not my present institution—we used to recruit people by saying you'll never have to teach composition here. So I carry, I think, some bitterness, which I think may be inappropriate right now, about literature.

LLG/SA So how do you now see the composition class? As utilitarian?

WBH Now I see the composition classroom as a place for learning how to use language and through using language—both reading and writing—connecting to your culture and empowering yourself, if that's the word, to operate in the culture and to understand more about your thinking process. I love to do that in the NIGHT course that I'm teaching. We keep talking about what happens when we write, whether we write on the kitchen table or in bed, very mundane things. One of the things we were talking about was where you get your ideas, and it came from them, not me, that the physical act of writing—physical and mental—generates ideas.

LLG/SA Writing as discovery, writing as learning?

WBH Writing is all of those things, and you can't separate it, I don't think, from your thinking. Language is it, as far as I'm concerned. It's also what separates us from the other animals. I used to say lower animals, now I say other animals. It's our ability to use language. I have almost a mystical admiration and respect for the word, which is the way the Bible started. In many religions it's the beginning of the word, which is language. And language is what separates us.

LLG/SA OK. Let's move on. What do you see as the "final analysis" of *Bridging the Gap?*

WBH I don't really know.

LLG/SA Of all your work, that one gets cited most often.

WBH If it does it's because it includes the work of many people. They're really impressive—Wayne Booth, Richard Lanham. That was my idealism. Start out with the most respected scholars in literature, who I knew taught composition, and get the connections that they see. The book started out as a session for MLA. I was in charge of the teaching and writing division program. The first person I called was Wayne Booth, and when I telephoned he was grading freshman themes. He started talking to me all about the paper he was grading. He wouldn't be on the program, but during the conversation I asked if he thought the program idea could be made into a book. He said, "Oh, it would make a wonderful book. The University of Chicago Press wants to publish more things like that. Be sure to call them." I had a call within two hours from the University of Chicago Press. Then when you call other people and say Wayne Booth is contributing, everybody says, "Oh Yes." To answer your original question, I don't know, really. Probably it is the work most cited.

LLG/SA It certainly is a point of departure in the current debate of lit/comp. Everybody starts with your book.

WBH I've been asked to give talks to strong literature departments. They're trying to get their people to be interested in composition, and I'm not sure I'm a good representative of that.

LLG/SA Let's talk about your most recent book, *Nineteenth-Century Scottish Rhetoric: The American Connection*. We see it as an introductory work inviting a structuralist approach that calls for a historical and social contextualization of nineteenth-century rhetoric studies. What do you perceive will be the long-term effects of your work on the history of nineteenth-century rhetoric? Do you see it shedding any light on problematic concepts of the period that now exist, and what directions would you suggest for future studies in this area?

WBH I hope it opens up a new area that proves to be very fruitful. This book will be followed by actual excerpts from three of those important people—Aytoun, Jardine, and Bain. I see new interest in the period, but again, I think it's got to be connected to what we're doing in the composition classroom today. I believe you must have a connection in history of rhetoric and composition studies. Getting back to the nineteenth-century, I think it's a crucial period if we are going to understand what we are doing in the classroom today, and understand composition theory. I think the mark of that is an increasing number of young scholars in this area. You two are the best examples of this. It's a wonderful feeling, and I think it will just open up new things. There's a lot of material just waiting to be looked at in Scotland and in this country, too. The

Scottish influence in this country needs to be explored more. I'm fascinated with why Jardine didn't have more influence. I want to hear more about that.

LLG/SA It's been said that your textbook *Rhetoric in the Classical Tradition* is perhaps the only truly classical rhetoric designed for beginning writers. Could you talk a bit about the conception and reception of that work?

WBH That was a very interesting and exciting project. It was very hard to write. At the first CCCC after it came out I was actually lionized. People would come up to me and say, "Oh, I love it!" These were professors, and one instructor said to me, "I got it right before I left and I put it in my drawer and locked it, so nobody would get it because I want to read it as soon as I get back." That's kind of the story of what happened to it. The instructors loved it, but they were afraid of it, afraid to teach it because they felt so unsure of their knowledge of classical rhetoric. It's never been a best seller, but it's had steady sales and now they are going up.

LLG/SA We would think so, now that you have a basis of practitioners who are educated in classical rhetoric.

WBH That's right. Students of rhetoric like it. The students say, "Why do I need this first chapter?" It sort of had a life of its own, and it's now picking up sales, and when you think of all the second-hand copies that are out there, that's sort of remarkable. This morning a man came up to me and said, "I'm using your textbook and I'm just thrilled with it. I think it's the best," and so forth and so on. He was using it in a graduate course. And of course that's what happened to Ed Corbett's book. It will be interesting to see how this new book by Sharon Crowley [*Ancient Rhetoric for the Contemporary Student* 1994], which follows in that tradition, fares.

LLG/SA I think it's interesting that the book is coming into its own, in a sense.

WBH Yes, because there are more people in the profession who have studied classical rhetoric. They're more comfortable with it. But I think I am known more through that book than for anything that I've done. People say to me, "Oh, I've read your work," and nine times out of ten that's the book they're talking about.

LG/SA What about your work with *Harbrace Handbook*? Harbrace is widely adopted because it gives us what we want, I mean we as a profession, but I don't see Harbrace making any great strides. That may be just my own bias. Do you see your other works influencing your work with Harbrace?

WBH That book has been changed markedly over the years. But we changed it in such a way as not to be offensive. That book has led the field in many ways, and people don't realize that. One of its strengths is that they don't realize it. Look at the example and exercises just two editions ago. That's only about six years? And look at the current one and you will be amazed. The examples are multicultural. We made a list of names, so that in the exercises we don't have John, Bill and Mary anymore. We have Drema, we have Sholanda. So it has changed, and we were one of the first handbooks to mention anything about sexist language. In fact, we were highly criticized when we said that "Everyone pick up their books" was acceptable. We got hot letters. The Harbrace is one of the most widely used handbooks in the field. It's not nearly as conservative as people think it is. It's also the way composition is taught by 90 percent of the people in the country who teach composition, and they're not here at CCCC.

LLG/SA They don't have the time or the money.

WBH They're teaching four and five and six classes of composition. They're teaching inner city kids. They're in a different, much more difficult world. They want and they need rules. Is it right or wrong? The instructors want to know that, and there is a lot of new stuff slipped in there. I think it has a tremendous influence for the good. The book got bad press.

LLG/SA It got bad press because of the way it's been employed or appropriated by practitioners who are not really able to change what they're doing. If you treat something like a Bible it becomes one.

WBH It also serves their purposes. They're not trying to teach people how to write great literature.

LLG/SA Just how to get a job or to get out of college.

WBH So I have always had trouble with that. I think CCCC does a very good job of serving a lot of those people, but there are a lot more that never get to CCCC. The Harbrace should probably be used as a reference. I have trouble with the rhetoric section. I tried to make a lot of improvements in that.

LLG/SA We know you were very conscientious about including more discussions of process pedagogy, things that practitioners are doing that relate to process pedagogy, in the book this time.

WBH Also we have introduced a rhetorical element very carefully. But we don't say that outright. We quietly incorporate it into a so-called rule.

LLG/SA Next question. You're a founding member of the coalition of women scholars in the history of rhetoric, which has been in existence for how many years?

WBH Just two or three.

LLG/SA How do you perceive your role in this organization? Tell us what the goals are.

WBH Our goals are twofold. One is to help younger women in the field get established by encouraging their publications. And secondly by helping them negotiate the political scene that everyone faces, and particularly women. So it's a kind of support group. I thought the other night we had wonderful perspectives on race and gender by four African-American women speakers.

LLG/SA I thought it interesting though that African Americans were all on the panel; few were in the audience.

WBH I sat next to an African-American man, but you're right. They outnumbered the ones in the audience. We don't have many African Americans in our profession. The difficulty if you're an African American is to study English literature and a standard European American language.

LLG/SA So how do you perceive your role in this organization. As a mentor?

WBH The mentor term bothers me, but just to help people when I can.

LLG/SA So people reading this article can contact you for guidance?

WBH We've made that very clear in the profession—that they can contact any of us, and I think you would truly find these people helpful. Andrea [Lunsford], Kathleen [Welch], we've all been through it and survived, so we have learned a few survival techniques. And the men have a little trouble with that. We are establishing a therapeutic old-girl network, borrowing the best part of the old-boy's network, if you can find a best part.

LLG/SA That leaves us with how has this organization affected the direction of your own work, if at all?

WBH I had a wonderful time at an all-day feminist workshop where I talked on Wednesday. I think I was asked to talk because I was a full professor; the title of the talk, which they gave to me, was "Full Professor Reflects on her Career." I came out of that session so revived and enriched, and it was because there were two full professors there and that was it. The rest of the participants were young people in the profession.

LLG/SA About fifteen people present?

WBH Yes. It was limited. We reached our capacity. But they were all young people, many of whom I did not know. That was a wonderful chance to get to know them, and we talked about political issues: What are you willing to do to survive before tenure? What are you willing to do, what must you do, what are you not willing to do, and how do you negotiate through those things?

LLG/SA What is your best advice to them?

WBH I think as Kathleen [Welch] was saying, read your department; you have to know your department. You have to be a good listener. And then you have to sort of negotiate. I think my advice is not to take on every issue. Save yourself for the big issues or you lose credibility. You just become a kind of a nag. I cringe when I hear people call me "dear," and I cringe when I hear "lady." But I finally realized that I shouldn't take up those issues. Wait until you can really do something or you'll lose your credibility.

LLG/SA Yes. We have friends who constantly call people on their language usage.

WBH I did that. The reason I know all these things is because I did them. Looking back, I know what a mistake it was. I also think women are inclined—I know this because I did it—to fuss up and down the halls and not take action. We should shut up and do our work. And you have to do some dumb things. And overlook some dumb things, even in yourself. When you make mistakes, you then pick yourself up and start over.

LLG/SA Try to regain credibility where you may have lost it, or hope nobody paid that much attention.

WBH That's right.

LLG/SA Another interesting part of your career is your international travel and involvement in international rhetoric. Over the last several years you've traveled extensively around the world, as the people-to-people ambassador to China, you've been to Italy—

WBH And I've been to Russia, strictly on tour.

LLG/SA But you spoke to people about rhetoric on the train?

WBH Undoubtedly I did. Don't you always? Actually I went with a group from the University of Missouri, so there was a lot of discussion. We had music on the boat every night. They were more interested in that than I was, Russian opera. But I love to travel. And when people are figuring out their research, they ought really to think about where they want to go. I have a colleague who's working on Mark Twain, and he "gets" to go to Hannibal, Missouri. Whenever I travel I feel somehow bigger, smarter. I get fascinated with the culture and the people.

LLG/SA Particularly when you go to observe as a recorder rather than a tourist?

WBH I've found traveling without some purpose is just deadly dull. Just one museum after another or one cathedral after another. I like to go with some design.

LLG/SA So what effect has your involvement in international rhetoric studies and your travel had on your perceptions of North American composition studies?

WBH In the history of rhetoric?

LLG/SA OK. Do universities in other countries that do not have composition programs have an advantage or a disadvantage over our system of education in this country.

WBH The places where I have been have the advantage that the schools and the universities are smaller. I just find this so cliché but tremendously broadening. When I came back from China I had always taught my course in the history of rhetoric, and then it became the history of western rhetoric. I realized, hey, I'm just teaching the rhetoric of a very small proportion of the world.

LLG/SA Has it humbled you, in a sense?

WBH Oh, yes. And it's made me realize how terribly provincial we are. In my class now I have a woman from Mexico and a woman from China, both extraordinarily intelligent. Whenever we talk about something in the teaching of composition, I say, "How do you do it in Mexico, and how do you do it in China?" And I really try to draw on those experiences, and the differences are always very interesting to me and other students. We need to enrich what we do.

LLG/SA We might be jumping around here now. You've done a great deal of work in writing across the curriculum. What insights can you offer someone interested in this area, and what is the future of writing across the curriculum, as you see it?

WBH I think writing across the curriculum is the way to go. And it's the philosophy behind it that I think is important, that we stop relegating the teaching of writing to one course, or two courses even, or to one department. Writing should be incorporated into every course in the university, and all professors should be responsible for the writing of their students. And if the students can't write about a subject, then they don't know it. I feel very strongly about that. In fact at one point Peter France at the University of Edinburgh said, "Oh, our students write so poorly. I think we ought to think about putting in a composition course," and I said, "don't." Because now all the professors in the university concern themselves with the writing of the students, and students will flunk the course if they can't write. They will flunk in biology and chemistry and history, whatever it is. If students can't write, they flunk.

LLG/SA You think that's good, to get back to the question of composition?

WBH I think that's the way it ought to be. I think too often students think that once they're past freshman composition they will never have to worry about writing again.

LLG/SA When do you think we will get there?

WBH I think we're heading in that direction. One of the problems is the political situation. The TAs are supported by the comp course, and that's why the English department will not give up composition. Otherwise they would not have their students in their Milton seminar. It is strictly economics. I am finally a Marxist.

LLG/SA Do you have any suggestions for how we might still keep the money in the English department by being more inclusive of other disciplines? Is that feasible, put graduate students from other disciplines in the English program?

WBH Some universities are doing that, and actually I think that's the way it should go, because I think we're turning out too many literature PhDs, and maybe we're getting to the point that we ought to watch how many rhetoric and comp PhDs we turn out. That's one of the reasons I left the university where I was. I was surrounded by graduate students who were not getting jobs. That was the first question I asked when I came to TCU—do students get jobs? They do. I made up my mind that I was not going to be associated with a discipline that turned out people who could not get jobs. I went to an MLA meeting one time when the department had gotten a room for our graduate students, where they could receive calls and hang their coats and stuff like that. A number of our students went there with no interviews and no papers to give. I saw those students sit in that room for four days in New York City waiting for a phone call. They never even got a phone call. I said then I am not going to have anything to do with this. As long as this economic situation continues, we will continue to turn out too many PhDs. The doctors are smarter than we are. They have limited the enrollment in med school. I think we need to do that in English.

LLG/SA We were talking on the telephone recently, and you told me that in an address at the TCU composition symposium, you stated that freshman composition should not emphasize the personal essay. What in your opinion should replace the personal essay in freshman composition and why?

WBH I think it should move from the personal essay to an argument, or whatever you want to call it. You have a thesis, a main idea and you support it. I think the temptation is that it's fun to teach the personal essay. In my night class for older students—

LLG/SA Auto/biography?

WBH It's just wonderful, because they don't have to produce arguments. Usually students can write much better in their personal voice. It's just natural; you're telling a story. So instructors and students hate to move out of that mode. That's the danger. It's just like literature. It's so attractive; it's so much fun. I love to teach the night course because their stories are interesting, and in that mode they realize they are doing well. I can talk to them about how to write better, and they pick it up right away. I like to read it, I like to hear it, they like to write it.

LLG/SA Because their subject is themselves.

WBH Or others—it's personal. You'd be interested to know, a third of them instead of writing autobiography are writing biography. Two of them are writing about friends. One of them is writing a biography of her daughter. Two of them are writing biographies of their grandparents. So the focus has shifted a little bit.

LLG/SA Oral histories, which we all find fascinating.

WBH That's right. And they love to do it, I love to hear it. It's much happier than trying to write an article supporting or not supporting a crime bill. That's just not that interesting usually.

LLG/SA So you're encouraging composition instructors to move away from the personal forms and tackle the argumentative—

WBH I think that's what they're going to have to do. Let's talk about the new book I'm writing; it's very germane to this. It's a reader, it's a textbook. It's going to have four sections. The first section will be diaries, then letters, then autobiography, and then biography—excerpts. It's based on two ideas. One is moving from your personal experience to objective examination, outside your own experience—and also reading your audience. The diary starts with your own personal experience and also yourself as a reader/listener/audience. With the letter you have one other person usually, and you're still talking about your own experience. In the autobiography you're still talking about your own experience, but you've moved out into a public audience. And then in the biography you have to go outside of your experience and your audience is a general one. I see that as a way in a writing course to move students out.

LLG/SA And you have students write essays based on those forms?

WBH Not yet, but I plan to start.

LLG/SA This would be a text for a composition course?

WBH I don't know whether it would be a course for freshmen or upper level students. My new interest is autobiography. One very interesting thing I've discovered about this book is that diaries and a lot of the letters are women's ways of writing.

LLG/SA Biographies are by men and about men?

WBH Yes. You've got this progression. I'm finding all sorts of diaries, by the way, published and in manuscript form. All sorts of letters, and you begin to get a few more men in letters. But they write a different kind of letter. You have a feeling that they might be published someday, beginning to see more of an audience—particularly the nineteenthcentury letter writers. But the women are really writing letters to one person, and then it moves out. You get more men writing autobiography, and then in biography, they're by and about men, for the most part. I'm interested particularly in women's autobiography. But I'm just starting.

LLG/SA And do you see yourself doing something historically? For example, are these going to be excerpts from a historical work?

WBH It'll be varied.

LLG/SA I think you ought to have a section on the way autobiography and journal writing and letter writing place into the development of our whole rhetoric of nature. Look at Selborn; all of our nature writing comes out of diaries, journals and letters. Have you got a publisher for this work?

WBH Yes. Blair Press.

LLG/SA What's the title of your new work. When can we look forward to seeing it?

WBH I'm not sure yet. Maybe *Life Writing*. I call my night course "auto/biography." But that doesn't quite cover this. Maybe *Moving Out*.

LLG/SA When can we expect to see your book?

WBH I'm supposed to have it finished by October.

LLG/SA So early next year. OK. This is our last question—a very generic one. What is the future of freshman composition studies? What should be the future, if there is a difference?

WBH I would see it moving out, in most schools, of its present location as a freshman course, and I would see the teaching of writing being spread across the curriculum and up and down the curriculum.

LLG/SA And you feel that's what it should be?

WBH Yes, I do.

LLG/SA What did we neglect to ask you?

WBH The question I get asked most often is, "How do you balance your personal life with your professional life?" I have seen that change so dramatically. I remember being approached by colleagues at one time when our graduate students had requested that their courses end when school let out because so many of them had children who they wanted to get home to. My colleagues' reaction to that was, "You must tell these women students not to ask for special consideration." I think that kind of thinking is gone, that both men and women should be given consideration to take care of children, elderly parents, a sick partner, or whatever. The old idea was never mention your personal life; don't mix it up with your professional life. I don't think we believe that anymore. I have a wonderful and supportive husband, but I never used to mention him. But I've changed that now. We just celebrated our fiftieth wedding anniversary, and I like to brag about that. His influence has not only helped me but in many ways made my career possible. We must make allowances for satisfying and fulfilling personal lives along with our professional lives for both men and women.

LLG/SA And the profession? Do you think if we've got happy people—

WBH Yes, of course. We'll help people stay in our profession. We can't continue to try and do it all and not speak about our personal lives. I see that trend going away. Again, men and women are entitled to personal lives, and in the end it will sustain and enrich our professional lives.

LLG/SA In looking back, what has been the most rewarding aspect of your career?

WBH I think the most exciting thing that has happened to me is seeing my students and other young scholars carry on the work I have started. For example, there is Paul Bator, Linda Ferreira-Buckley, and you two—building your work on the research that I started—the archival research in Scotland. And of course I built my work on the rich material of the scholars who came before me—Ed Corbett and Jerry Murphy. My students are carrying on my work just as I am carrying on their work. That is something that we all share. Finally it makes it all worthwhile—the digging through moldy manuscripts for days and weeks on end, the cold and rain in Scotland. That is the real reason for research and it's all bound up with teaching—the ongoing conversation between students and teachers, and among scholars and researchers all over the world.

Lynée Lewis Gaillet
Georgia State University
Atlanta, Georgia

Shelley Aley
Cottey College
Nevada, Missouri

Works Cited

Crowley, Sharon. *Ancient Rhetorics for Contemporary Students.* New York: Macmillan 1994. Print.

Enos, Theresa. "'A Brand New World': Using Our Professional and Personal Histories of Rhetoric." Festschrift *in Honor of Winifred Bryan Horner.* Carbondale: SIUP, 1993. 3-12. Print.

McDonald, Robert L. "Interview with Gary Tate." *Composition Studies* 20.2 (1992): 36-50. Print.

Composing With

Two Rooms

Jennifer Habel

My office lacks Virginia Woolf's prescribed lock on the door, but it is a room of my own, a room being one half of the "prosaic conclusion" she offered at the end of her famous essay (109). The other half is £500 a year or, approximately, $43,000 today. My office is on the second floor of my home, which I share with my husband and our two daughters. It is a small room with two windows that face our street, and contains more furniture per available square foot than any other room in our house: two bookcases, two file storage boxes, one cabinet, one table, one rolling cart, one desk. The tabletop is largely covered with objects, papers, and books, as is the top of the shorter bookcase, and the wall behind that bookcase is on its way to being covered—which is odd, because if I can be said to have a decorating style, it inclines toward sparseness.

Though different in almost every way—size, shape, palette, content—the room in the house most similar to my office is my daughters' bedroom. Like my office, their bedroom is far from sparse, and its contents are almost all of personal significance. In these rooms, my daughters and I keep, and in some cases display, prized belongings. We arrange them in privately meaningful ways and imbue them with power. The dolphin that hangs from the curtain rod over my youngest daughter's bed "watches out for [her]" in the night. The books that mean most to me in relation to my current project are carefully arranged on the leftmost side of the top two shelves of the bookshelf to my right.

Another similarity between these two rooms: they can be messy. When I am working well, my desktop becomes obscured by drafts and notes; other materials are scattered on the floor. That I don't mind this I experience as a victory. When the other rooms in my house are a mess, I feel oppressed, agitated—even angry. To keep a house with children in it neat, as I generally do, takes a discouraging amount of time, and I am discouraged by my need to do it. Disorder, Valéry claimed, "is the condition of the mind's fertility" (105).

At our previous home, my husband and I shared an office in a small shed we converted. I'd carry my laptop and a mug of tea or coffee out to the shed to work for—this seems remarkable now—45 minutes. My husband would watch our children who were then very young. As our children grew, my writing time, and that of my husband, who is also a writer, lengthened to an hour, an hour and a half…. Through the window in the office door I could see the set of French doors and through them the "family room" where my family most often was. I watched them as though they were a film without sound, and it was not unusual for whatever poem I was working on to be about them.

I would like to be able to describe my children's voices. The younger one has a slightly muffled or lisping quality that her sister's voice has lost. This morning, a Saturday, they are quiet: reading or drawing in their bedroom, which is diagonally across the hall from my office. My husband is reading in the room directly across the hall from me. I know this despite my door being closed, as it always is when I write, even when I am the only one in the house. I wish I did not *feel* my family's presence in the way I do, as a pressure at my back (I write with my back to the door, facing the windows), and I wish I did not feel so vexed when I hear "Mom!" / "Don't bother Mom"—at fault if I answer (this is my writing time) or if I don't (those are my children).

When the poet Christian Wiman was in the hospital for a bone marrow transplant, he found that "poetry died for [him] for a while." Wiman suffers from an incurable cancer of the blood that is in remission. The poems he eventually found useful were not those concerned with the ineffable, but ones that offered "reality rendered in such a way that you could see it again." A real poem, says Wiman, can "suddenly [make] the amount of reality that you have in your life greater." To find, collect, and communicate reality, says Woolf, is the writer's "business"; to do so, to work in a room of one's own, is "an invigorating life," it is to "live in the presence of reality" (114).

My daughters' room is the place they go most often—at night, of course, but also during the day. Despite the craft table and supplies in our large playroom, they choose to draw, cut, paste, color, stitch, bead, write seated on the rug in their much smaller bedroom. "I don't know why," they answer when asked. What is a room of one's own? Not a cocoon, which is to be grown out of; not a fortress, which too strongly suggests a war. One eats cereal there on Saturday mornings, or else pancakes with the others downstairs.

Works Cited

Valéry, Paul. "The Course in Poetics: First Lesson." Trans. Jackson Mathews. *The Creative Process: A Symposium*. Ed. Brewster Ghiselin. Berkeley: U of California P, 1954. 92-105. Print.

Wiman, Christian. "A Call to Doubt and Faith." *On Being with Krista Tippett*. On Being. 23 May 2013. Web. 10 Sept. 2014. <http://www.onbeing.org/program/a-call-to-doubt-and-faith-christian-wiman-on-remembering-god/4535.>

Woolf, Virginia. *A Room of One's Own*. San Diego: Harcourt Brace Jovanovich, 1929. Print.

Teaching with Love

Laura J. Davies

She stood there and looked at the empty chair. Her classmates, all cadets at the United States Air Force Academy, filed into the room, staring down at their spit-shined shoes. It was Monday afternoon.

I could see it in her eyes: she considered sitting there in spite of it all, and then rejected that idea at once. It was all there: anger, sadness, pain, resolve and despair competing for air. She crossed the room, sat in a different seat, and left her chair empty too.

I'm telling you about this moment – our first day of class after Nathan's[1] suicide last year – because it's one that I think about often as I drive through the Academy's North Gate and see the flag flapping in the gusts that blow down the Front Range of the Rocky Mountains. I remember the day the flag flew at half-staff for Nathan, a young man who sat in the front row of my first-year writing class, two seats left of center.

Every day in class, we pull a name from a stack of index cards, and the selected student goes to the front of the classroom. The student introduces himself, saying where he's from or what his major is. Then, we pepper him with questions. This exercise began for selfish reasons. I figured it would help me learn the names of the identically dressed cadets. But what it turned into is a daily moment of candor and community. It subtly emphasizes the theory that informs my understanding of teaching and of argumentation: that good argument and good pedagogy depend on good listening and honest engagement with others.

I remember the day Nathan's name was pulled. He told us about his prior enlisted service in the Air Force and his two little brothers back in Pittsburgh. I don't remember much more than that, besides his easy smile. He committed suicide the next weekend, just a month into the spring semester. He had sat in his seat – the seat now empty – maybe twelve times, but his death shook me.

Nathan's funeral was in Pittsburgh, but the Academy also held a memorial service for him. The morning of his memorial service, I walked across the Terrazzo and climbed the steps up to the chapel, the stinging February winds cutting through my coat, and saw his smile staring back at me as soon as I entered. Nathan's cadet picture, him looking sharp in his service dress and the flag draped behind him, was displayed on the steps leading up to the altar.

I left his service angry. The Air Force chaplain leading the service never pronounced his last name correctly and never mentioned why Nathan died. Nobody said "suicide" – even the official email from the Dean of Faculty failed to give a cause of death, leaving a gaping hole in the narrative we were able to construct about the loss of Nathan. The students from his squad who found him dead were met by institutional silence; the cadets who assembled together in the chapel to grieve were denied an opportunity to collectively consider and speak about the particular horror, tragedy, and shame of suicide.

I was angry at the chaplain and the institution at large, but I was also angry at Nathan. Part of the reason I was so mad was because I felt incapable of leading my class through their grief. We still had ten more weeks together: ten weeks where we'd meet three times a week for fifty-three minutes and feel the emptiness hang heavy in the air. I was searching for answers to his suicide just as my students were, even though we all knew there were no real answers. I had no comforting words of wisdom. Nathan's death cut us deep. My students in that section were not just his classmates, but also included his squad mates, his prep school roommate, and his best friend. At the end of that first week, I asked the class if they wanted to talk, and one cadet at the back of the room cried out, "No more talking! It's all they talk about! All I think about is Nathan! All I see is Nathan! Nathan, Nathan, Nathan! I want to get away!"

I wanted to get away too.

I've come to understand teaching as a risky business, and for all we talk about assignment sequences and scaffolding assessments, we talk little about what it means to us and to our students to *really* engage with one another, to be honest and vulnerable in each other's presence, to care about one another. What I mean by all of this is that teaching can be an act of love.

I've begun to appreciate the depth of what it means to teach with love in my struggle to teach through loss, as I deal with the consequences of Nathan's death. What do I do with his graded essay, filled with my comments and questions that will never be answered? What do I say to my students today, and the next class, and the next? What do I do for the student who can't finish her essay because she was revising that paragraph when her roommate came into the room and told her of Nathan's suicide? Do I draw a line through his name in my grade book, as if a stroke of blue ink could cross him out of my mind? Will anyone sit next to his empty chair?

At the heart of these questions is the idea that my classroom is a community, a community my students and I build through talk, listening, and little routines like our introduction exercise. This community is only successful when it is built on empathetic love, the kind of love that emerges from recognizing that we have a moral obligation to value other's lives and stories. My definition of love, then, arises from the idea of love as empathy, fellowship, respect, commitment, and yes, even love as risk, for real community love requires that we surrender control in anticipation of uncharted change.

My students take that risk in our little introduction exercise. I risked knowing Nathan, and his smile and his empty chair still remain with me. I can't get away. I've come to realize that a consequence of teaching through love is that I can't just forget about Nathan, no more than I can forget about the countless other students who have come to the front of my classroom and shared a part of their story while we all listen. That's what my classroom is really about: the community, the compassion, and the empathy that we build together.

Notes

1. Nathan is a pseudonym for my student. I have also changed the name of the student's hometown to protect anonymity.

Articles

A Plea for Critical Race Theory Counterstory: Stock Story versus Counterstory Dialogues Concerning Alejandra's "Fit" in the Academy

Aja Y. Martinez

This essay in counterstory suggests a method by which to incorporate critical race theory (CRT) in rhetoric and composition, as a contribution of other(ed) perspectives toward an ongoing conversation in the field about narrative, dominant ideology, and their intersecting influence on programmatic and curricular standards and practices. As a narrative form, counterstory functions as a method for marginalized people to intervene in research methods that would form master narratives based on ignorance and on assumptions about minoritized peoples like Chican@s. Through the formation of counterstories, or those stories that document the persistence of racism and other forms of subordination, voices from the margins become the voices of authority in the researching and relating of our own experiences. Counterstory serves as a natural extension of inquiry for theorists whose research recognizes and incorporates, as data, lived and embodied experiences of people of color. This essay argues it is thus crucial to use a narrative methodology that counters other methods that seek to dismiss or decenter racism and those whose lives are affected daily by it.

My story is grounded in research and experience acquired through my 28-year academic journey. I am Chican@,[1] student, professor, and am embedded in the academy. However, because I am Chicana[2], my path has been riddled with pain, anguish, and what Tara J. Yosso refers to as "survivor's guilt." Why me? Why did I "make it" out of the Southside of Tucson when so many of my classmates were left behind? "Why her?" is what I have painfully come to know others—peers, family, and colleagues—have wondered about me as well. During my time in the academy, I have met barriers of institutional racism, sexism, and classism in courses I have taken, courses I teach, and through interactions with colleagues and professors. Granted, prior to my time as a graduate student and as a faculty member in higher education, I was surely not beyond the reach of these various "-isms"; however, I have been awakened to an awareness of them through a combination of maturing into adulthood, taking courses in which literatures about social injustice and post-colonialism have been provided, and unrelenting experiences in the institution in which my race is continually targeted by colleagues, students, and professors as a personal and professional deficit when I struggle, and as an unfair advantage when I succeed.

I am compelled to describe these experiences coupled with knowledge provided by other scholars who have found it necessary to speak from marginalized spaces like mine. And because I come from a culture in which the oral tradition as taken from lived personal experience is valued as "legitimate knowledge" (Delgado Bernal and Villalpando 169), I must write this essay as testimony because I cannot continue to forge an academic career without documenting the persistence of racism in the field of rhetoric and composition and in the academy at large. Through a method of storytelling that "challenges mainstream society's denial of the ongoing significance of race and racism" (Yosso 10), this essay illustrates a composite portrait told through counterstory (a methodology of critical race theory (CRT)) to inform our field as it faces a major demographic shift. I focus my work on Chican@s because this is the fastest growing population in the academy (U.S. Department of Education), a group from which I feel I can draw upon my "cultural intuition" (11). However, the theoretical, pedagogical, and methodological strategies based on CRT can certainly be adapted to assist other historically marginalized and underrepresented groups in the academy.

The Pipeline: Reason for Concern

According to the 2010 United States Census, roughly fifty million or 16% of the United States population is Latin@ (Ennis et al.). Since the 2000 Census, the Latin@ population has grown 43%, with the largest growth occurring in the Chican@ community, which increased 54%. Currently, 65% of the now 16% United States Latin@ population are Chican@, making people of Mexican origin or decent the largest Latin@ population in the United States. College enrollment for Latin@s has jumped 65% since 2000; however, completion of degrees in higher education do not reflect this growth (U.S. Department of Education).

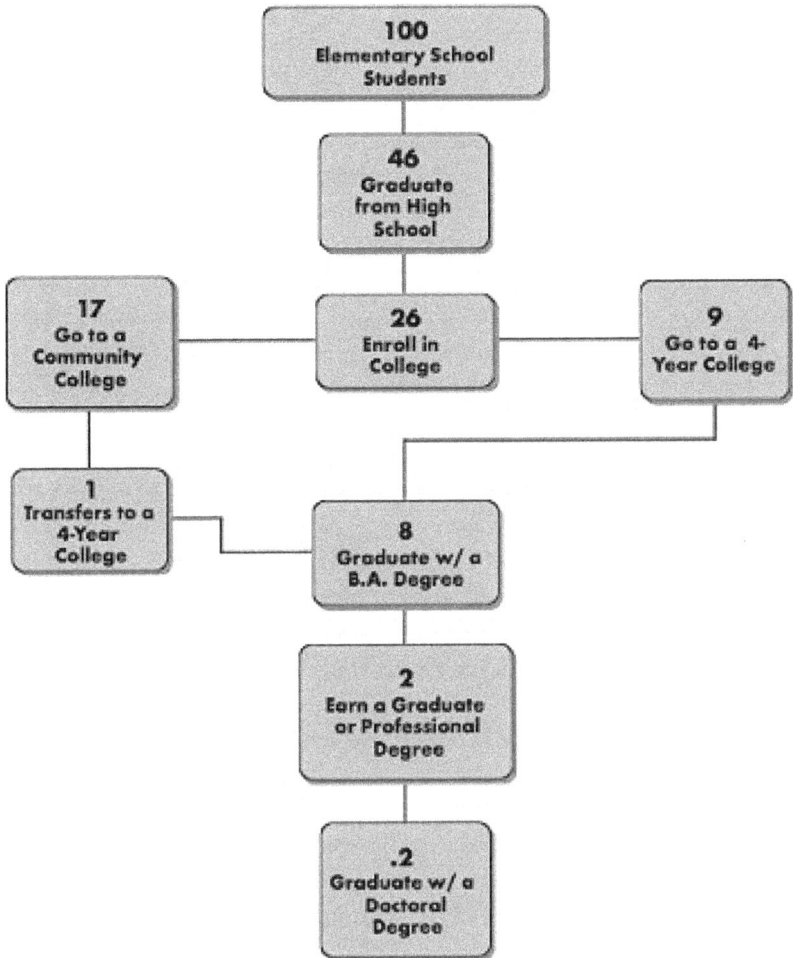

Fig. 1. The Chicana/o Educational Pipeline illustrating low academic outcomes at each point along the educational pipeline in 2000. (From Tara J. Yosso and Daniel G. Solorzano, *The Chicano and Chicano Educational Pipeline,* CSRC Policy and Issues Brief No. 13. Los Angeles: UCLA Chicano Studies Research Center Press, 2006).

In "The Chicana and Chicano Educational Pipeline," Tara J. Yosso and Daniel G. Solórzano illustrate the Chican@ educational pipeline as gathered from the 2000 United States Census (specific to the category "Hispanic," and disaggregated to account for Chican@s, see fig. 1). According to the 2000 Census, only 9% of Chican@s enroll in four-year colleges, 8% graduate with a bachelor's degree, and less than 1% of the latter graduate with a doctoral degree. In 2010 the United States Department of Education's National Center for Education Statistics released a report on enrollment and completion trends based on the 2010 United States Census. Eight percent of Latin@s completed bachelor's degrees in 2010, compared to the 6% of Latin@s who completed them in 2000, translating to a 2% increase in ten years. Three percent of Latin@s completed doctorates in 2000 compared to 4% in 2010. If this data were disaggregated to account for Chican@s as an isolated category, the 2010 data would likely not reflect a significant increase in completion reflective of enrollment trends.

In "On the Rhetoric and Precedents of Racism," Victor Villanueva cites field-specific numbers concerning Latin@s/Chican@s in rhetoric and composition. Villanueva reports that in 1995, 26 of the 1,373 individuals who earned doctorates in English language and literature were Latin@, which rounds out to 2% (651). In 2010 there were a total of 1,334 doctorates in this discipline with 40 earned by Latin@s, thus representing only 3% of the degrees conferred, so in all, a 1% increase in fifteen years (U.S. Department of Education). As a more representative sample of the demographics specific to rhetoric and composition, Villanueva details the break down of CCCC membership, reporting that in 1999 Latin@s accounted for 1% of all members. As of 2012, Latin@ membership has risen to 2%, reflecting a 1% increase in approximately 10 years (Suchor). If I were to break down any of these statistics further, I am sure that someone like me—a first-generation Chicana, single mother resulting from a teen pregnancy—is an anomaly. Because of the numbers reflecting enrollment of Latin@s that are disproportionate to their success and completion rates, institutions and individual programs urgently need to examine the disconnect preventing entire fields from serving this burgeoning student demographic. The statistics on Latin@ student success and retention, and my own personal experience, reflect the fact that higher education, and particular to this study, rhetoric and composition, are in need of theory, practice, and methods that better serve individuals from underrepresented backgrounds.

A Call for CRT

In "Working with Difference: Critical Race Studies and the Teaching of Composition," Gary A. Olson calls for greater attention in the field of rhetoric and composition on CRT so as to assist writing programs and their instructors to become better prepared, pedagogically and administratively, for underrepresented student populations (209). Olson contends that CRT provides our field with the tools by which to interrogate the effects of racial bias that actively impede success and retention in rhetoric and composition for marginalized students. Despite important contributions from scholars such as Keith Gilyard, Shirley Wilson Logan, and Jacqueline Jones Royster, Latin@s in this field have but two influences significantly referencing a theory on race scholarship concerning Latin@s—Gloria Anzaldúa and Victor Villanueva. Even so, as Olson suggests, "[rhetoric and composition] has witnessed no sustained examination of race, racism, and the effects of both on composition instruction and effective writing program administration" (209). Like Olson, I suggest we turn to CRT, but I extend this argument to focus on methodology, counterstory, in our field's pursuit of actively challenging the status quo with regard to institutionalized prejudices against racial minorities that proliferate in United States institutions of higher education.

Particular to CRT's counterstory, this method of research has potential for producing scholarship and informing pedagogy and mentorship in the field of rhetoric and composition. As an interdisciplinary method, CRT counterstory recognizes that the experiential and embodied knowledge of people of color is legitimate and critical to understanding racism that is often well disguised in the rhetoric of normalized structural values and practices. In this essay, I employ CRT counterstory as a hybrid form of scholarly inquiry and specifically rely on composite counterstorytelling as a writing genre. This form of counterstory differs from fictional storytelling by critically examining theoretical concepts and humanizing empirical data while also deriving material for counterstory's discourse, setting, and characters from sources. These include but are not limited to statistical data, existing literatures, social commentary, and professional/personal experiences concerning the topics addressed. As a writing form and a rhetorical methodology, I argue that counterstory has applications for both scholarly publication and craft in the composition classroom. However, the biggest hurdle to overcome in the present racialized era resides in programmatic and institutional recognition and acceptance of the ideology responsible for structural forms of inequality alive and well in the academy. In an effort to humanize this reality, this essay illustrates, through two tellings, a "stock story" and a counterstory, which serve as tellings of Chican@ experience along the educational pipeline, with a focus on the 0.2% completion rate of Chican@ PhDs. In an effort to provide talking points for our field to engage in pedagogical as well as programmatic planning (including admissions/hiring practices and mentoring), my counterstory contributes a perspective that expands dialogue and understanding as to why this completion rate of doctoral degrees for Chican@s is nearly non-existent.

Richard Delgado and Counterstory versus Stock Story

In his foreword to Richard Delgado's *The Rodrigo Chronicles,* Robert A. Williams, Jr., calls Delgado's stories outsider stories. Williams says these stories "help us imagine the outside in America, a place where some of us have never been and some of us have always been, and where a few of us…shift-shape, like the trickster, asking the hard questions…without answers, questions about what it means to be outside, what it means to be inside, and what it means to be in-between in America" (xii-xiii). Delgado characterizes counterstory as "a kind of counter-reality" created/experienced by "outgroups" subordinate to those atop the racial and gendered hierarchy. While those in power, or as Delgado offers, the "ingroup," craft stock stories to establish a shared sense of identity, reality, and naturalization of their superior position, the "outgroup aims to subvert that ingroup reality" ("Storytelling" 2412-13). Delgado describes stock stories as those that people in dominant positions collectively form and tell about themselves. These stories choose among available facts to present a picture of the world that best fits and supports their positions of relative power ("Storytelling" 2421). Stock stories feign neutrality and at all costs avoid any blame or responsibility for societal inequality. Powerful because they are often repeated until canonized or normalized, those who tell stock stories insist that their version of events is indeed reality, and any stories that counter these standardized tellings are deemed biased, self-interested, and ultimately not credible. Counterstory, then, is a method of telling stories by people whose experiences are not often told. Counterstory as methodology thus serves to expose, analyze, and challenge stock stories of racial privilege and can help to strengthen traditions of social, political, and cultural survival and resistance.

Delgado outlines several generic styles counterstories can take: chronicles, narratives, allegories, parables, and dialogues ("Storytelling" 2438). In this essay I extend his discussion of counterstory by crafting dialogues, with a nod to sophistic argument, that present two tellings of the same event. As a theoretical device, the dialogue is more than familiar in the field of rhetoric and composition and has been most notably employed by Plato to aid philosophical inquiry. Victor Villanueva reminds us that Plato's "writing is significant by virtue of its genre, an attempt at representation of dialogue, of storytelling…not as logocentric discourse but as representation of discourse *in action*" ("*Memoria*" 16; emphasis added). Also, Patricia Bizzell and Bruce Herzberg note the value Plato places on depicting oral exchanges because of their ability to respond "flexibly to *kairos,* the immediate social situation in which solutions to philosophical problems must be proposed" (81). Likewise, Delgado's specific method of placing two dialogues side-by-side provides him the opportunity to develop his ideas through exchanges between characters that represent and voice contending viewpoints on contemporary social issues. The audience is invited to first experience a version of the events from a status quo point of view, which in the case of this article's stock story represents that of the institution. Following the stock story, a counterstory is then presented to develop my marginalized viewpoint and to critique the viewpoint put forth by the stock story while offering alternative possibilities for the audience to consider. I call this method of placing two dialogues concerning the same events side-by-side "stock story versus counterstory."

Beyond the styles of counterstory outlined by Delgado, Tara J. Yosso also explains these styles as generally composed in the autobiographical, biographical, or composite genre (10). For this essay, I compose my counterstories as composite dialogues, and an important feature of composite counterstory is the composite character. Composite characters are written into "social, historical, and political situations that allow the dialogue to speak to the research findings and creatively challenge racism and other forms of subordination" (Yosso 11). Because these characters are written as composites of many individuals, they do not have a one-to-one correspondence to any one individual (Delgado, *The Rodrigo Chronicles* xix). In many cases, and as is the case for this particular stock story versus counterstory, the composite characters are abstractions representing cultural or political ideologies, and could mistakenly be read as overly-stereotyped depictions of certain ideologies and politics. However, in the case of Delgado's work, and mine as well, composite characters in stock stories and counterstories represent more than just a single individual and are intentionally crafted to embody an ideology, such as institutional racism or a Chican@ academic identity. Accordingly, the stock story and counterstory crafted in this essay feature dialogues conducted among composite characters that represent university professor stocktypes, Chican@ students, and parents of underrepresented students.

A Stock Story Discussing a Chicana Graduate Student's Status as Qualified to Proceed in her PhD Program

In the particular graduate program providing the setting for this story, a qualifying exam is conducted to assess students' potential for joining the professional conversation in the field of rhetoric and composition. This exam consists of a meeting between students and the program director during which the director engages in an assessment of each student's record in the program and the writing in her/his portfolio. The materials in the portfolio are meant to provide the director with a detailed sense of the student's analytical and writing skills. Aspects of the student's scholarship in the portfolio are evaluated based on a reflective essay and other academic writing (seminar papers) by the student. These writings indicate whether the student can step back from her/his writing and recognize her/his strengths and weaknesses as a scholarly writer and whether the student has developed a research trajectory indicative of her/his ability to perform graduate level work. In this story's program, the qualifying examination is intended as a mentoring opportunity for the student and program director to have useful conversations about the student's possibilities for writing and research. This particular step in the graduate school process was chosen because it serves a programmatic gatekeeping function for graduate students and can be especially problematic for underrepresented students, like the student discussed next.

The Stock Story

Setting. The program director and two professors are in a department conference room to discuss Alejandra Prieto, a Chicana graduate student who has failed her qualifying exam. In this program, as in others, if a student does not pass the qualifying exam, then a committee of professors will discuss the student, her portfolio, and her ability to continue in the program. The committee in this stock story consists of the program director and two professors, all of whom are white. The program director, D. Mosley, is male, from a middle class background, and tenured. One of the professors, F. Hayden, is male, from a working class background, and untenured, and the third professor, J. Tanner, is female, from an upper-middle class background, and tenured. Alejandra has completed her first full year of the PhD program after entering the program with a BA in sociology. The reasons for the committee's meeting are to discuss the student's failed attempt to pass her qualifying exam and faculty concerns about the student's research interests, writing ability, and an assigned final grade of C in a core program course (Cs in this graduate program constitute a failing grade; two Cs can result in expulsion.)

Mosley: Thank you for finding the time to meet today. I know the beginning of the semester is a busy time for us all, so I'm glad we could all decide on a time at last. Now I know you are unfamiliar with this sort of meeting, but it's official procedure after a student has failed his/her qualifying exam.

Tanner *[teasing]*: Yes, Mosley, I went ahead and double-checked the program handbook to see that this meeting was a legitimate way to proceed, considering we've *never* experienced a student failing her qualifying exam, at least not in the sixteen years I've been program faculty, not to mention the four additional years I served as chair.

Hayden: Well, that's not exactly true; I recall other faculty saying some students have been of questionable qualifying status before, but I hear they usually leave the program before we have to come to this stage of committee discussion.

Mosley: Either way, Alejandra's progress and status in the program have become a concern for those of us in the room today. After reviewing her course schedules for the past two semesters, I see that she's taken all but one of her courses from each of us, all courses in rhetorical theory and one in composition pedagogy with Dr. Burton. Of the four courses she's taken so far, Alejandra's grades are three A's, and one C, which Tanner assigned her. Now I met with Alejandra earlier this week regarding her qualifying exam and let her know concerns had been raised about her performance in class and her writing. I also had specific questions for her about the C she earned in your class, Tanner, to which she did not have an adequate answer. So I guess I'd like to start there with what happened in your class; what's your assessment of this student?

Tanner: Well, to be honest, she's a sweet girl, she really is. You know she even brought some sort of Mexican cake to class one day to share with everyone. Sweet girl. However, as I recall, I raised a major concern about this student when we were in committee meetings about new admits, and it's the same concern I'm raising now: Is this student a good *fit* for this program? You both served on the program admissions committee with me back when we were forming Alejandra's cohort and you both…

Hayden: Yes, Tanner, we remember how you objected to her admission because she would be starting the doctoral program with only a BA in what you deemed an unrelated field. But I also remember that she was one of a very few minority applicants that year, and, as an undergraduate, had impressive experience documented on her CV as a research assistant on nationally funded projects. Plus, with the direction our field needs to go concerning the changing demographics of student and faculty populations, it couldn't hurt to admit a student whose focus is on social issues related to race and education, rather than the mostly literature and creative writing folks we usually get. We need to be more interdisciplinary, you know that.

Tanner: That aside, Hayden, we're a top-five-ranked program, and we demand a lot from our students. Our curriculum is rigorous, and our students need to be the best and the brightest *in our field*, and it does nobody any favors to admit students who can't even tell you who and what the major theorists and journals of our time are!

Mosley: Okay, there's no reason to raise our voices. What we need is to return to the reason for this meeting, Alejandra's status as a student in this program. Talking about whether or not she should have been admitted is pointless because she's here, she's in the program, and we need to move forward and decide whether she should remain or go. Now, when I met with Alejandra for her qualifying exam, she was pretty emotional and not able to coherently discuss her progress in the program to this point. She even asked me outright if we admitted her as some sort of "affirmative action" recruit!

Tanner: [*mumbles something incoherent under her breath*]

Hayden: She didn't really ask that, did she? What did you say?

Mosley: She most certainly did, and I denied it, of course. This program, because of its ranking and rigor, is strictly merit-based, and I told her as much. Curiously she somehow knew she wasn't a first priority admit and was on our second list of admits.

Hayden: Well, I always thought it a bad idea to have grad student reps on admissions committees. They gossip too much, and sometimes damaging information falls into the ears of those never meant to hear it.

Mosley: Yes, well, back to the original question: Tanner, what happened in your class that resulted in this C on Alejandra's record?

Tanner: Right, well, did you ask her?

Mosley: I did, but I'd like to hear your perspective on the issue as well.

Tanner: Well, as I've said, again and again, Alejandra is just not a good fit for this program. She rarely spoke in my class, and the few times she did, her comments always drew the material back to her comfort zone of social oppression, particular to race. I mean sure, race is an issue, but it's all she wants to talk about! And then her writing! Her seminar paper was just not on par with the rest of the students, not in content or quality. She tried, in my opinion unsuccessfully, to tie everything she read and studied in my course back to what I feel are likely recycled papers from sociology courses or projects. That aside, this attempt she makes to fuse her old discipline and ours comes across as awkward, at best, in her prose. It's just not clear writing; there's no focus and no connection or contribution to the field. Plus, she doesn't even use MLA and seemingly makes no attempt to do so. I stand my ground and still contend she is not a good fit for this program. She *earned* that C in my course.

Hayden: Ouch, Tanner, a C may as well be an F in this program, but I hear what you're saying regarding her participation in class. I experienced the same thing in the course she took with me. She rarely ever spoke, which made me begin to question whether or not she read and, more so, if she even comprehended the material. I mean she was practically silent the whole semester.

Mosley: Did she ever miss class?

Tanner and Hayden: No.

Mosley: Yeah, she never missed a day of my course either, but I recall her silence as well. So Tanner, did you ever speak to her regarding your concerns about her classroom performance or her handling of course materials?

Tanner: She knew as well as any other student that I hold an open door policy. I am *always* happy to assist students in any way possible, and I set office hours and appointments with students whenever needed.

Mosley: Yes, I asked her during our meeting whether she ever visited you concerning her progress in your course or if she ever discussed her grade with you. She said she hadn't.

Tanner: No, she didn't, and as I've said, my door is *always* open to students.

Mosley: Well as the handbook states, the official purpose for this meeting is for us to discuss whether the student has made satisfactory progress, maintained a 3.5 grade point average, or had other problems in the program. We need to assess Alejandra's potential for joining the professional conversation in our field, and this is based on her record in the program, her writing in coursework, and her meeting with me as program director. After hearing both of your concerns, I'm pretty sure she shouldn't continue on toward the PhD. I'll be meeting with her again next week for a follow-up to her exam, and she and I will discuss a plan of what she should do next. I'm thinking it'll be in *her* best interest to just take the Master's and go. Are there any last topics either of you would like to discuss?

[*Tanner shakes her head no.*]

Hayden [*tentatively*]: You know, Mosely, I feel as if I'm pointing out the obvious, but I'm surprised this hasn't come up and that you're already considering she not continue in the program; despite Alejandra's C in Tanner's course, she did earn three A's in yours, mine, and Burton's courses. Does this not count as satisfactory progress? And come to think of it, for all the lack of contributions she made to course discussions, she did write really thoughtful, provocative reflection essays each week to the assigned reading in my course, so it was wrong of me to say and assume she didn't read or comprehend course material. And from what I remember, her seminar paper, while rough, was not any worse than those written by other first-years who came in with their BAs and, in fact, wasn't too far off the mark from what some MAs turn in. But Tanner, I think what makes her work…what's the word…difficult? Yes, I think her work is difficult for us to wrap our minds around because it's unconventional, probably by and large due to the fact that she approaches it from a perspective we're not trained in or accustomed to…

Mosley: Yes, Hayden, I hear exactly what you're saying. In fact, she did speak at least once in my course, and it was to ask what the "Eastern canon of rhetoric" is? [*laughing*] Different perspective indeed!

Hayden: So then, maybe it's not that she doesn't show potential for joining the professional conversation in our field, but perhaps it's that she has potential to say things we're uncomfortable with because her research interests are beyond our areas of expertise and her approach is something we've just not experienced before. Potential…I think she has it but just requires a better investment in mentoring—on our part.

Mosley: Tanner?

Tanner [*shrugs*]: I'm just not interested in her work. I don't understand it. And to be perfectly honest, I feel we've all done the most we can to help this student be successful. Her difficulties and failures in this program are hers, not ours. And Hayden, for all the positives you point out, do they in all honesty outweigh this student's shortcomings? Are you seriously suggesting we all, as faculty, shoulder the responsibility of teaching her *how* to be a student, a scholar, and a professional in *our* field. It's a little late in the game for her to play catch up in that regard, and I'm not paid enough to take on this task. You're either ready or not. You're a good fit, or you're not, and from what I've seen, she's not prepared to jump in and be the graduate student our program has such a successful record of bringing to degree and placement. So what does taking on Alejandra's lack of preparedness mean for us? More work. You, Hayden, of all people should be wary of this situation, what with your teaching load and the fact you still have quite a publishing quota to meet before you go up for tenure in a couple years. Do you honestly have the time it's going to take to mentor an underprepared student like Alejandra? Can you truly commit to mentoring this individual and showing her the ropes of this profession while also juggling the responsibilities you have to your own career and to the students who *are* prepared and *truly* need you? A student like Alejandra is unfair to us as professors who are pressed for time as it is. As I've already said, I'm not paid enough to teach someone how to be a student, and even if I were, I just don't have the time, none of us do.

Hayden: I never really looked at it that way…but how about if we…

Mosley [*interrupting*]: Good points Tanner, I believe Hayden and I hear you loud and clear [*winks at Hayden*] [*Hayden shrugs, shakes his head and looks down*], and we share your concerns. There's never quite enough time or money, now is there? [*chuckles*] Okay, I'd like to thank you both for taking the time to meet with me, and I'll take what you both have to say into serious consideration before meeting with Alejandra next week.

A Counterstory in which a Chicana Graduate Student and Her Mother Discuss her Status as Qualified to Proceed in her PhD Program.

Setting. Alejandra has just left the office of D. Mosley, program director, after their follow-up meeting. The meeting consisted of Mosley recounting various talking points from the committee meeting (described in the stock story) and asking for Alejandra's response to the concerns raised by each professor in that meeting. The meeting lasted nearly an hour and resulted in Mosley suggesting that Alejandra consider finishing the program with the MA and perhaps seeking the PhD in another program or field. Tearfully, Alejandra calls her mother to discuss the meeting.

Alejandra: *¿Hola Mami, como estas?*

Mami [*concerned*]: *Bien. ¿Estás llorando mija? ¿Qué paso?* Was it your meeting?

Alejandra [*defeated*]: Yes...

Mami: Why, what happened?

Alejandra: He told me I should just take the Master's and go—

Mami: What?! And go? Go where? *¿Qué te dijo?*

Alejandra: I don't even know if it's worth getting into because he's right. I don't think I'm cut out for this program, maybe not even for grad school, I don't know...

Mami: Bullshit. *No es cierto mija.* You've worked too damn hard to start telling yourself "no" now...

Alejandra: I'm not telling myself "no" Mom; they are.

Mami: You have every right to be in that program, and no *pendejo* has the right to tell you that you can't...

Alejandra: But they're kicking me out.

Mami: Kicking you out? What exactly did he say?

Alejandra: Well, Dr. Mosley met with two of my professors to discuss my "progress and potential" in the program.

Mami: Which professors?

Alejandra: I've only taken four courses so far, and Dr. Burton is in Brazil for the semester, so beside Dr. Mosley, it had to be Dr. Hayden and Dr. Tanner.

Mami: Tanner? That *babosa* who gave you a C?

Alejandra: Yes, her…

Mami: Oh great.

Alejandra: So anyway, he said they all talked about my work in the program, and he told me they all "really like me as a person," and mentioned that Dr. Tanner had said how sweet I was because I brought Mexican cake to class one day to share with everyone…

Mami: That's nice *mija*, you did that?

Alejandra: No, I didn't; it was left-over cornbread from a barbeque place I went to the night before. And you raised me not to waste food, so I brought it in to share rather than throw it away.

Mami: What?! And because you're Mexican she assumes it's "Mexican cake"? Didn't you tell me once she's from the South? How can she not recognize cornbread when she sees it?

Alejandra: I don't know *Mami*; I think Dr. Mosley was just trying to give me a compliment before dropping the bomb.

Mami: Okay, so besides the cake, what else did he have to say?

Alejandra: He said each professor had specific concerns about my writing, my research interests, my classroom participation, and my overall "fit" for the program.

Mami: "Fit," what do they mean by that?

Alejandra: I don't know. Dr. Mosley's concerns about my research interests were really confusing. First, he asked how I think the fields of sociology and rhetoric and composition are related, but before he let me answer, he asked, "Do you really think the discussion of 'race' *still* has a place in this field?" Which I guess was his way of saying this field has already discussed race?

Mami: And so by "fit," is he saying your research interests in "race" aren't a fit for this field?

Alejandra: I don't know, but if you remember, one of the most racist things that ever happened to me was in Dr. Mosley's class.

Mami: *¿Qué?* Refresh my memory…

Alejandra: He gave us a list of fifteen theorists from this book called *The Rhetorical Tradition,* for the fifteen of us in the class to choose from and present to the rest of the class on their major contributions to our field. I don't know if people of color gravitate toward likeness, but the two of us in Dr. Mosley's class (me and this guy from St. Lucia) sat in the back corner, and by the time the list got to us, we looked at who was left and then both looked at each other with ironic grins. Guess who was left for us "colored" folks to choose from?

Mami: Who?

Alejandra: Frederick Douglass and Gloria Anzaldúa. You know who Douglass is right?

Mami: *Sí,* the black abolitionist, but I've never heard of Anzaldúa. *¿Es Mexicana?*

Alejandra: *Tejana,* and she identifies as Chicana, but isn't that crazy?

Mami: I know you're brown and got the *Tejana,* so does that mean the person who got Douglass is black?

Alejandra: Yep, Chev looks like what we'd classify as "black," but he's not African American. He's from the Caribbean, and me, well, I'm definitely not *Tejana,* and I've never called myself Chicana…

Mami: Right, you're Mexican. Your dad's Mexican, I'm Mexican, so you're Mexican.

Alejandra: Well, so I thought, but funny enough it was Dr. Mosley who called me "Chicana" today during our meeting. He said, "with your working class Chicana identity, you should have a wealth of cultural experiences to share and write about."

Mami: Why did he assume you're working class? If brown, then poor?

Alejandra: I know Mom; that's my point—it's all about assumptions in this program. No one bothers to ask me anything; they all just assume to know things about me, and it's like they all speak above me or around me, like I'm not here, as if it's easier for them to ignore me, unless I'm "sharing my wealth of cultural experiences"…

Mami: Like the Mexican cake?

Alejandra [*chuckles*]: Yeah. Exactly.

Mami: So let me get this straight: Mosley doesn't want you to talk about race as it relates to his classroom or the field, but instead prefers that you talk about your culture? What's wrong with this picture? Only talk about race if it has to do with happy topics like *tamales, mariachi,* and *folklórico*? *No cambian las cosas.*

Alejandra: I feel like my presence makes the professors and students uncomfortable.

Mami: Okay, so I can see *they* don't understand the "fit" of your research interests, but what was all this *cagada* about your participation being a concern?

Alejandra: Oh that. Dr. Mosley said the faculty is worried because I never speak up in class.

Mami: You don't speak in class?

Alejandra: No, not really, but here's why: in Dr. Tanner's course, for example, I genuinely tried to engage the material because I really identified with the gender and socioeconomic class issues brought up by the theorists she had us read, but when I would ask in class why race wasn't part of the discussion, since I know race, class, and gender are so interconnected in this country, Tanner would shut me down, every time. She'd say things like "well that's not really rhet/comp material you're referring to," when I'd cite sociologists who discussed the same issues but with race as a focus. I felt unwelcome in her class, like the knowledge I brought with me, from sociology and from my personal perspective concerning race, was always automatically dismissed, because, according to her, I wasn't really using a rhet/comp perspective.

Mami: So you didn't feel like you could make a contribution to the conversation? But I thought they brought you into the program because of your sociology background, because it was—what was the word?

Alejandra: Interdisciplinary. Right, that's what I was told too, but now Dr. Mosley's saying they're unsure if I'm a good "fit." And maybe I'm not a good fit. In Tanner's class I just felt defeated. So silence became my refuge; it seemed like my only immediate option for survival.

Mami: Mija, I'm sorry, that sounds terrible, I had no idea...

Alejandra: It's alright, *Mami*. But what I guess I don't understand about the students I'm in class with is this constant chatter they engage in—and that, according to Dr. Mosley, they're expected to engage in. But it happens in every class I take, so I guess I understand the professors' concern that I don't speak, but Dr. Mosley actually asked if my silence was due to the fact that maybe I had trouble comprehending the material?

Mami: What?! What a terrible assumption to make!

Alejandra: *Mami*, to them silence equals lack of comprehension. And it wasn't that I didn't "get it"; I just wasn't prepared to contribute to half of the discussions taking place because I'm new to the field. I'm still learning. And the few times I did speak, I was either shut down or given strange looks as if I said something disturbing. So I decided silence would be my best strategy for the time being. It's as if there's some cultural standard in grad school that I don't understand and am completely out of place in.

Mami: It sounds more like a foreign country than just school, but what I don't fully understand yet is how you got to the point in the conversation where Mosley said you should take the Master's degree and go.

Alejandra: Oh right, well, he brought up the C in Dr. Tanner's course and said Dr. Tanner claimed I never spoke to her about it and never sought her out during the semester for help in the course. But I basically told Dr. Mosley I'm terrified of Dr. Tanner, that she was so hostile, unwelcoming, and discrediting toward me in her class that the last thing I wanted to do was put myself in a vulnerable position like office hours with her, especially after the heinous grade she assigned me. *Mami*, a C in this program is pretty much an F, and an F-U, for that matter. I hope never to work with her again and will avoid her at all costs.

Mami: So what did Mosley have to say about that?

Alejandra: Well, Mosley didn't like that I haven't attempted to resolve this grade issue with Dr. Tanner and pretty much concluded the meeting with his recommendation that I finish the Master's and perhaps look into other programs for doctoral work.

Mami: And how do you feel about his recommendation? I've noticed you're not crying anymore…

Alejandra: Well, to be honest *Mami*, now that I've had the opportunity to talk about it, I don't feel sad anymore. I'm kinda pissed. It makes me mad that these professors would rather be rid of me than face working with a student who is unconventional and is then what? Scary? Threatening? A waste of time? What is it they dislike about me?

Mami: It's not that they dislike you; they don't *get* you.

Alejandra: And I guess that would make sense; it's not like there are any other Latina/os or Chicana/os in the program, not as students or faculty, so their discomfort has to be about more than just the fact that I come from another field. I think it's because I'm the first Latina/Chicana/Mexicana they've ever had in their program, and they don't know what to do with me.

Mami: Yes, as if accepting you into their program was all the work they needed to do to diversify. But what about making sure you succeed? No, apparently your success is not their problem and helping you succeed is definitely not what they're prepared to do.

Alejandra: I'm not gonna let them tell me "no." I'm going back to Dr. Mosley's office tomorrow for another meeting. We need to discuss what it's going to take for me to succeed in this program. I'm going to talk about race, I'm going to be interdisciplinary, and I'm going to make these people *see* me.

Mami: Good *mija*, that's what you need to do—get mad and get to work. Call me tomorrow to let me know how it goes; I've got to hang up and get *cena* going…

Alejandra: Mmmm, what are you making?

Mami: *Pues*, "Mexican cake," of course!

A Plea for Narrative: A Place for Counterstory in Rhet/Comp

When commenting on the conventions of academic discourse, Victor Villanueva notes the strength of *logos* but the pronounced weakness of *pathos* in academic exchanges ("*Memoria*"). This leaning toward logic and reason to best communicate "serious" thought, and the pitting of logic against the assumed unreliability and volatility of emotion reaches far back into Aristotle's original suspicions that a too-heavy reliance on *pathos* leads the audience away from truth—the kind verifiable by facts and "proof." But as Villanueva argues, the personal, too often tied to emotions beyond logic and reason, "does not negate the need for the academic; it complements, provides an essential element on the rhetorical triangle, an essential element in the intellect—cognition *and* affect" ("*Memoria*" 13-14; emphasis in original). For people of color, the personal as related through narrative provides space and opportunity to assert *our* stories within, and in many instances counter to, the hegemonic narratives of the institution.

Solórzano and Yosso characterize these hegemonic narratives as "majoritarian" stories that emerge from a legacy of racial privilege and naturalize racial privilege (27). These stories privilege whites, men, the middle and/or upper class, and heterosexuals by naming these social locations as natural or normative points of reference. A majoritarian story distorts and silences the experiences of people of color and others distanced from the norms such stories reproduce. A standard majoritarian methodology relies on stock stereotypes that covertly and overtly link people of color, women of color, and poverty with "bad," while emphasizing that white, middle and/or upper class people embody all that is "good" (Solórzano and Yosso 29).

Narratives counter to these majoritarian or stock stories, then, provide people of color the opportunity to validate, resonate, and awaken to the realization that we "haven't become clinically paranoid" in our observations and experiences of racism and discrimination within the institution (Villanueva, "*Memoria*" 15). In fact, as Villanueva points out, it is almost shocking to realize in the academic institution, where the sheer numbers of people of color are as exceptional as they are, how "our experiences are in no sense unique but are always analogous to other experiences from among those exceptions" ("*Memoria*" 15). What's more, as these experiences are narrated through spoken and increasingly written and published work, people of color come to realize not much by way of diversity and inclusiveness in the institution has changed. Thus, my work in narrative counterstory within this essay is inspired by narratives specific to rhetoric and composition, such as Anzaldúa's *Borderland/La Frontera*, Villanueva's *Bootstraps*, Gilyard's *Voices of the Self*, Vershawn Ashanti Young's *Your Average Nigga*, and Frankie Condon's *I Hope I Join the Band*. Each of these scholars uses a narrative voice to relate racialized experiences, and as a necessary function of counterstory, these narratives serve the purpose of exposing stereotypes, expressing arguments against injustice, and offering additional truths through narrating authors' lived experiences. My work extends this narrative trend already in use in rhetoric and composition by crafting counterstory, but deviates from more familiar forms of autobiographical or biographical narrative through using a composite approach to the formation of these narratives, an approach most notably employed by critical race theorists Derrick Bell, Richard Delgado, and Tara J. Yosso, and constitutes the methodological basis for my greater body of work (Martinez "Critical Race").

As noted in my reference above to Condon's work, whites can and do tell counterstories, and people of color in contrast, can and do tell majoritarian stories (Bonilla-Silva 151; Martinez, "The American Way" 586). The keepers and tellers of either majoritarian (stock) stories or counterstories reveal the social location of the storyteller as dominant or non-dominant, and these locations are always racialized, classed, and gendered. For example, Ward Connerly is African-American, from a working class background, male, and a prominent politician and academic. From his racialized position, Connerly is a minority, but speaks and represents himself from dominant gendered and classed locations. From the position of an upper class male, Connerly crafts stock stories to argue against affirmative action and to deny racial inequities. Alternatively, Condon's work narrativizes embodied whiteness and individual responsibility as a white ally. Although Condon is white, she is also a woman who speaks from a non-dominant social location, while as a white ally, she uses her dominant racialized location to craft critical race narratives that disrupt "discourses of transcendence" often responsible for leading audiences of white anti-racists to believe they are somehow "absolved from the responsibility of doing whiteness" (13).

Condon makes an especially powerful case for the necessity of narrative by stating, "We need to learn to read, to engage with one another's stories, not as voyeurs but as players, in a dramatic sense, within them, and as actors who may be changed not only by the telling of our own stories, but also by the practices of listening, attending, acknowledging, and honoring the stories of our students and colleagues of color as well" (32). In my crafted dialogues above, I take up Condon's call to write and invite audiences into a dramatic engagement with these dialogues in hopes that through the detailing of the stock story versus counterstory, my audience will locate their own subjective identities within the characters and thematic focuses of the text. Although I write the above narratives to commune with an audience of people of color whom I assume will identify with and have academic experiences similar to those of Alejandra, this audience in not my primary target. My primary audience is the audience Condon herself identifies as the more difficult to persuade: "academics…who hope to join in the work of antiracism [who] need to stop minimizing the complexity and significance of narrative, stop depoliticizing the personal, and start studying the rich epistemological and rhetorical traditions that inform the narratives of people of color" (33).

Thus, I position my work in counterstory within social scientific interests with an active Humanities perspective, maintaining three main objectives: First, raise awareness of issues affecting the access, retention, and success of Latin@s in higher education, particularly in rhetoric and composition. Second, I hope this work will motivate discussion of strategies that more effectively serve students from non-traditional backgrounds in various spaces and practices, such as the composition classroom, mentoring, and graduate programmatic requirements so as to *achieve* access, retention, and success. And third, I offer this demonstration of stock story versus counterstory as a guide for counterstory not previously theorized by CRT, but which I believe will resonate with scholars in rhetoric and composition who are familiar with narrative forms spanning from Plato to contemporary scholars, and who seek options and variety in narrative forms to employ in the composition classroom and to publish work about these important issues.

As a narrative form, counterstory functions as a method for marginalized people to intervene in research methods that would form master narratives based on ignorance and on assumptions about minoritized peoples like Chican@s. Through the formation of counterstories or those stories that document the persistence of racism and other forms of subordination told "from the perspectives of those injured and victimized by its legacy" (Yosso 10), voices from the margins become the voices of authority in the researching and relating of our own experiences. Counterstory serves as a natural extension of inquiry for theorists whose research recognizes and incorporates lived and embodied experiences of people of color (Solórzano and Delgado Bernal 314). It is thus crucial to use a narrative methodology that counters other methods that seek to dismiss or decenter racism and those whose lives are affected daily by it. I have used personal stories as counterstory throughout this work to raise awareness about ongoing and historic social and racial injustices in the academy, combining reflection on lived experiences with literature and statistics (Yosso 10). This essay in counterstory suggests a method by which to incorporate CRT in rhetoric and composition, contributing to ongoing conversations in the field about narrative, dominant ideology, and their intersecting influence on programmatic and curricular standards and practices. I offer this essay as an argument for using narrative in our field, and as an invitation to those who would continue the story.

Acknowledgments

I want to thank Jaime Armin Mejía, Cruz Medina, Adela C. Licona, and the Smitherman/Villanueva Writing Collective for providing feedback and encouragement with this essay through its very many various stages and drafts. I want especially to thank my mother, Ana Patricia Martinez, who took the time to sit with me and co-craft the Mami-Alejandra dialogue. The voices of the mother-daughter exchange would not/could not be genuine without my mother's touch.

Notes

1. @: Sandra K. Soto states that her use of the "@" ending in Chican@ "signals a conscientious departure from the certainty, mastery, and wholeness, while still announcing a politicized collectivity" (2). This "@" keystroke serves as an expression of the author's "certain fatigue with the clunky post-1980s gender inclusive formula-

tions" of the word and announces a "politicized identity embraced by man or woman of Mexican descent who lives in the United States and who wants to forge connection to a collective identity politics" (2). It also serves to unsettle not only the gender binary but also the categories that constitute it.

2. Chican@ and Chicana/o are used in my work synonymously with Mexican-American. These terms are used in my work to refer to women and men of Mexican descent or heritage who live in the United States. According to Yosso, "Chican@ is a political term, referring to a people whose indigenous roots to North America and Mexico date back centuries" (16). Also see Acuña for more on the history and origins of this term.

Works Cited

Acuña, Rudolfo F. *Occupied America: A History of Chicanos*. 7th ed. New York: Pearson Longman, 2010. Print.

Anzaldúa, Gloria. *Borderlands/La Frontera: The New Mestiza*. 3rd ed. San Francisco: Aunt Lute, 2007. Print.

Bell, Derrick. *And We Are Not Saved: The Elusive Quest for Racial Justice*. New York: Basic Books, 1987. Print.

---. *Faces at the Bottom of the Well*. New York: Basic Books, 1992. Print.

Bizzell, Patricia, and Bruce Herzberg. *The Rhetorical Tradition: Readings from Classical Times to the Present*. 2nd ed. New York: Bedford/St. Martin's, 2001. Print.

Bonilla-Silva, Eduardo. *Racism without Racists: Color-Blind Racism and the Persistence of Racial Inequality in the United States*. 2nd ed. Boulder: Rowman & Littlefield, 2006. Print.

Condon, Frankie. *I Hope I Join the Band: Narrative, Affiliation, and Antiracist Rhetoric*. Logan: Utah State UP, 2012. Print.

Connerly, Ward. *Creating Equal*. San Francisco: Encounter Books, 2000. Print.

Delgado Bernal, Dolores, and Octavio Villalpando. "An Apartheid of Knowledge in Academia: The Struggle over the 'Legitimate' Knowledge of Faculty of Color." *Equity and Excellence in Education* 35.2 (2002): 165-80. Print.

Delgado, Richard. *The Rodrigo Chronicles: Conversations about America and Race*. New York: New York UP, 1995. Print.

---. "Storytelling for Oppositionists and Others: A Plea for Narrative." *Michigan Law Review* 87.8 (1989): 2411-41. Print.

Ennis, Sharon R., Merarys Ríos-Vargas, and Nora G. Albert. "The Hispanic Population: 2010." U.S. Department of Commerce: Economics and Statistics Administration, U.S. Census Bureau, May 2011. Web. 19 Dec. 2011. <http://www.census. gov/prod/cen 2010/ briefs / c2010br-04.pdf>.

Gilyard, Keith. *Voices of the Self: A Study of Language Competence*. Detroit: Wayne State UP, 1991. Print.

Logan, Shirley Wilson. *"We Are Coming": The Persuasive Discourse of Nineteenth-Century Black Women*. Carbondale: SIUP, 1999. Print.

Martinez, Aja Y. "'The American Way': Resisting the Empire of Force and Color-Blind Racism." *College English* 71.6 (2009): 584-95. Print.

---. "Critical Race Theory Counterstory as Allegory: A Rhetorical Trope to Raise Awareness About Arizona's Ban on Ethnic Studies." *Across the Disciplines* Fall (2013). Web. 12 Nov. 2013. <http://wac.colostate.edu/atd/race/martinez.cfm>.
Olson, Gary A. "Working with Difference: Critical Race Studies and the Teaching of Composition." *Composition Studies in the New Millennium: Rereading the Past, Rewriting the Future*. Eds. Lynn Z. Bloom, Donald A. Daiker, Edward M. White. Carbondale: SIUP, 2003. 208-21. Print.
Royster, Jacqueline Jones. *Traces of a Stream: Literacy and Social Change Among African American Women*. Pittsburgh: U of Pittsburgh P, 2000. Print.
Solórzano, Daniel, and Dolores Delgado Bernal. "Examining Transformational Resistance Through Critical Race and LatCrit Theory Framework: Chicana and Chicano Students in an Urban Context." *Urban Education* 36.3 (2001): 308-42. Print.
Solórzano, Daniel, and Tara J. Yosso. "Critical Race Methodology: Counter-Storytelling as an Analytical Framework for Education Research." *Qualitative Inquiry* 8.1 (2002): 23-44. Print.
Soto, Sandra K. *Reading Chican@ Like a Queer: The De-Mastery of Desire*. Austin: U of Texas P, 2010. Print.
Suchor, Kristen. "FW: CCCC Demographics." Message to author. 14 Dec. 2011. E-mail. U.S. Department of Education, National Center for Educational Statistics. Integrated Postsecondary Education Data System. "Completions Survey." Washington: US Department of Education. 2010.
Villanueva, Victor. *Bootstraps: From an Academic of Color*. Urbana: NCTE, 1993. Print.
---. "*Memoria* Is a Friend of Ours: On the Discourse of Color." *College English* 67.1 (2004): 9-19. Print.
---. "On the Rhetoric and Precedents of Racism." *CCC* 50.4 (1999): 645-61. Print.
Williams, Robert A., Jr. "Forward." *The Rodrigo Chronicles: Conversations about America and Race*. New York: NYU P, 1995. Print.
Yosso, Tara J. *Critical Race Counterstories Along the Chicana/Chicano Educational Pipeline*. New York: Routledge, 2006. Print.
Yosso, Tara J., and Daniel G. Solórzano. "The Chicana and Chicano Educational Pipeline." *CSRC Policy and Issues Brief* 13 (2006): 1-4. Print.
Young, Vershawn Ashanti. *Your Average Nigga: Performing Race, Literacy, and Masculinity*. Detroit: Wayne State UP, 2007. Print.

Geneva Smitherman: Translingualist, Code-Mesher, Activist

Russel K. Durst

This article examines the work of Geneva Smitherman, its contribution to the development of composition studies, and its relation to recent scholarship on translingualism and code-meshing. Analyzing her prodigious output in relation to these contemporary studies of language diversity and writing instruction, the article considers Smitherman's achievements in three areas: the study of African American English, composition pedagogy, and political activism on behalf of language minority students.

In her 2000 book *Talkin That Talk: Language, Culture, and Education in African America*, Geneva Smitherman cites a list of so-called "speech demons" that a mayor of New York and his chancellor of public schools waged a public campaign to eradicate in the late 1980s. The list included such locutions as "He be sick" and "May I axe a question?" (152). Some African American students in college classes that I teach use nonstandard forms to varying degrees in their own speech and writing. Over the years, I have wrestled with the issue of standard versus nonstandard usage in school and workplace, wondering just how important it is to use Standard English and why. On the one hand, my studies in linguistics make it clear that African American English is a bona fide language form with its own grammar, phonology, and lexicon, and I can understand these students whether they use standard forms or not. On the other hand, I know that some people in a position to make decisions about the students' advancement might view their dialect use more negatively, and I need to prepare students for that possibility.

Questions of standard versus nonstandard language use are currently under discussion in composition studies. Min Zhan Lu and Bruce Horner propose a framework that would replace *monolingualism*, the view that language is "discrete, stable, internally uniform" and that American students should use Standard English exclusively (583), with *translingualism*, "a disposition of openness and inquiry toward language and language differences" that encourages study and strategic use of linguistic variation (585). Translingualism "recognizes difference not as deviation from a norm of 'sameness' but as itself the norm of language use" (584). In a 2011 essay, Horner, Lu, Jacqueline Jones Royster, and John Trimbur call for a translingual paradigm that "encourages . . . respect for perceived differences within and across languages" and "acknowledges that deviations from dominant expectations need not be errors; that conformity need not be automatically advisable" (304). Working within this framework in an empirical study of a college class that employed a translingual pedagogy, Suresh Canagarajah found that multilingual and monolingual students productively negotiated meaning as writers and readers across language varieties. A related strand of scholarship examines code-meshing, in which multilinguals mix nonstandard and standard forms to create hybrid texts. Vershawn Young discusses and illustrates the meshing of African American and Standard English in his own discourse and that of others. A 2011 collection by Young and Aja Martinez explores meshing of standard forms with dialects of the southern United States, Spanish, Hawaiian Creole, and international versions of English. In addition to elucidating language practices, these new studies, in the words of Lu and Horner, aim to counter "the continuing denigration of subordinated groups through attacks on their language" (583).

Cited as an influence in the literature of translingualism and code-meshing, but not discussed in detail, is the work of Geneva Smitherman. In Keith Gilyard's words, while Smitherman is known primarily for her "immense and profound" contribution to the study of African American English and language diversity in education and in society more broadly, "rhetorical considerations are at least as important as linguistic ones in order to best understand her overall research program and her impact" (161). Beginning in the early 1970s and focusing primarily on the language of African Americans, Smitherman articulated many of the key ideas embodied in the above approaches: urging full acceptance of minority dialects of English, advocating closer attention to language diversity in education, calling for the mixing of Standard and Nonstandard English, and combining in her own writing different codes in rhetorically effective ways. While best known for her research, writing, leadership, and community work on the language and education of African Americans, Smitherman also played a critical role in the development of composition studies, and her ideas and efforts continue to influence the field. She has been a leading explicator of African American English, detailing not only its distinctive vocabulary and grammar but also its discourse structures. She has been a major force in helping define views on questions of standard versus nonstandard language forms. And, she has helped complicate the field's understanding about what makes a text effective, going beyond a focus on surface correctness and "proper form" to consider rhetorical and stylistic elements.

In light of the current focus on language and dialect issues in composition studies and ongoing concerns about fairness for speakers and writers of other variants of English, this essay reexamines Smitherman's work, its contribution to composition studies, and its relation to scholarship on translingualism and code-meshing. Through the lens of these contemporary studies, I discuss

Smitherman's innovative work in three areas: research on African American English, composition pedagogy, and political activism. I argue that, although writing several decades earlier, Smitherman anticipated many of the most important insights of translingualism and code-meshing. In addition, I suggest that what most sets her work apart from today's approaches is its public dimension. While her research and pedagogy have contributed substantially to composition studies, Smitherman never limited herself to academic audiences. She moved beyond scholarly publication and presentation in her efforts as an activist in courtrooms, political debates, education policy making at all levels, and national consideration of the language and schooling of African American and other minority students. I conclude by arguing that the current work on language in composition, while admirably seeking to understand minority language users and find ways to help them, would benefit significantly from a more public, activist dimension along the lines that Smitherman pursued, going beyond the academy, in order to have greater impact.

Smitherman as Academic

Now retired, Smitherman has for decades been an active and influential scholar with widely ranging research. She examined African American English in considerable depth, presenting her work for both scholarly and lay audiences. In addition to numerous articles and book chapters, she published several single-authored books with major presses that provide among the most detailed discussions of the lexicon, grammar, semantics, sounds, and functions of African American English. Two books, *Black Language and Culture: The Sounds of Soul,* published by Harper in 1975, and *Talkin and Testifyin: The Language of Black America*, published in 1977 by Houghton Mifflin, not only brought Smitherman herself to public attention throughout the country, but also resulted in greatly enhanced visibility for her area of expertise. In the immediate aftermath of the civil rights movement, the inner-city upheaval following the assassination of Martin Luther King, Jr., the Vietnam War protests of the 1960s and early 1970s, and the era of student unrest, the exigencies of life for African Americans, including their language, became a subject of intense public scrutiny throughout the nation as never before. During this time period, due in part to public protests and other efforts to gain legitimacy in society, the field of Afro-American studies came into existence. Scholars throughout humanities and social science disciplines were exploring all aspects of black life, and for the first time with institutional support as well as an interest that extended beyond university campuses. Smitherman's work is best understood as part of this broader outpouring of intellectual inquiry itself made possible by the political activity of many. With rigorous preparation, a willingness to confront entrenched attitudes, a sense of style and humor, an astute understanding of what would appeal to her readership, and impeccable timing, Smitherman labored for the better part of a decade to produce detailed, thorough works of scholarship on what was then generally called Black English. Yet by design she also produced books accessible to a much wider public.

Part of Smitherman's standing as a scholar of African American English rests in the fact that she was the first African American to study and publish prominently on the dialect. In addition, she was among the first authors to publish on the topic with a larger public audience in mind. However, the language of African Americans had received serious study from white scholars since at least the mid-twentieth century. Linguist and folklorist Melville Herskovits in 1941 published a sympathetic and perceptive study of black American culture, including language analysis, entitled *Myth of the Negro Past*. Sociolinguist William Labov published a book in 1972 called *Language in the Inner City*, which devoted considerable space to an examination of the structures and functions of African American English. That same year, the scholar of American dialects, J. L. Dillard, came out with a book entitled *Black English: Its History and Usage in the United States*, which comprised a brief discussion of the dialect's development.

These works offer a range of scholarly perspectives on black dialect. Along with the many scholarly articles these authors produced, they shed light on the language of African Americans and take it seriously as a legitimate, rule-governed, culturally appropriate dialect spoken by millions across the country. However, such had not always been the case, for the history of work in this area is mired in racism and the perpetuation of negative stereotypes about African Americans. As Smitherman herself discovered in her research and wrote about in an essay entitled "Discriminatory Discourse on Afro American Speech," up to the mid-twentieth century writing about the language of African Americans in the United States, invariably produced by white authors, presents members of this ethnic group as ignorant, unintelligent, and incapable of complex or systematic language use. Operating from a view of culture as biologically determined, with people of African origin occupying the lowest position in terms of human development, they present African American English as closer to child language or animal communication than to the language of more evolved people of European or Asian ancestry. For example, she cites southerner and amateur linguist J. A. Harrison's 1884 article, "Negro English," in which the author asserts, "The humor and naivete of the Negro are features which must not be overlooked in gauging his intellectual caliber and timbre; much of his talk is baby talk . . . the slang which is an ingrained part of his being as deep-dyed as his skin" (234).

Such overt racism was barely evident in mainstream scholarship by the mid-twentieth century, particularly after African American linguist Lorenzo Dow Turner (1949) presented a powerful case linking Gullah, a dialect spoken on islands off the coast of Georgia and South Carolina, to West African languages and offered evidence of other such links to African languages among black Americans more broadly. However, vestiges of racism remained in even some of the most respectable social science inquiry well into the twentieth century. For instance, prominent psychologists and sociologists in the 1960s popularized the concepts of "verbal deprivation" and "linguistic impoverishment," creating a deficit theory to explain low school achievement. Such studies were used to justify the creation of Head Start and other programs benefiting African American and other low-income children. In "Discriminatory Discourse," Smitherman quotes Carl Bereiter, a leading educator, social scientist, and policy maker during the 1960s, who questioned the ability of many young African American students to use language "as a tool of thought" (202). Given this legacy, it is especially important to emphasize that Smitherman was the first African American to publish major books intended for not only a scholarly but also a lay audience, in her effort to replace these pejorative views with analysis and documentation that revealed African American English in all its complexity and sophistication.

Talkin and Testifyin: The Language of Black America became both a critical and commercial success in 1977. The book is written in a lively and informal manner, with regular doses of humor, succinct explanations, and examples of language forms drawn in many cases from the author's own primary research and life experience, as well as from popular fiction, journalism, memoir, poetry, theatre, and song. Smitherman employs her African American dialect strategically throughout the book, particularly at the end of paragraphs and longer units when she wishes to hammer home an important point, further exemplifying the nature, intelligibility, and appropriateness of African American English even in a nationally published book directed at a wide audience of educated readers. Moreover, she does not shy away from consideration of the many, often colorful uses obscene terms can play in discourse.

The book appeared at a time when most linguists showed a marked reluctance to move beyond questions of sound, word, phrase, and syntax, the traditional core areas of linguistics and the primary foci of the dominant Chomskyan approaches, in their language analysis. Smitherman accordingly provides several chapters of discussion on these core areas of linguistics early in her text. She details prominent structural rules of African American English, such as final consonant deletion ("test" becomes "tes"), the initial "th" sound becoming "d" ("this" becomes "dis"), deletion of the linking verb ("He big."), and other more obscure patterns. Yet at the same time, she goes well beyond the sentence in her analysis and devotes a great deal of her discussion to such larger topics as history; global aspects of discourse; and the social, political, and educational contexts surrounding language use. She analyzes characteristic everyday verbal performances of African Americans such as playing the dozens, styling, and signifying, showing how varied, sophisticated, complex, and adaptable the dialect is.

Many of the findings from Smitherman's scholarship, as well as the conclusions she draws from them, have found a place in current work on translingualism and code meshing. She did not develop a language theory that casts doubt on the idea of a standard form, as in translingualism, nor study specific classroom approaches that encourage blending of Standard and Nonstandard English, as in code-meshing, but in other ways her work aligns closely with recent studies. For instance, like Horner, Lu, Jones Royster, and Trimbur, she casts doubt on the notion that Standard English is applicable in all situations, including formal, professional settings, and she illustrates this point not only through incorporating both standard and nonstandard forms in her own published prose, but through examples drawn from other writers such as Langston Hughes. She also demonstrates, as do Lu and Horner, that usages departing from Standard English are not necessarily errors and can even be more rhetorically effective than can more standard usage, depending on both content and context. And Smitherman was also the first scholar to show that distinct language forms, such as African American and Standard English, can be blended together in rhetorically effective ways in a single text. Smitherman asserted these ideas long in advance of the more recent discussions; current scholars have employed them as foundational concepts in translingualism and code-meshing.

Smitherman as Composition Specialist

Most germane to a consideration of Smitherman's contribution to the field of composition studies is the final chapter of her 1977 book *Talkin and Testifyin*, entitled "Where Do We Go from Here? TCB! Social Policy and Educational Practice." In an effort to "take care of business," she argues that African American English is a legitimate language form with a distinguished history, a systematic grammar, lexicon, and sound system, and a wide range of functions; that white Americans often assume wrongly that speakers of African American English are stupid; and that the dialect should be accepted as such in the United States, just as New England or Southern dialects generally are. Finally, she puts forward the view, quite radical for the mid-1970s, that educators are often far too quick to condemn students who use African American English and consign them to failure, when they could achieve better results by focusing less on surface features of form and more on the strengths of the points students are making. To understand how unusual this view was in 1977, consider that Mina Shaughnessy's *Errors and Expectations*, published the same year and heralded at the time for its progressive approach to instruction for minority writers, is striking today for its strong emphasis on the teaching of Standard English.

To support her assertions, Smitherman gives examples provided by the linguist William Labov comparing a perceptive argument by a teenaged speaker of African American English to a rambling, vague, and self-contradictory statement by an educated, middle-class, middle-aged speaker of Standard English to support the view that insightful points, intelligible to mainstream Americans, can indeed be made in the dialect. But Smitherman's most effective illustration of skillful use of African American English throughout the book is her own language. She regularly deploys incisive, pithy statements in dialect to make her most important points, and in no case is her meaning obscured. Indeed, this moving back and forth between African American and Standard English is very effective rhetorically, both in helping her support her overarching argument and in allowing her to write an informative, entertaining, and stylish text. Her typical strategy is to write a paragraph using Standard English but then to finish the paragraph with a rhetorical and stylistic flourish, stating an emphatic comment in African American dialect. For example, on the very first page of *Talkin and Testifyin*, she writes,

> Before about 1959 (when the first study was done to change black speech patterns), Black English had been primarily the interest of university academics, particularly the historical linguists and cultural anthropologists. In recent years, though, the issue has become a very hot controversy, and there have been articles on Black Dialect in the national press as well as in the educational research literature. We have had pronouncements on black speech from the NAACP and the Black Panthers, from highly publicized scholars of the Arthur Jensen–William Shockley bent, from executives of national corporations such as Greyhound, and from housewives and community folk. I mean, really, it seem like everybody and they momma done had something to say on the subject! (1)

In moving her argument to the area of education, she provides an example of a short, badly written essay by an African American college student about the legitimacy of the Vietnam War, an essay that makes an assertion without backing it up, a very familiar problem in the writing of first year college students in general, not just those speakers of nonstandard dialects. Yet the student's teacher responded to the essay only with the comment, "Correct your grammar and resubmit." Smitherman incisively points out that "the problem with such writing instruction is that it fails to deal with the basic problems of most student writers, be they black or white. Namely, weaknesses in organization, content, logic, coherence, use of supporting details, and communicative power" (213). This is her larger point: educators are essentially wasting their time and holding students back by focusing inordinately upon surface features and "proper" form, when they could be helping students much more to develop intellectually and linguistically by centering instruction on more fundamental features of student writing and thinking, such as those she mentions in the above quote. She asserts that African American students will, over time, learn standard forms through practice and exposure, but as they are learning, they should be permitted, even encouraged, to use their home dialect. She is by no means arguing here that Standard English should not be taught, and nowhere states that view in the book. Rather, she simply believes formal correctness is often overemphasized, particularly in the education of low-income minority children, those already most at risk for academic problems. Her thinking here corresponds to and supports that of such emerging composition specialists of Smitherman's era as Peter Elbow and Janet Emig, who inveighed against the near-obsessive sentence level emphasis of too many composition instructors. Emig, for example, in her landmark 1971 monograph on secondary students' composing processes, *The Composing Processes of Twelfth Graders*, declared that, with its overemphasis on minor sentence level mistakes, "the teaching of composition in American high schools is essentially a neurotic activity" (99).

Like these other composition specialists, too, Smitherman emphasizes the importance of revision, advocating that students write multiple drafts to make sure their ideas are fully worked out before even beginning to turn their attention to sentence level concerns of grammar, mechanics, and style. In her 1994 essay, "The Blacker the Berry, the Sweeter the Juice: African American Students and the National Assessment of Educational Progress," Smitherman speaks directly to teachers, urging them to "de-emphasize your and your students' concerns about BEV grammar; overconcentration on these forms frequently suppresses the production of African American discourse and its rich, expressive style" (95). She elaborates:

> As cultural norms shift focus from "book" English to "human" English, the narrativizing, dynamic quality of the African American Verbal Tradition will help students produce lively, image-filled, concrete, readable essays, regardless of rhetorical modality—persuasive, informative, comparison-contrast, and so forth. I am often asked "how far" does the teacher go with this kind of writing pedagogy. My answer: as far as you can. Once you have pushed your students to re-

write, revise; rewrite, revise; rewrite, revise; and once they have produced the most powerful essay possible, then and only then should you have them turn their attention to BEV grammar and matters of punctuation, spelling, and mechanics. (95)

Language conservatives such as cultural critic John Simon, discussed later in this essay, have lambasted Smitherman for promoting, even celebrating, the beauty, expressive power, and cultural significance of African American English, and for concomitantly deemphasizing the importance for minority children of learning Standard English. She truly does argue for the equal status of African American and Standard English, suggesting that the latter should not be privileged over the former, in society generally or in the schools, and that educators should be at the forefront of this move to spread awareness and understanding of minority dialects. Indeed, she believes that *all* students, not only African Americans, should learn about African American English in school, not simply that African American students should learn Standard English. For this reason, Smitherman not only critiques those who believe that African American English is deficient as a dialect and that its speakers themselves in many cases have serious educational deficiencies. She also critiques advocates of bidialectalism, holders of a more mainstream view which supports students' maintenance of their home dialect but urges that students also receive serious instruction in Standard English, and, most important, learn which situations require which form of language. While not necessarily opposed to such dialectal variation, known as code-switching, Smitherman argues that this approach, like the deficit model that came before it, actually devalues African American English and its speakers, because, in her words,

> Although the difference-bi-dialectal theorists proceed from a linguistically sound and seemingly more humane premise than deficit theorists, they are unable to reconcile the obvious paradox in pedagogy which speaks to the regularized, functional quality of black speech, at the same time that it exhorts mastery of a set of "prestige" language norms in order to "succeed" in the "larger" society. . . . Thus blacks quickly perceive that Black Dialect must not be all that systematic or beautiful, for after all, they is gon to have to give it up when they bees moving on up in "higher" social and economic groups. And, to add insult to injury, we all know that there ain no cultural enrichment or "language programs for the disadvantaged" in white, middle-class schools. That is, it is only upon blacks that the virtues and greatness of bi-dialectalism are inflicted. (*Talkin and Testifyin* 207–08)

Therefore, in Smitherman's view, subsequently articulated by advocates of translingualism and code-meshing, educators should strive to promote language variation and increase the understanding and acceptance of minority Englishes, rather than just concentrating on teaching minority children Standard English. She eschews the term "nonstandard dialect" and instead uses "African American Language" to describe the language form used by the majority of Americans of African descent, thereby giving it a status equal to what is commonly known as Standard American English. Moreover, she argues strongly, paving the way for advocates of code-meshing such as Young and Martinez, that the—at first glance—progressive-seeming concept of code-switching actually favors the dominant group, because users of minority language forms are asked to switch to Standard English in formal or professional discourse, while users of the Standard need never code switch. Drawing on Smitherman, recent publications employing current approaches highlight pedagogies encouraging writers to draw on language varieties, while assessing their appropriateness and rhetorical effectiveness in particular discourse situations, such as Theresa M. Welford's essay on working with Appalachian students. In addition, composition authors now regularly mesh African American and Standard English in their own publications, as in Staci Perryman-Clark's article examining minority college student writers' rhetorical uses of their home dialect in assigned writing.

Smitherman as Activist

Smitherman has long worked for social, political, and educational change, as she discusses in her essay, "From Ghetto Lady to Critical Linguist" (*Talkin That Talk*). She entered Wayne State University at age 15, the first member of her family to go beyond the seventh grade. However, along with many others, she found herself barred from the education program after failing a mandatory speech test for prospective teachers. As a speaker of African American English, she was accustomed to such pronunciations as 'mouf' instead of 'mouth' and 'foe' instead of 'four.' She was surprised that nearly all of the failing students were African American dialect speakers. Smitherman was and, more than half a century later, remains outraged that she and her fellow dialect speakers were thus stigmatized. She learned Standard English, went on to pass the test, and subsequently distinguished herself as a college student. At the same time, she learned that there existed "a bias against this different sounding American English emanating from the margins" (2). After college, Smitherman taught high school English and Latin in Detroit public schools, then earned a doctorate in sociolinguistics and education at the University of Michigan in 1969. Hired as assistant professor of English and education by her undergraduate alma mater, Wayne State University, she soon led a successful fight to abolish the gatekeeping speech test with which she and others had been forced to contend, beginning her long career as an activist.

Early in the 1970s, Smitherman became a major participant in discussions on dialect and English instruction through her scholarship and willingness to get involved in language policy decisions as well as grassroots activism. One of the most important projects she spearheaded came out of her work with the Conference on College Composition and Communication (CCCC), a subgroup of the National Council of Teachers of English (NCTE), on their groundbreaking policy statement regarding the education of nonstandard dialect speaking students, which she helped to create. *The Students' Right to Their Own Language* was a resolution adopted by the CCCC by majority vote at the annual business meeting in Anaheim, California in 1974, after several years of preparation, internal discussion, and intense policy debate within the organization. The resolution, controversial in the field of English, called for faculty at all levels to accept students' nonstandard ways of speaking and writing as legitimate forms of English rooted in history and to focus more on the content as opposed to the superficial structural features of students' messages. Smitherman, as a young professor and relatively new member of CCCC, was asked in the early 1970s, along with a group of mainly senior figures in the organization, to join a committee exploring the development of a policy on standard versus nonstandard language concerns regarding the education of students whose primary language or dialect was not Standard English. At the time, she had recently been named to the organization's Executive Board as well.

The evolution and repercussions of this policy statement are examined in detail in two major and contrasting sources. The first is a 1999 article by Smitherman herself in the journal *CCC* entitled, "CCCC's Role in The Struggle for Language Rights." In this article, she provides a critical but laudatory participant-observer's view, approximately 25 years after its passage, of the long and drawn out process of creating the policy statement, the events leading up to the organization's decision to put forward a resolution, the personalities who took part and their varied motivations and roles on the committee, reactions to the resolution from both inside and outside the organization, and long term achievements of their work. The second source, a 2000 book by Stephen Parks entitled *Class Politics: The Movement for the Students' Right to Their Own Language*, places the dialect issue in larger political, cultural, and historical contexts as an outgrowth of 1960s activism. He traces the rise and fall of a group of professors of English and other disciplines, from inside and outside CCCC, who in the 1960s formed the New University Conference (NUC) that tried to radicalize CCCC and other professional organizations at their annual national conventions through proposing resolutions and offering talks and teach-ins, with the goal of making the groups much more active than they had been in contemporary anti-war, civil rights, and economic redistribution movements. Parks openly laments that the larger CCCC membership rejected the more broadly political approach of the NUC and elected to keep its interests focused on issues traditionally associated with writing instruction and scholarship.

The two authors thus have different agendas and perspectives regarding the *Students' Right* document. Smitherman, on the one hand, sees a document that made the strongest possible political and pedagogical statement about the legitimacy and acceptability of nonstandard dialects that could be accepted by the membership at the time; that succeeded in passing despite a lack of support by the parent organization, NCTE, and active opposition by many CCCC members; and that had a beneficial, if regrettably limited, impact on instruction and attitudes nationwide. Parks, on the other hand, critiques the final version of the resolution as one that had been shorn through compromise of its most radical economic and political elements, recommendations that went well beyond questions of dialect use to address more fundamental aspects of social justice. Parks perceives the final iteration of the text as emblematic of the profession's move away from serious, wide-ranging attacks on race- and class-based inequities to a more limited and, in his view, regrettable focus on language forms and classroom instruction. However, despite their differences, both sources are invaluable documents for understanding just what took place, what was at stake, and what the initiative and its aftermath mean for students of English, the history of composition, and American education more broadly. The *Students' Right to Their Own Language* resolution of 1974 reads as follows:

> We affirm the students' right to their own patterns and varieties of language—the dialects of their nurture or whichever dialects in which they find their own identity and style. Language scholars long ago denied that the myth of a standard American dialect has any validity. The claim that any one dialect is unacceptable amounts to an attempt of one social group to exert its dominance over another. Such a claim leads to false advice for speakers and writers, and immoral advice for humans. A nation proud of its diverse heritage and its cultural and racial variety will preserve its heritage of dialects. We strongly affirm that teachers must have the experiences and training that will enable them to respect diversity and uphold the right of students to their own language. (1)

The above resolution should be seen as a fairly radical document and a genuine departure from its usual approaches for an organization historically charged with instructing college students in the nuances of Standard English. It represented an attempt not just to change educational practice but to educate and alter the public's attitudes toward and understanding of dialect issues.

The Committee that created the resolution was chaired by Melvin Butler of Southern University in Baton Rouge, Louisiana, who died tragically before its passage, and in addition to Geneva Smitherman consisted of such luminaries as Richard Lloyd-Jones of the University of Iowa, Elisabeth McPherson of Portland State University, and Ross Winterowd of the University of Southern California, as well as other college composition specialists. The CCCC Executive Committee unanimously approved the resolution before it was submitted to the membership for a majority vote. In her 1999 essay, Smitherman cites three related goals that the Committee sought to achieve in putting forward the resolution:

> (1) to heighten consciousness of language attitudes; (2) to promote the value of linguistic diversity; and (3) to convey facts and information about language and language variation that would enable instructors to teach their non-traditional students—and ultimately all students—more effectively. (359)

Toward these ends, the Committee supplemented the paragraph-length resolution with a booklet-sized discussion of language and dialect issues intended to clarify for the membership and the larger public the linguistic, political, and pedagogical aspects of standard versus nonstandard dialects. Specifically, they wished to convey the substantial and well-respected findings from the linguistic, sociolinguistic, and educational research of such scholars as William Labov that all dialects are systematic and rule governed, that nonstandard language users are capable of complex thought and expression, and that disparagement of nonstandard dialects and their users amounts to nothing less than a prejudice.

While it nowhere advocates that students *should not* learn Standard English, and in the supplemental discussion does indeed acknowledge the value for students from the margins of learning standard forms, the main focus of the *Students' Right to Their Own Language* is on accepting student dialect use, on exposing students to a multiplicity of language varieties, and on promoting a sense of language effectiveness that goes beyond a narrow concern with superficial correctness to consider seriously larger rhetorical, argumentative, and stylistic features. The document also conveys its authors' view that, over time, students will learn Standard English through exposure and gentle instruction even while permitted, and even encouraged, to express themselves through their home dialects. In addition, it argues that students who do not know nonstandard forms will benefit from classroom exposure to them. Society as a whole, it asserts, has for far too long been holding students back by rejecting their valid language forms, and the Committee wanted to do what it could, using its own bully pulpit, to change the prevailing attitudes while promoting the achievement of minority and other nonstandard dialect speakers.

Before the 1974 meeting, the booklet containing the resolution and accompanying documents was sent to the entire CCCC membership for its consideration. At the business meeting of the annual convention, the resolution passed, but with a vote of only 79 in favor and 20 opposed, given the low attendance at the meeting. Afterwards, an entire issue of the organization's journal, *CCC*, would be devoted to an explication and discussion of the resolution. However, this relatively small number of votes in support of *Students' Right* later came back to haunt CCCC. Leaders of the organization, Committee members who produced the resolution, and other supporters worked hard to convince the larger NCTE to support it. But the Council, with its primary focus on elementary and secondary students and with its leaders feeling both internal and external pressure to ensure mastery of Standard English as a key task of English instruction, would not budge. They passed a much weaker resolution calling for a basic respect for all language varieties, but at the same time coming out most strongly for the continued emphasis on Standard English as the primary language form all students should be learning.

Ultimately, as Smitherman points out in her 1999 article, this move by the much larger NCTE overshadowed and limited the scope and effectiveness of the CCCC resolution. However, she is far more concerned that NCTE has not subsequently taken more of a leadership role in the quest for acceptance of nonstandard language forms and the students who speak and write them. She spent 1977 to 1979 as the chief advocate and educational consultant for the plaintiffs in the widely publicized Ann Arbor Black English case in Federal Court, a lawsuit filed against the Ann Arbor, Michigan School Board for neglecting the needs of young, impoverished speakers of African American English, an inordinate number of whom had been placed in special education. The court ruled for the plaintiffs, resulting in more attention to such students and more regard by school officials toward their dialect. Smitherman also led a successful effort within CCCC in 1987 to pass a national language policy statement advocating respect for and instruction in minority languages and dialects even as students learn Standard English, the language of wider communication. Despite such efforts, the larger, more visible NCTE could still clearly have followed the lead of CCCC and done more in courting public opinion, but Smitherman argues that the resolution still had its uses. It initiated a major discussion about dialects and minority students that had been largely lacking in the composition community. It helped to educate writing instructors and, to some extent, the larger public about dialect issues. Finally, numerous teachers shifted their pedagogy as a result of these efforts toward a more sensitive and productive approach in working with speakers and writers of dialects other than the standard.

Yet, after the initial controversy surrounding passage of the *Students' Right to Their Own Language*, the resolution receded from public view, becoming more of an historical artifact marking a distinctive period of educational activism and optimism before the conservative turn of the Reagan era. But it is no accident that such a resolution came out of the field of composition in the 1970s rather than from a discipline such as literature or linguistics. The idea of accepting student use of nonstandard language fit very well within the zeitgeist of the emerging field of composition, with its emphasis on meeting students where they are, not where faculty might wish them to be; on celebrating what students know while encouraging them to continue learning; on providing access to college for previously excluded groups; and on the responsibility of faculty to make the world a better place through their work.

In addition to her concerted efforts to promote educational fairness for all students through policy changes in the CCCC, Smitherman took other public stances, appealing to both academic and nonacademic audiences. Her works on African American English sold widely, earning her appearances on network television shows such as *Today* and *Dick Cavett* as well as articles in important newspapers around the country. On *Cavett*, Smitherman and linguist James Sledd heatedly debated conservative critics who decried the decline of the English language and the prevalence of dialects. In Sledd's words, she "eviscerated John Simon," author of *Paradigms Lost* and a well-known elitist advocate of a fixed standard form for English (3). As well, Smitherman has led initiatives to protect the interests of poor and minority youth across the United States. She cofounded and directed a nationwide mentoring program for young African American males known as My Brother's Keeper. She served as an expert advisor on the Oakland, California Ebonics initiative, a much discussed case in which parents of young African American students along with a team of nationally known educators successfully convinced the school district to adopt a policy of greater acceptance of African American English, the home dialect of a large percentage of the district's students (Smitherman, "Ebonics"). Finally, she has mentored generations of young academics of color all over the country, earning widespread recognition along with the nickname "Dr. G."

Work in translingualism and code-meshing is still at an early point in its development. Its proponents call for societal changes in attitudes toward and policies governing the teaching, assessment, and use of nonstandard dialects in schools, workplaces, the media, and elsewhere. They have created a working group "to articulate and enact translingual approaches to writing" (Horner, Lu, Jones Royster, and Trimbur 309). In addition, they have begun to develop curricula in which language varieties are encouraged and valued. However, these calls have appeared only in professional publications and presentations and have been directed exclusively to other academics. To be sure, such efforts are proactive, praiseworthy, and necessary steps, but for major change to be possible, academics will also need to work beyond the academy, as Geneva Smitherman did and as I will discuss below.

Conclusion

What can we as literacy educators do to help writers and speakers of nonstandard dialects? In his 2005 book, *Writing at the End of the World*, Richard Miller critiques the tendency of academics to work toward political change solely within the confines of academia. He states, "In the right setting, we can forget that we are the individuals vested with the responsibility for soliciting and assessing student work; we can imagine that power has left the room. . . . The students, however, never forget where they are. . . ." (130). Likewise, as teachers and scholars, we can adopt programmatic policies and develop curricula supporting students' use of Nonstandard English. But if we do so without also venturing outside the academy to work for changes in entrenched attitudes and policies, then we risk doing students a disservice by preparing them for a world that exists only in our classrooms. Smitherman labored for decades to effect change at local, regional, and national levels. Comparable work needs to be done today in school districts, courtrooms, professional organizations, think tanks, and the world of politicians at all levels who pass laws and enact policies. To take the next step, let us follow her example.

Works Cited

Bereiter, Carl. "Academic Instruction and Preschool Children." *Language Programs for the Disadvantaged: Report of the NCTE Task Force on Teaching English to the Disadvantaged*. Ed. Richard Corbin and Muriel Crosby. Champaign: NCTE, 1965. 195-203. Print.

Canagarajah, A. Suresh. "Negotiating Translingual Literacy: An Enactment." *Research in the Teaching of English* 48.1 (2013): 40-67. Print.

Conference on College Composition and Communication. *Students' Right to Their Own Language*. Spec. issue of *CCC* 25.3 (1974): 1-32. Print.

Dillard, J. L. *Black English*. New York: Random, 1972. Print.

Elbow, Peter. *Writing without Teachers*. New York: Oxford UP, 1973. Print.

Emig, Janet. *The Composing Processes of Twelfth Graders*. Urbana: NCTE, 1971. Print.

Gilyard, Keith. "Geneva's Quartet: Notes on Linguistics, Aesthetics, Rhetoric, and Policy." *True to the Language Game*. Ed. Keith Gilyard. New York: Routledge, 2011. 161-71. Print.

Harrison, J. A. "Negro English." *Anglia: Journal of English Philology* 7 (1884): 232-79. Print.

Herskovits, Melville. *Myth of the Negro Past*. Boston: Beacon, 1941. Print.

Horner, Bruce, Min-Zhan Lu, Jacqueline Jones Royster, and John Trimbur. "A Translingual Approach to Language Difference in Writing." *College English* 73.3 (2011): 221-42. Print.

Labov, William. *Language in the Inner City*. Philadelphia: U of Pennsylvania P, 1972. Print.

Lu, Min-Zhan, and Bruce Horner. "Translingual Literacy, Language Difference, and Matters of Agency." *College English* 75.6 (2013): 582-608. Print.

Miller, Richard E. *Writing at the End of the World*. Pittsburgh: U of Pittsburgh P, 2005. Print.

Parks, Stephen. *Class Politics: The Movement for the Student's Right to Their Own Language*. Urbana: NCTE, 2000. Print.

Perryman-Clark, Staci M. "African American Language, Rhetoric, and Students' Writing: New Directions for STROL." *CCC* 64.3 (2013): 469-95. Print.

Shaughnessy, Mina P. *Errors and Expectations: A Guide for the Teacher of Basic Writing*. New York: Oxford UP, 1977. Print.

Sledd, James. "Race, Class, and Talking Proper: The Ebonics War Continues." *Texas Observer*. Texas Observer, 21 July 2000. Web. 17 July 2014. <http://www.texasobserver.org/779-race-class-and-talking-proper/>.

Smitherman, Geneva. *Black Language and Culture: The Sounds of Soul*. New York: Harper, 1975. Print.

---. "The Blacker the Berry, the Sweeter the Juice: African American Student Writers and the National Assessment of Education Progress." *The Need for Story: Cultural Diversity in Classroom and Community*. Ed. Anne Haas Dyson and Celia Genishi. Urbana: NCTE, 1994. 80-101. Print.

---. "CCCC's Role in the Struggle for Language Rights." *CCC* 50.3 (1999): 349-76. Print.

---. "Discriminatory Discourse on African American Speech." *Discourse and Discrimination*. Ed. Geneva Smitherman and Teun van Dijk. Detroit: Wayne State UP, 1988. 144-75. Print.

---. "Ebonics, King, and Oakland: Some Folk Don't Know Fat Meat is Greasy." *Journal of English Linguistics* 37.2 (1998): 97-107. Print.

---. *Talkin and Testifyin: The Language of Black America*. Boston: Houghton Mifflin, 1977. Print.

---. *Talkin That Talk: Language, Culture, and Education in African America*. New York: Routledge, 2000. Print.

Turner, Lorenzo D. *Africanisms in the Gullah Dialect*. Chicago: U of Chicago P, 1949. Print.

Welford, Theresa M. "Code-Meshing and Creative Assignments: How Students Can Stop Worrying and Learn to Write Like Da Bomb." Young and Martinez 21-54. Print.

Young, Vershawn A. *Your Average Nigga: Performing Race, Literacy, and Masculinity*. Detroit: Wayne State UP, 2007. Print.

Young, Vershawn A., and Aja Y. Martinez, eds. *Code-Meshing as World English: Pedagogy, Policy, Performance*. Urbana: NCTE, 2011. Print.

Immodest Witnesses: Reliability and Writing Assessment

Chris W. Gallagher

This article offers a survey of three reliability theories in writing assessment: positivist, hermeneutic, and rhetorical. Drawing on an interdisciplinary investigation of the notion of *witnessing*, this survey emphasizes the kinds of readers and readings each theory of reliability produces and the epistemological grounds on which it rests. Positivist reliability, positing an *a priori* reality and objective truth, produces "modest witnesses" (Haraway) who generate consistent, "true" scores. Hermeneutic reliability, which views "truth" as socially constructed though dialogue, produces communal witnesses who generate consensus, agreed upon readings. Rhetorical reliability, which views "truth" as a rhetorical effect of testimony, produces embodied witnesses who generate a range of perspectives, including articulated differences. While many writing assessment scholars, both in composition studies and in educational measurement, reject positivist reliability and embrace hermeneutic reliability, I suggest that the challenge for our field and our writing programs is to articulate a rhetorical theory of reliability and to design writing assessment systems that align with our prevailing conceptions of writing and reading as rhetorical activities.

For many writing program administrators, the assessment concept *reliability* presents considerable challenges. We may shy away from what seems to be a dauntingly complex psychometric concept requiring sophisticated statistical analyses. We may worry that achieving consistency in scoring requires us to simplify what we assess, thereby narrowing our construct of writing. We may fear that the norming traditionally employed to ensure consistent scoring inhibits meaningful, engaged reader responses to student writing. Certainly as a writing program administrator I have had these concerns. And my response has been, I think, typical: I have held my nose and calculated and reported reader agreement rates.

We may think of such a response as acceding to a stringent psychometric expectation, but this narrow insistence on inter-rater reliability is likely to confound psychometricians. The psychometric concept of reliability, even in its most traditional form, is far broader than inter-rater agreement. It also includes *intra*-rater agreement: the extent to which a single rater scores consistently. And it considers instrument reliability, which measures internal consistency and consistency among parallel forms of assessments.[1] Ironically, then, we in our writing programs tend to focus on a narrower approach to reliability than we may feel has been imposed on us.

Moreover, the general acceptance in writing programs of inter-rater reliability tethers us to a classical psychometric tradition in which reliability is defined as consistency. Although teachers and scholars in our field tend to view writing and reading as rhetorical acts, many of our programs operate on assessment concepts and practices that demand highly controlled, *a*rhetorical approaches to reading and writing. Most writing programs I have taught in and visited use some variant of the holistic scoring model developed by the Educational Testing Service (ETS) in the 1970s: design a rubric; train scorers to apply it to student work using "anchor" papers (or portfolios) and practice sessions; double score some or all of the student artifacts; reconcile discrepant scores; calibrate as necessary (see Neal; White; Wilson). The goal, though often framed in terms of fairness, is really consistency: scorers should arrive at the same score, irrespective of their own reading preferences and habits (Huot 88). This concession to reliability-as-consistency may be a gesture of self-preservation: certainly I have felt that my writing programs could not afford to be perceived as *un*reliable. But if we believe that writing and reading are fundamentally rhetorical acts, we should ask if arhetorical reliability-as-consistency comes at too high a price.

Fortunately, as I will show, reliability-as-consistency is not our only option. Reliability is a rich and multivalent concept within and across various disciplinary discourses, and it need not be jettisoned or grudgingly accepted. Indeed, an interdisciplinary inquiry into theories of reliability begins to yield a theory of *rhetorical reliability* that is consonant with widely held beliefs in composition studies about the nature of reading and writing. This theory, I believe, can reinvigorate our assessment work and allow us to frame (to borrow Peggy O'Neill's term) reliability in ways that articulate and advance rhetorical understandings of writing and writing assessment.

Although writing program administrators and writing assessment scholars need to think beyond inter-rater reliability, I take this concept as my focus in this article both because it has mesmerized writing assessment in composition studies (see Broad *What*; Elliot; Huot; O'Neill; White) and because even this narrow but important concept requires more careful theoretical investigation than we have devoted to it. In our programs and in our writing assessment literature, we tend to think of inter-rater reliability as a scoring problem: How can we achieve sufficiently high agreement rates? I propose that we re-theorize reliability as a perceptual and representational problem: What and how do we see when we observe students and their writing? How do we—singly and together—arrive at judgments about what we see? What are the nature, status, and function of our accounts of what we see?

These questions prompt me to turn to the notion of *witnessing*, especially as it emerges in feminist science studies, trauma studies, legal studies, and critical theory generally. Witnessing focuses our attention on *who* is observing and *how* they observe, and so it provides a useful analytical tool for framing a survey of theories of reliability. Further, witnessing is helpful for our purposes precisely because it provokes ongoing debates about reliability, and in particular our ability to apprehend and represent "truth." It allows us to distinguish between and among theories of reliability according to those theories' epistemological beliefs and assumptions about what makes a witness (in this case a scorer or a reader) reliable.

Because the first two theories of reliability I survey—positivist and hermeneutic—will be familiar to most readers, I treat them briefly. The third theory, rhetorical reliability, receives more attention, as it is less familiar, and also because it is more amenable to the ways we tend to understand reading and writing in our field. This survey, I emphasize at the outset, is not intended to be a history: though we can identify some historical trends, writing assessment is not a linear journey from one theory to the next. Nor is the survey exhaustive. Rather, my aim is to offer an interdisciplinary theoretical investigation that affords composition studies new ways of thinking and talking about the vexing concept of reliability.

On Witnessing

Readers might find it odd that I would turn to the concept of witnessing to make sense of the act of writing assessment. Isn't there something positivist about the very idea of witnessing? Do we even believe in accurate perception and representation anymore? In fact, theorists from a range of disciplines have rescued witnessing from positivism and reclaimed it as a rhetorical act.

Poet Carolyn Forché, for instance, theorizes a twentieth-century "poetry of witness" in which poetry-as-testimony to personal and social extremity

> cannot be judged by simplistic notions of "accuracy" or "truth to life." It must be judged by its consequences, not by our ability to verify its truth. In fact, the poem might be our only evidence that an event has occurred; it exists for us as the sole trace of an occurrence. As such, there will be nothing for us to base the poem on, no independent account that will tell us whether or not we can see a given text as being "objectively" true. Poem as trace, poem as evidence.

For Forché, the poet-as-witness can never offer a direct, transparent representation of an *a priori* Real, but she can produce "evidence" of what she has observed and perceived. As a rhetor, the poet's credibility is grounded not in accuracy—how her account accords with what happened—but instead in what her testimony *does* (leaves a trace).

While legal studies may seem far afield from Forchéan poetics, legal and literary scholar Jan-Melissa Schramm dismisses the commonsense conflation of legal witnessing and positivism and suggests that in fact the law acknowledges the profoundly rhetorical nature of witnessing, placing a premium on credibility. According to Schramm, the law's many attempts throughout the Enlightenment and nineteenth century to establish rules of admissibility (competency, voluntariness, etc.) recognize both the power of storytelling and the limits of human perception, memory, and representation. For all its rules and procedures, Schramm insists, the law ultimately must approach witnessing as "transactional"—that is, rhetorical, as opposed to purely rule-governed (479). Indeed, modern law generally has moved away from "complex rules of exclusion" of testimony, leaving judges and juries to evaluate the credibility of witnesses (494).

Like Forché and Schramm, rhetorician and human rights scholar Wendy Hesford challenges the commonsense notion that witnessing provides unmediated access to reality (*Spectacular* 49). Hesford recognizes the potential dangers of witnessing: problems of identification (assimilation, colonization), spectaclization, appropriation, and voyeurism (13). But these dangers inhere not in witnessing itself, but rather in what Hesford calls "objectivist oracular epistemology" (3). This epistemology—essentially the idea that seeing is believing—underwrites "the visual field of human rights internationalism" (3). Hesford's theoretical intervention is a rhetorical witnessing that is understood as mediated by material, embodied, cultural, and ideological artifacts, discourses, and forces. It is never innocent, and it is always situated and historically contingent. It is partial and located—always a view from somewhere, some body (see also Hesford, "Documenting").

Readers familiar with the work of feminist science scholar Donna Haraway will hear echoes here of her devastating accounts of the effects of the "view from nowhere," that peculiar god-trick of Western science whose avatar she dubs "the modest witness" ("modest_witness"). But like Hesford, Haraway is unwilling to abandon vision; rather, she re-theorizes it: "I do not turn from vision, but I do seek something other than enlightenment" ("Promises" 65). For Haraway, vision itself is a "siting/sighting device," but instead of ensuring distance and impartiality, it produces "effects of connection, of embodiment, and of responsibility" (64). Like Hesford's rhetorical witness, Haraway's viewer is "*anything* but disembodied" (68).

Even this brief treatment shows that what binds these diverse theorists together is the conviction that the rhetorical effect of credibility is more relevant than ever in light of broad acceptance of the notion that we can never achieve unmediated access to transcendent Truth. To be sure, the shift away from positivism across academic disciplines and subsequent crisis of representation (Kamberelis and Dimitradis), the retreat from certainty in science (Peat), the unspeakable genocidal atrocities of the twentieth and twenty first centuries (Bernard-Donals, "Ethos," "The Rhetoric"; Felman and Laub), and widespread postmodern anxiety and instability (Bauman; Giddens) have shaken our faith in our ability to perceive and represent events accurately. But these theorists suggest that in a post-Cartesian world, we must not retreat from truth telling, but instead we must confront witness testimony in rhetorical terms. Severed from positivist epistemology, witnessing is reclaimed as a material and embodied rhetorical act.

Figured this way, witnessing has the potential to guide rich investigations into the nature of perception and truth telling. It is with this hope that I offer the following survey of theories of reliability in writing assessment. I contend that each theory of reliability invites readers/assessors into a particular witnessing relation, depending on the theory's construction of truth and its epistemological grounds. Each theory generates a different kind of reader, and these readers produce different kinds of artifacts. Figure 1 provides an overview.

	Reader Role	Theory of Truth	Ground	Artifact
Positivist reliability	Modest witness	Truth as "out there," located in independent a priori reality	Objectivity	Ascertained score (consistency: agreement)
Hermeneutic reliability	Communal witness	Truth as socially constructed via dialogue	Community standards	Achieved consensus (consistency: agreement)
Rhetorical reliability	Embodied witness	Truth as an effect of testimony	Perceived credibility	Achieved consensus + Articulated difference (agreement + disagreement)

Fig. 1. Theories of Reliability

This chart represents different ways to understand, frame, and evaluate reliability in writing assessment—*any* writing assessment, whether teachers evaluating essays in classrooms, teachers and administrators conducting program assessment by evaluating student portfolios against a rubric, or a group of trained raters (or perhaps machines) at a testing firm scoring selected response "writing" tests. The chart is intended to have heuristic value. Leaders of and participants in any writing assessment can ask themselves, What kind of reader does this assessment produce? What theory of truth underwrites it? On what epistemological grounds does it rest? What do the readings produce?

While charts tend to convey representational purity and certainty, I acknowledge that surveying, too, is an embodied and material rhetorical act. I hardly offer "the view from nowhere." This body—my body, with its history as a testing industry worker, a writing teacher and program administrator, and a composition scholar—has a situated perspective to offer. That perspective—definitely partial, certainly arguable—is this: positivist reliability has had a deleterious influence on the development of writing assessment theory and practice and has no place in writing assessment; hermeneutic reliability is sometimes useful but also problematic and has a limited role to play in writing assessment; and rhetorical reliability should prevail whenever possible in writing assessment because it is most consistent with the way our field understands what happens when people read and write.

Positivist Reliability and the Modest Witness

The traditional psychometric notion of reliability is the brainchild of English psychologist and psychometrician Charles Spearman, (in)famous for his theory of general intelligence, "Spearman's g" (Cherry and Meyer). Rooted in the twentieth-century "natural science" of measurement, this traditional conception of reliability rests on the positivist belief that an independent, *a priori* reality can be apprehended and measured under the right conditions. Thus, reducing measurement error, including human error, is central to reliability (Berlak; White; Williamson).[2] The idea is to ascertain, and minimize, the distance between an examinee's "true" score and her assigned score. Again, although positivist reliability is framed as a matter of ensuring "fairness," it has been concerned primarily with attaining *consistency* in scoring (Huot 88). And because reliability has been construed traditionally as a "necessary but insufficient" condition for validity, the perceived need to produce consistent scores has functioned to circumscribe the kinds of assessments that have been attempted (Cherry and Meyer; Elliot; Moss; Slomp and Fuite; Wiggins).

Indeed, positivist reliability has fixated on human error—"the serpent to be stamped out of the garden," in Edward White's terms (98). In writing assessment, at least in recent years, this preoccupation tends to manifest in the ceaseless quest for inter-rater reliability (Huot; Huot and Neal; O'Neill; White). At issue in this conception of reliability, then, is not just the production of consistent scores, but also the production of a certain kind of reader—a certain kind of witness to writing. This reader is what Haraway calls "the modest witness," the ideal modern scientist: a bodiless, transparent, detached spectator of the world who observes, describes, measures, and explains. "Self-invisibility," Haraway contends, "is the specifically modern, European, masculine, scientific form of the virtue of modesty" ("modest_witness" 224).

Of course, disembodiment is easier to achieve for some than for others:

> the kind of visibility—the body—that women retain glides into being perceived as "subjective," that is, reporting only on the self, biased, opaque, not objective…Colored, sexed, and laboring persons still have to do a lot of work to become similarly transparent to count as objective, modest witnesses to the world rather than to their "bias" or "special interest." (Haraway, "modest_witness" 232)

According to positivist reliability, if people with their pesky bodies—say (women/feminized) teachers—must participate in scoring, rigorous norming must be employed to ensure that, to the extent possible, their subjectivity is erased and they are able to occupy the "view from nowhere." This phenomenon is described in painful detail in Todd Farley's *Making the Grades: My Misadventures in the Standardized Testing Industry*, in which the author chronicles his experiences as a "scoring monkey" who is trained right out of his capacity for human response to student writing. This same phenomenon was poignantly captured for me in a poster on the wall of the testing firm for which I once worked: featuring an image of Jiminy Cricket, it read, "Always Let the [Scoring] Guide Be Your Conscience."

In recent years, we have seen growing interest—and growing investments by the testing industry—in a "total solution" to the embodiment problem: machine-scoring. While I don't have space to explore automated essay scoring (AES) or "robo-grading" here, it is worth noting that the machine is the apotheosis of the modest witness. Although many composition scholars have shown that even the most sophisticated machines can't *read*—can't, that is, understand writing as doing rhetorical work for particular audiences in specific rhetorical contexts—machine-scoring is touted by vendors (such as ETS and Pearson) and some in the educational measurement community (e.g., Shermis and Burstein) as an efficient way to produce consistent scores. (For an overview of research findings on AES, visit humanreaders.org.)

But positivist reliability and the modest witness are not confined to high-tech or high-stakes testing. They are operative any time a writing program uses norming to require readers to stifle their experiences as readers in favor of producing scores that are similar to or (ideally) identical with those of other scorers and then treats the results as "true scores." The primary task of the modest witness—the "god-trick"—is to disappear, to become transparent. The goal is not to make readers *credible*; it is to efface them, rendering the question of credibility irrelevant. Consistency ensures accuracy because it indexes the absence of human error. The assessment is reliable because the participants' inherent unreliability has been minimized or removed.

Hermeneutic Reliability and The Communal Witness

While some psychometricians, policymakers, and test purveyors continue to subscribe to positivist reliability, much writing assessment theory over the past couple decades—both in composition studies and, increasingly, in educational measurement—has sought to move beyond it. One important thrust of this effort theorizes a post-positivist (often social constructionist) hermeneutic reliability.

Hermeneutic reliability holds that there is no such thing as a "true score"—only value-laden judgments. We are not measuring an independent, *a priori* reality, but rather constructing a version of reality through our necessarily partial powers of apprehension and representation. Because any version of reality is mediated by human interpretation, it must be contextualized by the situation in which it is constructed and the subjects who construct it. Judgments about writing, then, are necessarily informed by communal values, beliefs, assumptions, and conventions, and these must be accounted for by any act of assessment. Unlike positivist reliability, hermeneutic reliability maintains that those who are most knowledgeable about the learning and assessment situation—teachers, usually—are most qualified to conduct assessment.

Measurement expert Pamela Moss's hermeneutic framework is the theoretical touchstone for hermeneutic reliability. In her influential "Can There Be Validity Without Reliability?," Moss frames her hermeneutic approach in opposition to a traditional psychometric approach. Whereas a psychometric approach involves independent raters scoring student work without access to contextual information about students, teachers, or teaching and learning conditions, a hermeneutic approach

> would involve holistic, integrative interpretations of collective performances that seek to understand the whole in light of the parts, that privilege readers who are most knowledgeable about the context in which the assessment occurs, and that ground these interpretations not only in the textual and contextual evidence available, but also in a rational debate among the community of interpreters. (86)

Moss emphasizes that traditionally conceived reliability is one way, but not the only way, of warranting knowledge claims (92). Depending on the purposes and uses of an assessment, a hermeneutic approach might be perfectly appropriate and valid. Under the hermeneutic approach, "[i]nitial disagreement among readers would not invalidate the assessment; rather, it would provide an impetus for dialogue, debate, and enriched understanding informed by multiple perspectives" (89).

While Moss's model has been influential in composition studies (see Broad, "Pulling" and *What*; O'Neill, Moore, and Huot), composition theorists have proposed hermeneutic models of reliability on their own terms. For example, William L. Smith's "expert reader" model, which he reported on in 1992 and 1993 book chapters (Moss's essay appeared in 1994), emerged from his recognition that traditional reliability "misses the point" ("Assessing" 185). As Smith notes, "[t]o assume that there are only 4 or 12 categories of students or texts seems untenable. Some students (or essays), regardless of the number of points on the scale, will not fit neatly into that scale, and thus disagreements must be expected" (185). In his study of disagreements in a set of placement studies at the University of Pittsburgh, Smith found that the scoring splits were often themselves consistent. Using a "rater-set" method, Smith concluded that placement ratings may be "reliable even when the raters disagree" (173). This finding led Smith to a new method: asking teachers to determine only whether students should or should not be placed in the courses that the teachers most recently taught. When he organized raters this way, he found very high agreement rates among teachers teaching the same course (90-96%)—without formal training or norming (198). In effect, their experience teaching the course trained them to interpret student writing in similar ways. While Smith's model includes no official norming, rubrics, or scores and only limited double-readings of student essays, it retains the yoking of reliability and consistency. His innovation is placement that is valid *and* reliable, with reliability defined as agreement.[3]

More recent reliability theory in composition studies builds on the notion that what Moss calls "initial disagreement among readers" (89) can be a positive feature of community building. Bob Broad contends that "only by openly discussing, debating, and negotiating evaluative differences can a writing program move genuinely and with integrity toward increased evaluative coherence" (*What* 128). Brian Huot's "(re)articulated" reliability is "a critical standard with which communities of knowledgeable stakeholders make important and valid decisions" (101). Similarly, Patricia Lynne—while rejecting the term reliability—insists "that the process for assessment be dialogic, that the goal be consensus about the assessment decision, and that rational argumentation be the means by which such consensus is reached" (137). Though they disagree on many points, these theorists agree that assessment should involve dialogue and debate aimed at generating shared understandings rooted in community values. And they believe that articulating differences in readers' interpretations can be an important means by which to forge consensus. If positivist reliability's reliable witness is a compliant rater whose subjectivity has been systematically removed through norming, hermeneutic reliability's reliable witness is a rational participant in the interpretive community who upholds the community's critical standards and engages in the debates that shape those standards.

Hermeneutic reliability provides ways of talking about reliability without subscribing to positivism. It has ties to a philosophical tradition that is amenable to composition studies; most composition scholars were trained by humanists and qualitative social scientists versed in hermeneutics. Because hermeneutic reliability insists that assessment decisions are best made by those knowledgeable about the teaching and learning context, it provides writing teachers and administrators a warrant for conducting their own assessments. At its most robust, this approach may even become a "form of participatory democracy," for "key to building consensus is a shared willingness to appreciate other perspectives" (Kalikoff 109, 120).

Still, we should recognize the limitations of hermeneutic reliability. Like all consensus-driven processes, it risks marginalizing, or managing away, outlier views and dissent in favor of shared understandings and normed judgments. As writing studies scholarship dating back three decades has established, even the most inclusive dialogic process can assimilate or subsume individual and cultural diversity into the consensus framework of the community (Harris; Myers; Trimbur). Hermeneutic reliability does not reckon with the institutional realities that make free and open dialogue untenable in many assessment situations. Even our field's most vocal critic of positivist reliability, Patricia Lynne, does not adequately address this problem because she subscribes to "an ethical structure based on Habermas's 'communicative ethics,' which advances the notion that communities reach ethical decisions based on rational argumentation" (15). While rejecting Habermas's utopian ideal speech situation, she embraces a "limited speech situation" based on the premise that "participation be grounded in expertise and accountability" (135). But placing limitations on who participates in writing assessment does nothing to counter the problem that within the imagined speech situation, we must assume that sovereign subjects conduct rational exchanges on a level playing field. Lynne imagines the "fullest consideration possible for all involved" (138), but does not discuss how "all involved" are situated within multiple, sometimes conflicting discourses, ideological forces, institutions and other social structures—and how all of these may constrain the kinds of dialogues she imagines.

So while hermeneutic reliability acknowledges reader differences, we must wonder to what extent they are likely to emerge in the first place given the pressure exerted by the consensus mandate imposed by the very complex and politically charged institutional community that surrounds any educational assessment. Further, because these differences are put in service of arriving at consensus, we must wonder whether they are ever allowed to reach their full expression or to inform the assessment process in transformative ways. Finally, we must wonder if these differences are seriously engaged, given that they are ultimately erased, submerged in favor of achieved agreement.[4]

We are confronting here the limitations of identification-based, consensus-driven Enlightenment rationality—the target of much of Donna Haraway's work. Her cyborg, for instance, stands in antagonistic relation with "the tradition of reproduction of the self from the reflection of the other" ("Cyborg" 8). The cyborg is an attempt to theorize political coalition without identification (indeed without identity) and without appropriation. It is a celebration of difference and the unassimilated and "inappropriate/d" self and other ("Ecce"). After all, assimilation and appropriation, too, are god tricks of sorts—disappearing acts.

Haraway doesn't oppose collectivity—the cyborg is after all "a kind of disassembled and reassembled, post-modern collective and personal self" ("Manifesto" 23). But she insists on coalition politics through "affinity, not identity" (14), which is to say that she insists on retaining unassimilated, inappropriate/d difference. She writes, "We do not need a totality in order to work well" (31). We do need language, of course, but we must "struggle against perfect communication, against the one code that translates all meaning perfectly" (34). Hers, she says, is a dream "not of a common language, but of a powerful infidel heteroglossia" (39).

While hermeneutic reliability acknowledges that difference exists, its consensus imperative ultimately provides no room for the unassimilated, inappropriate/d self or other. Communal witnesses, if not exactly transparent or effaced (like modest witnesses), are assimilated, appropriated. Their singular perspectives and the "powerful infidel heteroglossia" to which they might otherwise give voice are subsumed into consensus. A formal norming apparatus is replaced with a no less potent pressure to conform to community standards. While hermeneutic reliability, to its considerable credit, values conversation and debate and at least *initially* values diverse views, it ultimately produces agreement, and agreement is still the guarantor of, if not Truth, at least "truth." Reliability still hinges on consistency; the consistency is just achieved differently.

Rhetorical Reliability and the Embodied Witness

Reliability-as-consistency, whether rooted in positivism or hermeneutics, ultimately denies the rhetorical nature of assessment. Instead of expecting assessors to read student writing and present their readings differently depending on their particular, embodied perspectives, we expect them, in the end, to produce identical readings and judgments, as if their rhetorical situatedness did not matter. Indeed, writing assessment protocols and procedures based on norming often go to great lengths—including, for instance, frequent calibrations—to control the variables that might cause the kinds of discrepant readings that are routine when readers read writing.

By contrast, thinking about reading and writing—and assessing—as rhetorical means thinking about them as embodied. Accounting for embodiment, for corporeality, entails, among other things, "becom[ing] answerable for what we learn how to see" (Haraway, "Situated" 583). Because we learn how to see with our bodies, we must confront the ways in which our perspectives, like our bodies, are complex and contradictory—and therefore partial (in both senses of the word: incomplete and biased). The rhetorical witness—the opaque, subjective, immodest witness—seeing always from her body cannot gain unmediated access to the Truth. But she can tell the (partial) truth as and from where she sees it.

Rhetorical reliability solicits witnesses' embodied testimonies—accounts of *what and how they see*. Its goal is not to ascertain a "true score" in the name of objectivity or to achieve consensus in the name of community standards, but rather to articulate (that is, to state, but also to put in meaningful relation) a range of unassimilated, inappropriate/d perspectives: to retain, indeed to cultivate, heteroglossia. Rhetorical reliability not only acknowledges, but also embraces and preserves reader differences. These differences are not merely a vehicle for arriving at consensus; indeed, consensus is not insisted upon. Nor are they an index of how much "reader error" is in play. The differences stand because they are an expected and meaning-full result of rhetorical interactions between situated, embodied readers and writers.

Despite composition studies' understanding of the rhetorical nature of writing and reading, the articulation of reader differences is often figured in the field's writing assessment literature not as reliability, but rather as its limit. For instance, in *Rethinking Rubrics in Writing Assessment,* Maja Wilson offers an impassioned case for preserving dissensus in writing assessment. Arguing that "agreement can… keep us from understanding" (54), she advances a rhetorical approach to assessing writing that "help[s] students to wade through conflicting views of their work, honoring disagreement without getting lost in it" (60). She lauds scholarly review processes in which disparate perspectives are taken into account and used to guide writers to new insights (61-64). But then Wilson suggests that if we are to mount a similar approach to assessing student writing, "we will need principles other than reliability to guide us" (64). For Wilson, embracing discrepant readings requires us to dismiss reliability because that psychometric concept is conflated with consistency.

At the same time, one can discern in recent writing assessment scholarship an incipient theory of reliability that does admit discrepant readings. Michael

Neal, for instance, at once embraces reliability and pushes it away. Like many in rhetoric and writing studies, Neal is devoted to a rhetorical approach to writing pedagogy: "The rhetorical nature of reading and writing is the hill on which teachers of writing should make our stand against the pervasive notion that machines can do the work of assessing student writing and that they can do it better since they are objective and reliable" (67). Neal agrees that machines can *score* more consistently than humans, but he insists that they cannot in any meaningful sense *read* texts. And "[b]ecause subjectivity will necessarily exist in any human interpretation of a text, it is better to acknowledge it and include it in the overall assessment rather than attempt to ignore it" (113). Here Neal seems to gesture toward a new approach to reliability: "Reliability can serve an important purpose, but we must reframe what that is and acknowledge that consistency plays out in a variety of ways in any assessment technology and that not all are equal or even necessary" (114). It is not clear here whether Neal wishes to expand the very notion of reliability (as the word "reframe" suggests) or to jettison it, at least sometimes. Nor is it clear how consistency would "play out in a variety of ways" without edging into inconsistency. But it is clear that Neal values inconsistency: "It is at these points of dissonance [differences in interpretation] that some of the most valuable work within writing assessment can take place" (116). Ultimately, though, like Wilson, Neal does not disentangle reliability from consistency, leading him to conclude that "reliability plays into the strengths of mechanistic assessment technologies" (115). While he comes close to offering a reframing of reliability that would meaningfully account for reader differences, he ultimately reverts to the familiar claim in composition studies that we must "prevent reliability from gaining undue influence" over writing assessments (115).

Carl Whithaus, in his *Teaching and Evaluating Writing in the Age of Computers and High-Stakes Testing*, moves us closer to a reframed reliability by advocating assessment methods that are interactive, descriptive, situated, and distributive (xxxii). Whithaus' approach to teaching and assessing writing, like Neal's, is rhetorical; because he sees writing as interactive and situated communication, he advocates assessment systems that have these qualities as well (41). In particular, he advocates the provision of multiple, descriptive reader reports of student writing that articulate a range of responses. Whithaus mostly describes classroom methods such as involving students in setting classroom criteria and involving peers in distributive assessment, but he also points to some program and institutional assessment systems, such as the electronic portfolio assessments of the sort developed at Alverno College. According to Whithaus,

> If individuals are encouraged to record their responses, and these responses are then associated with the compositions in a database

that is available to the instructor and other evaluators, it is possible to build a situated evaluation of a student's composition. This evaluation acknowledges that writing, composing, and communicating are localized social activities by incorporating disparate responses from teachers, student-authors, peers, and outside audiences. Unlike the commonly used 1-to-6 point holistic reading or the more detailed rubric-based multitrait scoring systems, a distributive assessment system does not insist that all readers read alike. (88)

Here Whithaus glimpses a reframed reliability for writing assessment that, rather than involving a trade-off with validity, serves to increase it: "It is in these movements toward an amorphous, new type of 'reliability,' toward 'descriptive' evaluations, and toward the application of situated and negotiated evaluation criteria that I sense a foundation for accurate, valid, and useful methods of writing assessment" (98). In other words, Whithaus begins to imagine here a *rhetorical* reliability whose credibility derives not from consistency but rather from the provision of a range of readings, which may well be inconsistent.

Although Neal and Whithaus move us toward a new theory of reliability, the assessment principles and practices under discussion here are not, in fact, new. We just have not been accustomed to thinking about them in terms of reliability. In his WPA-CompPile research bibliography on "Distributive Evaluation," for instance, Whithaus demonstrates that distributive evaluation has a long history in composition studies, dating back at least as far as Peter Elbow's 1968 *College English* article "A Method for Teaching Writing." While distributive evaluation begins from the premise that "different readers read differently," WPAs, writing faculty, and scholars have each responded in various ways to this phenomenon. Some have implemented norming to obtain consistent scores, some have designed consensus processes, and some—the minority, to be sure—have embraced reader differences (Whithaus, "Distributive"). Those in the last category have not necessarily framed their work in terms of reliability, but distributive evaluation that values differences opens the door to theorizing rhetorical reliability—*if* we can sever reliability from consistency and allow discrepant readings to stand.

Take, for instance, Richard Haswell's 1991 discussion of a certain junior-level diagnostic essay in his book *Gaining Ground in College Writing*. The essay he discusses received the following scores from teacher-raters using an eight-point scale: 1, 4, 5, 5, 6, 7, and 8 (342). While the spread of scores is extreme, it cannot come as a complete surprise to those of us familiar with Paul Diederich's discussion in *Measuring Growth in English* of Diederich, French, and Carlton's famous ETS study, which found extremely low rates of reader agreement on student writing. What may be surprising is that instead of seeing the disparate judgments as a *problem*, as the bulk of writing assessment theory has, Haswell views them as warranted and appropriate. To Haswell's eye, the essay itself is uneven, inconsistent: "If we judge the language ability of this author, the effort probably deserves the 8, but if we ask whether she got a point across and convinced us of it in the fifty minutes, the effort probably deserves the 1" (343). Haswell suggests the discrepant scores represent a developmental reality: this writer has learned to do some things well and has yet to learn to do other things well. The spread of scores tells us something important about the essay: "the seven rates of 1, 4, 5, 5, 6, 7, and 8 describe the essay more accurately than any less varied set. They are more truthful, and therefore more useful to any pedagogical effort to help the student" (347).

As Haswell indicates, the issue is not just that readers read differently, but also that writers write differently—sometimes in the same piece. Writing development is uneven, and depending on where readers look, they will see different things. Haswell doesn't reject holism out of hand or deny that we must sometimes make placement decisions, but instead insists on the "root dishonesty" (347) involved in claiming that single ratings are truthful representations of student writers or their writing. At the same time, Haswell argues for something more, or other, than normed, multitrait scoring. He advances multiple, unreconciled readings as truthful because they capture more of the complexity involved in both writing and reading. Indeed, we should expect meaningful writing to provoke a range of responses.

This is not to say that rhetorical reliability makes a fetish of *in*consistency or to deny that shared community values do, and should, influence readers. But rhetorical reliability insists that these values are always evolving and multiply interpretable. When important decisions must be made, they should be arrived at through deliberation in light of these shared, public values. Electronic portfolio expert Darren Cambridge's description of the "deliberative assessment" model at New Century College (NCC) suggests what this might look like. In this assessment system, students develop personalized eportfolios in the context of institutional expectations, articulated as competencies necessary for graduation. But while student eportfolios are required for graduation, "[t]here are no set criteria for judging what graduate-level [competencies] look like" (74). Instead, various members of the NCC community, including students, read and evaluate the eportfolios in light of those competencies, which are "both defined in a broad enough way that they can accommodate a wide range of interpretations and defined clearly enough that they make multiple interpretations mutually intelligible" (74). Rather than scoring eportfolios through the narrow lens of predetermined criteria, the eportfolios prompt ongoing deliberation about the qualities of a well-educated graduate. According to Cambridge, "decision makers are committed to taking into account the varied interests and ideas shared" by various readers of the eportfolios (75). Decisions are made *in light of* the range of readings, discrepant or not; no one is asked to retract or change their reading in accordance with a perceived true score or community standards.

In a rhetorical reliability framework, the range of relevant, informed readings is itself the marker of the trustworthiness, the reliability-as-credibility, of the assessment system because we know writing worth reading provokes a range of readings. Although it may be difficult to imagine a form of reliability in which discrepant readings are not a liability, the notion that evaluative systems may gain rather than lose credibility by accounting for discrepant views is hardly novel, even when high stakes decisions must be made. Decisions based on scholarly peer review, as Wilson notes, rely upon the judicious consideration of multiple, relevant, informed points of view. The same is true of academic review in general; the most important decisions we make—about whom to hire, which graduate student applicants to admit, whether to tenure or promote—rely on multiple, unnormed and often unreconciled perspectives. For instance, by the time a typical tenure file makes its way to the highest level of academic administration, a large number of perspectives—those of the candidate, disciplinary colleagues, departmental colleagues, college colleagues, a dean, a provost—are represented. Often those perspectives differ. While we might prefer perfect unanimity, its absence is not an indication that the tenure process is not working and lacks credibility; on the contrary, the process *derives* its credibility, its reliability, from the generation and consideration of a range of perspectives from various vantage points. Theoretically—certainly I recognize that the tenure process does not always work this way in practice—we trust a process that motivates and records as testimony the considered judgment of an array of variously situated, relevant, informed witnesses.

Consider also the mechanism of the dissenting opinion in Supreme Court cases. According to eminent legal scholar Lawrence Douglas, the Court legitimates itself precisely through routine public confessions of its inability to function as a modest witness. Douglas asserts, "the law presents its efforts at constitutional exposition in a rhetorical form that orchestrates this performance through measured subversion, namely, by presenting a majority opinion along with its systematic refutation in the form of a dissent" (258). The dissent, then, is not an indicator of a process gone awry, and it is not only an opportunity for a minority voice to be heard. Rather, it is "a critical constituent of a rhetoric of legitimation that empowers the Court's project of Constitutional exposition…through a public declamation of the Court's *awareness* of the impossibility of ultimately demonstrating the correctness of its readings and privilege of readership" (259, emphasis in original). Interpretive authority is established and legitimated by "a complex display of the impossibility of the hermeneutic task" (259).

Assessment of student writing, academic review, and legal decision making are different in many ways. But they are usefully analogous: they are all review and evaluation processes in which participants are tasked with viewing materials and providing some form of witness testimony (a score or reader report, a review and a publication or tenure recommendation, a legal opinion). Participants in these distributive evaluation processes are asked, "What do you see from where you are? How do you judge what you see?" And then sense must be made of the varying perspectives in order to arrive at a high stakes judgment.

So we are quite familiar with distributive evaluation processes that account for and document discrepant perspectives even when high stakes decisions must be made. In these processes, there is no attempt to norm witnesses away from their subjectivity by getting them all to interpret what they observe in the same way; testimonies stand, whether or not they agree with the views of the majority or the ultimate decision-maker. When this happens, we do not say there are no operative standards or criteria; we acknowledge that those standards or criteria are interpreted and/or applied differently. Instead of conveniently forgetting this fact when it comes to writing assessment because we are afraid our credibility will be damaged if we don't bow to a narrowly conceived reliability-as-consistency—or because we have acceded to the specious argument that fairness is guaranteed by consistent scores—composition studies needs to elaborate a theory of reliability-as-credibility that is rooted in our rhetorical approach to writing (and reading).

And we need to build assessment systems that are consistent with that theory. Whithaus, Neal, Haswell, Wilson, and Cambridge help us imagine how to design the kinds of interactive, descriptive, situated, and distributive (Whithaus) classroom and program assessment methods it requires. I agree with Whithaus and Cambridge that electronic portfolios provide a particularly rich avenue of investigation. As is already the case at Alverno College, LaGuardia Community College, Indiana University-Purdue University Indianapolis, Portland State, and elsewhere, student-generated electronic portfolios may be read and evaluated by a range of audiences inside and beyond institutions (see Cambridge; *Diagnostic Digital Portfolio*; Enyon; Hughes; Light, Sproule, and Lithgow). But whether or not students generate eportfolios, rhetorical reliability might ask a range of witnesses—instructors, administrators, advisors, professionals (including potential employers), other community members, and students themselves—to provide reader reports from their particular vantage points. While we would dispense with traditional norming, we would involve participants in the collaborative design, piloting, and use of reading protocols that guide these variously situated readers. Such activities would surely generate rich, contextualized discussions of how to define, value, and assess writing—and thus provide meaningful professional development for writing teachers and administrators. Depending on the scale of the assessment (classroom, program, institution, inter-institution, etc.), the audiences for the results (students, teachers, administrators, accreditors, etc.), and various factors such as timeframe and available resources, the assessors could offer some mix of selected response and narrative responses; the assessment could be largely descriptive, largely evaluative, or a balance of both.

The key to rhetorical reliability is not the scale or the instrument; rather, it is how readers are asked to function, what they are asked to produce, and what is done with what they produce. In rhetorical reliability, there is no expectation that readers will observe, perceive, and narrate in the same ways; indeed, both the value and the credibility of the assessment system hinge on the provision of testimony from various perspectives, various bodies. Reliability is "calculated" not by attending to agreement rates, but by evaluating the credibility of witnesses: Are their perspectives relevant to what the assessment is attempting to learn? Are they useful to students, teachers, programs, and/or institutions? Are their perspectives adequately described and explained? Do the accounts engage in productive ways with the texts? Do they indicate something meaningful about those texts? Do they appropriately engage (but not slavishly adhere to) community values? Do they identify other values that inform their accounts? If these questions are appropriately addressed, there is no need to reconcile discrepancies; rather, those differences become sites for mining meaning, opportunities to understand the interactions among writers, readers, and texts in contexts of reception.

Any assessment system that derives its reliability from making productive use of credible situated reader accounts, even and especially where they differ, is operating on rhetorical reliability. Systems of this kind have enormous potential to be of direct use to students; as Haswell and Wilson suggest, learning to write entails learning how to negotiate multiple, often conflicting responses to one's writing. But as Broad has shown—and I have seen this as well in my program assessment work—inquiring into reader differences can have significant value for curricular, pedagogical, and professional development. In any case, assessment systems must be designed to reflect the values and meet the expectations of their local contexts. To be sure, some programs will be more constrained than others, particularly in terms of what they publicly report. But even in highly constrained contexts, the reader differences that rhetorical reliability documents internally may be fed back into the program. In programs where arguments for rhetorical reliability are already taking hold, such as the eportfolio assessment programs described above, new public reporting protocols must be developed. One of the challenges for writing assessment in the years ahead will be to articulate reliability in ways that engage policymakers within and beyond our institutions and reflect, sustain, and advance our disciplinary values.

Conclusion

This new articulation of reliability should build on the nascent reconceptualizations of reliability proposed by Whithaus and others, as well as the historical and emerging writing assessment practices I pointed to in the previous section. But this articulation begins with the recognition that reliability is a multivalent and contested concept across a range of discourses. We can draw on these discourses, including educational measurement, to craft new theories of reliability for writing assessment. As Peggy O'Neill demonstrates, there are diverse views on reliability within the educational measurement community; indeed, some psychometricians (e.g., Cherry and Meyer; Haertal) reject the kinds of adjudication of discrepant readings that are common in inter-rater reliability calculations.

However, as O'Neill also suggests, "[w]e need to think carefully about what values reliability taps into and how they connect to the values we hold about teaching writing and learning to write." In my view, we need to break with those psychometricians whose notions of reliability, rooted in classical test theory, hew to the overriding value of consistency, and continue to learn from those who can help us shift our thinking to rhetorical conceptions of reliability (see Parkes) and to the value of credibility. Credibility, as we have seen, need not depend upon either consistency with known facts (accuracy) or consistency among witnesses (agreement, consensus). Indeed, the credibility of evaluative systems is sometimes enhanced, rather than undermined, by the inclusion of multiple perspectives from variously situated observers. In the case of writing, we know that readers read differently and that writers write inconsistently; reader differences might be the only window into these phenomena. Because we value the rhetorical nature of writing and reading, we must value *in*consistency, even dissensus.

The time has come to break the link between reliability and consistency and to advance new interdisciplinary reliability theory and practice rooted in rhetoric. Instead of conceiving dissensus as an embarrassing problem or threat, we might better understand it, in Thomas Rickert's formulation, as "a series of multivalent practices that are not merely critical but productive, joyous, and inventive" (32). Productivity, joy, inventiveness: these are values composition studies should be able to get behind.

Acknowledgements

The author wishes to thank Shari Stenberg, Beth Britt, Patricia Lynne, the anonymous *Composition Studies* reviewer, and Laura Micciche for their invaluable help with this essay.

Notes

1. The concept of inter-rater reliability itself is more complex in educational measurement than we tend to recognize. See, for instance, Stemler's discussion of three categories of inter-rater reliability: consistency estimates, consensus estimates, and measurement estimates. Stemler's work is particularly interesting because it attempts to account for discrepant readings. Consistency estimates adjust for rater differences before providing summary scores and measurement estimates calculate rater differences in order to identify raters who need to be retrained (consensus estimates average scores of multiple judges once consensus has been reached).

2. For the most recent and authoritative treatments of reliability in educational measurement, see the 2014 *Standards for Educational and Psychological Testing* (American) and Haertel. See also Huot; Llosa; Parkes.

3. See also Haswell and Wyche-Smith's version of an expert rater model, a two-tiered rating procedure. Like Smith, Haswell and Wyche-Smith offered new ways to think about and achieve rater reliability, while still hitching it to consistency.

4. In my experience as a rater both for a private assessment firm and for university and K-12 assessment processes, rater trainings *appear* to be a process of consensus-building, but they often are really an exercise in learning to apply a rubric, or scoring guide, to arrive at a "true score." In practice, then, what looks like hermeneutic reliability often functions as positivist reliability.

Works Cited

American Educational Research Association, American Psychological Association, and National Council on Measurement in Education. *Standards for Educational and Psychological Testing*. Washington: American Psychological Association, 2014. Print.

Bauman, Zygmunt. *Liquid Times: Living in an Age of Uncertainty*. Malden: Polity Press, 2007. Print.

Berlak, Harold. "The Need for a New Science of Assessment." *Toward a New Science of Educational Testing and Assessment*. Ed. Harold Berlak, Fred M. Newman, Elizabeth Adams, and Thomas A. Romberg. Albany: SUNY P, 1992. 1-21. Print.

Bernard-Donals, Michael. "Ethos, Witness, and Holocaust Testimony: The Rhetoric of *Fragments*." *JAC* 20.3 (2000): 565-82. Print.

---. "The Rhetoric of Disaster and the Imperative of Writing." *Rhetoric Society Quarterly* 31.1 (2001): 73-94. Print.

Broad, Bob. "Pulling Your Hair Out: Crises of Standardization in Communal Writing Assessment." *Research in the Teaching of English* 35 (2000): 213-60. Print.

---. *What We Really Value: Beyond Rubrics in Teaching and Assessing Writing*. Logan: Utah State UP, 2003. Print.

Cambridge, Darren. *Eportfolios for Lifelong Learning and Assessment*. San Francisco: Jossey-Bass, 2010. Print.

Cambridge, Darren, Barbara Cambridge, and Kathleen Yancey, eds. *Electronic Portfolios 2.0: Emergent Research on Implementation and Impact*. Sterling: Stylus, 2009. Print.

Cherry, Roger D., and Paul A. Meyer. "Reliability Issues in Holistic Assessment." Williamson and Huot 109-41. Print.

Diagnostic Digital Portfolio. Alverno College. 11 Feb. 2012. Web. 5 Feb. 2014. < http://ddp.alverno.edu/ >.

Diederich, Paul B. *Measuring Growth in English*. Urbana: NCTE, 1974. Print.

Diederich, Paul B., John W. French, and Sydell T. Carlton. *Factors in the Judgment of Writing Quality*. Princeton: Educational Testing Service, 1961. Print.

Douglas, Lawrence. "Constitutional Discourse and its Discontents: An Essay on the Rhetoric of Judicial Review." *The Rhetoric of Law*. Ed. Austin Sarat and Thomas R. Kearns. Ann Arbor: U of Michigan P, 1994. 225-60. Print.

Elbow, Peter. "A Method for Teaching Writing." *College English*. 30.2 (1968): 115-25. Print.

Elliot, Norbert. *On a Scale: A Social History of Writing Assessment in America*. New York: Peter Lang, 2005. Print.

Enyon, Bret. "Making Connections: The LaGuardia Eportfolio." *Electronic Portfolios 2.0: Emergent Research on Implementation and Impact*. Ed. Darren Cambridge, Barbara Cambridge, and Kathleen Yancey. Sterling: Stylus, 2009. 59-68. Print.

Farley, Todd. *Making the Grades: My Misadventures in the Standardized Testing Industry*. San Francisco: Berrett-Koehler Publishers, 2009. Print.

Felman, Shoshana, and Dori Laub. *Testimony: Crises of Witnessing in Literature, Psychoanalysis and History*. NY: Routledge, 1991. Print.

Forché, Carolyn. "Twentieth-century Poetry of Witness." *The American Poetry Review* 22.2 (Mar.-Apr. 1993). 9+. Print.

Giddens, Anthony. *Runaway World: How Globalization is Reshaping Our Lives*. NY: Routledge, 2000. Print.

Haertel, Edward H. "Reliability." *Educational Measurement*. 4th ed. Ed. Robert L. Brennan. Westport: American Council on Education/Praeger, 2006. 65-110. Print.

Haraway, Donna. "Ecce Homo, Ain't [Ar'n't] I a Woman, and Inappropriate/d Others: The Human in a Post-Humanist Landscape." Haraway, *The Haraway Reader* 47-61. Print.

Haraway, Donna. *The Haraway Reader*. NY: Routledge, 2004. Print.

---. "A Manifesto for Cyborgs." Haraway, *The Haraway Reader* 7-45. Print.

---. "modest_witness@second_millennium." Haraway, *The Haraway Reader* 223-50. Print.

---. "The Promises of Monsters: A Regenerative Politics for Inappropriate/d Other." Haraway, *The Haraway Reader* 63-124. Print.

---. "Situated Knowledges: The Science Question in Feminism and the Privilege of Partial Perspective." *Feminist Studies* 14.3 (1988): 575-99. Print.

Harris, Joseph. "The Idea of Community in the Study of Writing." *CCC* 40.1 (1989): 11-22. Print.

Haswell, Richard H. *Gaining Ground In College Writing: Tales of Development and Interpretation.* Dallas: SMUP, 1991. Print.

Haswell, Richard H., and Susan Wyche-Smith. "A Two-Tier Rating Procedure for Placement Essays." *Assessment in Practice: Putting Principles to Work on College Campuses.* Ed. Trudy W. Banta, Jon P. Lund, Karen E. Black, and Frances W. Oblander. San Francisco: Jossey-Bass, 1996. 204-207. Print.

Hesford, Wendy. "Documenting Violations: Rhetorical Witnessing and the Spectacle of Distant Suffering." *Biography* 27.1 (Winter 2004): 104-44. Print.

---. *Spectacular Rhetorics: Human Rights Visions, Recognitions, Feminisms.* Durham: Duke UP, 2011. Print.

Hughes, Julie. "Becoming Eportfolio Learners and Teachers." Cambridge, Cambridge, and Yancey 51-58. Print.

Huot, Brian. *(Re)Articulating Writing Assessment for Teaching and Learning.* Logan: Utah State UP, 2002. Print.

Huot, Brian, and Michael Neal. "Writing Assessment: A Techno-history." *Handbook of Writing Research.* Ed. Charles A. MacArthur, Steve Graham, and Jill Fitzgerald. NY: Guilford P, 2006. 417-32. Print.

Kalikoff, Beth. "Berlin, New York, Baghdad: Assessment as Democracy." *Journal of Writing Assessment* 2.2 (2005): 109-24. Print.

Kamberelis, George, and Greg Dimitriadis. *On Qualitative Inquiry: Approaches to Language and Literacy Research.* NY: Teachers College Press and National Conference on Research in Language and Literacy, 2005. Print.

Light, Tracy Penny, Bob Sproule, and Katherine Lithgow. "Connecting Contexts and Competencies: Using Eportfolios for Integrative Learning." Cambridge, Cambridge, and Yancey 69-80. Print.

Llosa, Lorena. "Building and Supporting a Validity Argument for a Standards-Based Classroom Assessment of English Proficiency Based on Teacher Judgments." *Educational Measurement: Theory and Practice* 27.3 (Fall 2008): 32-42. Print.

Lynne, Patricia. *Coming to Terms: A Theory of Writing Assessment.* Logan: Utah State UP, 2004. Print.

Moss, Pamela A. "Can There Be Validity Without Reliability?" O'Neill, Moore, and Huot 81-96. Print.

Myers, Greg. "Reality, Consensus, and Reform in the Rhetoric of Composition-Teaching." *College English* 48 (1986): 154-73. Print.

Neal, Michael. R. *Writing Assessment and the Revolution in Digital Texts and Technologies.* NY: Teachers College P, 2011. Print.

O'Neill, Peggy. "Reframing Reliability for Writing Assessment." *Journal of Writing Assessment* 4.1 (December 2011): n.pag. Web. 5 Feb. 2014. < http://journalofwritingassessment.org/article.php?article=54>.

O'Neill, Peggy, Cindy Moore, and Brian Huot. *A Guide to College Writing Assessment.* Logan: Utah State UP, 2009. Print.

Parkes, Jay. "Reliability as Argument." *Educational Measurement: Theory and Practice* 26.4 (Winter 2007): 2-10. Print.

Peat, F. David. *From Certainty to Uncertainty: The Story of Science and Ideas in the Twentieth Century*. Washington: Joseph Henry P, 2002. Print.

Rickert, Thomas. *Acts of Enjoyment: Rhetoric, Žižek, and the Return of the Subject*. Pittsburgh: U of Pittsburgh P, 2007. Print.

Schramm, Jan-Melissa. "Testimony, Witnessing." *Law and the Humanities: An Introduction*. Ed. Austin Sarat, Matthew Anderson, and Cathrine O. Frank. NY: Cambridge UP, 2010. 478-95. Print.

Shermis, Mark, and Jill Burstein, eds. *Handbook of Automated Essay Evaluation*. NY: Routledge, 2013. Print.

Slomp, David H., and Jim Fuite. "Following Phaedrus: Alternate Choices in Surmounting the Reliability/Validity Dilemma." *Assessing Writing* 9.3 (2004): 190-207. Print.

Smith, William L. "Assessing the Reliability and Adequacy of Using Holistic Scoring of Essays as a College Composition Placement Technique." Williamson and Huot 142-205. Print.

---. "The Importance of Teacher Knowledge in College Composition Placement Testing." *Reading Empirical Research Studies: The Rhetoric of Research*. Ed. John R. Hayes, Richard E. Young, Michele L. Matchett, Maggie McCaffrey, and Cynthia Cochran. Norwood: Ablex, 1992. 289-316. Print.

Stemler, Steven E. "A Comparison of Consensus, Consistency, and Measurement Approaches to Estimating Inter-rater Reliability." *Practical Assessment, Research & Evaluation* 9.4 (2004): n.pag. Web. 5 Feb. 2014. <http://pareonline.net/getvn.asp?v=9&n=4>.

Trimbur, John. "Consensus and Difference in Collaborative Learning." *College English* 51.6 (1989): 602-16. Print.

White, Edward M. "Holistic Scoring: Past Triumphs, Future Challenges." Williamson and Huot 79-108. Print.

Whithaus, Carl. "Distributive Evaluation." WPA-CompPile Research Bibliographies. No. 3. Feb. 2010. Web. 13 Feb. 2014. <http://comppile.org/wpa/bibliographies/Bib3/Whithaus.pdf>.

---. *Teaching and Evaluating Writing in the Age of Computers and High-Stakes Testing*. Mahwah: Lawrence Erlbaum Associates, 2005. Print.

Wiggins, Grant. "The Constant Danger of Sacrificing Validity to Reliability: Making Writing Assessment Serve Writers." *Assessing Writing* 1.1 (1994): 129-40. Print.

Williamson, Michael M. "An Introduction to Holistic Scoring: The Social, Historical, and Theoretical Context for Writing Assessment." Williamson and Huot 1-43. Print.

Williamson, Michael M., and Brian A. Huot, eds. *Validating Holistic Scoring for Writing Assessment*. Cresskill: Hampton Press, 1993. 142-205. Print.

Wilson, Maja. *Rethinking Rubrics in Writing Assessment*. Portsmouth: Heinemann, 2006. Print.

Yancey, Kathleen Blake. "Looking Back as We Look Forward: Historicizing Writing Assessment." *CCC* 50.3 (1999): 483-503. Print.

Disability Studies in the Composition Classroom

Ella R. Browning

Although attention to disability is becoming more apparent in first-year composition curricula, too often disability is simply "tacked on" to existing courses. Scholars have argued that composition instructors interested in fully integrating a disability studies perspective into their curriculum would do well, instead, to think critically about every aspect of their classroom spaces, the subject matter they teach, and the ways in which they teach it. This can seem, however, like an overwhelming task, even for instructors interested in incorporating a disability studies perspective into their pedagogy. This may be especially challenging for instructors working within standardized composition programs without much flexibility in the curricula they are asked to teach. Using as an example a sample first-year composition curriculum at a large public university, this article explores how a disability studies perspective can be incorporated into a composition classroom in meaningful, productive ways, without altering the curriculum itself. In so doing, the article provides readers with a number of theoretical approaches to disability studies that may be helpful in reconsidering pedagogical strategies in a composition classroom, and also provides readers with suggestions for concrete, practical applications of such reframing strategies within the context of this particular sample curriculum.

Issues of disability matter in composition studies and classrooms, first, because we have a long, proud history of making the invisible visible and of examining how language both reflects and supports notions of Other. Second, we also rightly pride ourselves on our attention to practice—and on our refusal to separate it from the theoretical assumptions that explicitly or implicitly inform it. Third . . . because we already challenge the binaries of theory/practice, writing/thinking, and self/other, we should be well equipped—even eager—to embrace the critique of the (false) abled/disabled binary.

—Brenda Jo Brueggemann, Linda Feldmeier White,
Patricia A. Dunn, Barbara Heifferon, and Johnson Cheu

At the Computers & Writing 2014 conference the three keynote speakers addressed issues of inclusion, accessibility, and ethics. These are not unusual topics in the field of rhetoric and composition. Since the late 1990s and early 2000s, issues of disability and disability studies (DS) have emerged in a number of journals and conferences within our field, and more and more composition scholars have incorporated disability into their research and pedagogy. The focus of the keynote speakers at Computers & Writing demonstrates that disability and accessibility are still, and will continue to be, important issues within the field of rhetoric and composition. More specifically, as Margaret Price has noted, "disability has become more apparent in first-year writing pedagogies." However, she continues, "'apparent' is often the operative word" ("Accessing Disability," 54). Price and other DS scholars have noted that too often, disability is added to first-year composition (FYC) in the form of a single reading, or simply tacked on to the end of the race-class-gender triad of intersectional subjectivities to form race-class-gender-ability. Nirmala Erevelles has called this method of adding disability to a curriculum the "add-and-stir policy that once used to haunt race, feminist, and queer theory" ("Rewriting Critical Pedagogy," 66). Deb Martin explores this notion further in "Add Disability and Stir: The New Ingredient in Composition Textbooks," her chapter in Cynthia Lewiecki-Wilson and Brenda Jo Brueggemann's *Disability and the Teaching of Writing: A Critical Sourcebook*. Martin lays out a number of overly simplified or unproblematized ways in which disability is often represented in textbooks and curricula, such as adding a single text about disability or a single text by an author who identifies as a person with a disability. Composition instructors interested in fully integrating a DS perspective into their curriculum and avoiding the "add-and-stir" approach would do well to think critically about every aspect of their classrooms:[1] the physical space, the pedagogical techniques in use, the projects and assignments students are asked to complete, the technology students are required to use, and the subject matter instructors suggest that students discuss.

Thinking critically about and potentially transforming every aspect of a classroom and course can seem, understandably, like an overwhelming, time-consuming, and unwieldy task for instructors, even if they are interested in incorporating a DS perspective into their pedagogy. Should instructors, then, simply forgo incorporating disability into their classrooms because they do not have the time or freedom to do so as thoroughly as possible? The answer to that question is, in a word, no. But how might instructors bring a DS perspective into a composition classroom space without altering the curriculum itself and without devoting a full course to a disability theme, as many instructors do not have the opportunities to make these kinds of changes? And can this kind of integration of a DS perspective be done meaningfully, avoiding the add-and-stir approach? Using as an example a FYC curriculum at a large public university, this article explores how a DS perspective can be incorporated into a composition classroom in meaningful, productive ways, without altering the curriculum itself. According to recent census data, there were approximately

56.7 million people with some kind of disability living in the United States in 2010. This number is an increase by 2.2 million from the data collected in 2005. As I will demonstrate later in this article, students come into our classrooms with an awareness of disability; they see it in the news, in movies, on television; they have experienced it with friends, family, loved ones; perhaps they live it in their daily lives. As composition instructors, we occupy a powerful space: the composition classroom. Within this space, we can provide opportunities for undergraduate composition students to consider, explore, and articulate nonnormative embodied experiences in meaningful ways, even within a standardized composition curriculum.

Background

Although DS theory and research is becoming more and more prevalent within the field of rhetoric and composition, this article may serve as an introduction to DS for some *Composition Studies* readers. Because of this, I want to provide readers with some background on DS and a brief exploration of how some scholars pursuing this kind of work understand the notion of disability within larger social and cultural frameworks. Understanding these relationships is an important first step in problematizing undergraduate students' expectations and assumptions about disability and incorporating a DS perspective into a composition classroom.

The relationship between place, space, and the social construction of the dis/ability system is one that has been explored extensively within DS scholarship (Erevelles, "The Color of Violence"; Garland-Thomson; Lewiecki-Wilson and Brueggeman; Price, "Access Imagined"; Wilson and Lewiecki-Wilson). At the core of this scholarship has been a differentiation between two models of disability: the "medical model of disability" and the "social model of disability" (Lewiecki-Wilson and Brueggeman).[2] The medical model of disability, historically, has been consistent with the ways that our society (de)values individuals with disabilities. The medical model of disability understands disability as something wrong with the body, something abnormal, something tragic, something that needs to be fixed. One of the ways we can see the medical model of disability at play is in the many "overcoming narratives" circulating in popular culture. "Overcoming narratives" assume that disability is something that can and should be overcome, consistent with the idea that disability is something that needs to be "dealt with" through accommodations (Lewiecki-Wilson and Brueggeman). "Overcoming narratives" often further the notion that if a person has a disability he or she cannot live a full and fulfilling life. Overcoming narratives support the belief that the only way for a person with a disability to be happy is to "overcome" or "triumph over" his or her disability in some way. Instead of seeing disability as something to be overcome, DS scholars see disability as simply a different way of living in and experiencing the world, an expression of physical- or neuro-diversity[3] that should be acknowledged and valued.

Many efforts at accommodating individuals with disabilities, though often well intentioned, coincide with a medical model of disability in that accommodations are simply added on to existing structures and systems. These might manifest as a ramp added to a building that previously was only accessible via stairs, or it might mean that in a computer lab classroom there is only a single computer that offers accessible technologies for students who need them. Jay Dolmage has referred to this practice as "retrofitting" and explores the ways in which physical structures, as well as curricula, are often "retrofitted" to accommodate individuals with disabilities. While these additions are important in providing accessibility for individuals with disabilities, they do little to change the ways that disability is viewed by our typically ableist society. Accommodations like these further the idea that it is people with disabilities who have the "problems," not the structures or institutions that have been constructed with a too-narrow understanding of what a body is or how it functions. The solution, then, is to produce systems and institutions, including classroom pedagogies, with disability in mind already, so that disability and nonnormative bodies are always already a part of our society and of the structures that support and reflect our cultural ideologies.

In opposition to the medical model of disability is what is commonly known as the "social model of disability." As a field, DS is concerned largely with the social model of disability and the ways that language and culture create and sustain what Rosemarie Garland-Thomson has articulated as the "the dis/ability system." In their introduction to *Disability and the Teaching of Writing: A Critical Sourcebook* editors Cynthia Lewiecki-Wilson and Brenda Jo Brueggeman explain that "disability studies asks us to think carefully about language and its effects, to understand the role of the body in learning and writing, to view bodies and minds as inherently and wonderfully divergent, to consider issues of access and exclusion in policies and in the environment, and to reengage with theories of difference and diversity" (1). Integrating a DS perspective into a composition classroom thus means thinking carefully about the issues above within the context of a specific writing classroom or within a specific university writing curriculum. This might be done in a number of ways depending on classroom space, curricular requirements, technology usage, and the instructor's own interests, values, expectations, and goals, as well as the larger university structure that supports this particular classroom environment.

Many of the ways we can hope to rebuild our universities, and thus help our students "rebuild" rather than "retrofit" (Lewiecki-Wilson and Brueggemann) their understanding of dis/ability, is through what and how we teach those students. In "Mapping Composition: Inviting Disability in the Front Door" from the edited collection *Disability and the Teaching of Writing,* Jay Dolmage argues that "[i]f the composition teacher wants to treat students ethically and respectfully, she must consider the spaces where she teaches in terms of disciplinary attitudes, but also in terms of bricks and mortar, walls and steps that exclude bodies. The disciplinary and the institutional, the discursive and the physical, must be considered always in interaction" (16). Rather than simply retrofitting our universities, our classroom spaces, and our pedagogies, we must actively integrate disability, in thoughtful and critical ways, into all aspects of our teaching. This can seem like an overwhelming task, but a number of DS scholars have suggested ways that instructors might utilize a DS perspective to transform their classrooms and their curricula. These suggestions are especially beneficial for those instructors with the time and freedom to customize their courses as they see fit.

Rather than providing two separate sections below, one exploring a brief literature review of DS theory and one showing a sample, standardized curriculum that could be reframed using a DS perspective, I have woven the two together. In the epigraph with which this article begins, Brueggemann, White, Dunn, Heifferon, and Cheu explain, "…we also rightly pride ourselves on our attention to practice—and on our refusal to separate it from the theoretical assumptions that explicitly or implicitly inform it" (371). Following these scholars' lead, I have crafted the following discussion to do three things: (1) showcase an example of a standardized FYC curriculum and explore how and where a DS perspective might be integrated into such a curriculum; (2) provide readers with a number of theoretical approaches to DS that could be helpful in reconsidering pedagogical strategies in a composition classroom; and (3) expand on those theoretical approaches by providing readers with suggestions for concrete, practical applications of such reframing strategies within the context of this particular sample curriculum. Perhaps most importantly, I will highlight the ways that students enter our classrooms with preconceived notions of what disability is and what it means by analyzing the ways one particular student articulates how infants might be affected by the risk of premature birth. I explore how we as composition instructors might respond to such exigencies by using students' preconceptions about disability as tools for pedagogical change.

Discussion

In "An Enabling Pedagogy: Meditations on Writing and Disability" Brenda Jo Brueggemann explores what she calls an "enabling pedagogy," or "a theory and practice of teaching that posits disability as insight" in three classroom spaces (795). For the purposes of this project I will focus on the third course

Brueggemann includes in her essay, a FYC honors course she designed around the theme "Abilities in America."[4] As part of this course, students were asked to read "race, class, gender, sexuality, and a whole host of other cultural and academic concerns . . . through the lens of disability" (806). One activity Brueggemann did with her students early in the term helps to contextualize what this might mean. Brueggemann asked students to brainstorm "hot issues in America," which she then wrote up on the board in the classroom. Next, she asked students to pick one of those topics, and they chose "date rape." Brueggemann asked her students how date rape and disability might be related, and when she was met with blank stares, she explained "how statistics on sexual abuse record alarmingly high numbers among disabled, institutionalized persons, both young and old" (807). She continued, reminding her students "how disabled people are more often than not perceived as either asexual or abnormally sexual" (807), and how this perception often results in an increased potential for abuse. Then, Brueggemann asked her students to get into groups and do the same exercise with a different "hot issue" written on the board. As an invention activity, this has the potential to open up an extraordinary number of topics for students to focus on for writing projects. This invention activity also has the potential to complicate students' understanding of issues they might otherwise think of as rather clear-cut.

ENC 1102 at the University of South Florida (USF) is the second of a two-semester FYC program. ENC 1102's curriculum consists of three distinct but interconnected writing projects, each one building off the previous one. The overarching relationship between the three projects, and a brief description of them, is as follows:

> Students will select a controversial, current issue to analyze throughout the semester. The major projects in 1102 ask students to consider this issue from a rhetorical perspective by analyzing visual arguments from various stakeholders (Project 1), arguing for a solution to the issue while negotiating common ground between various stakeholders (Project 2), and [using both written and visual arguments] inviting a non-engaged stakeholder to take action for the given issue in a concrete way (Project 3). (First Year Composition at USF)

In this curriculum, students complete a variety of writing exercises and visual mapping assignments to choose a topic prior to writing Project 1. Topic selection is a key aspect of this particular curriculum because, as the description above mentions, students are encouraged to trace and explore their topics from various perspectives throughout the entire semester. Brueggemann's invention exercise, connecting "hot issues" in the United States to disability, could be one such exercise to help students choose a topic that will be complex, dynamic and engaging enough for them to explore for an entire semester. Introduced early in the semester, Brueggemann's invention exercise could accomplish a number of goals: (1) help students think about possible topic ideas; (2) help students complicate topic ideas they may already have in mind; and (3) introduce the notion of disability as one worth approaching critically, similar to the ways students may have already been introduced to critical discussions of race, class, and gender in this or other courses.

One invention exercise that students in ENC 1102 are currently asked to complete is a prewriting exercise in which they "map out" their chosen topic and the various stakeholders[5] involved with or related to that issue. For the purposes of this article I will refer to this prewriting exercise as a "stakeholder visualization" exercise, and it will be the focus of my analysis. Figures 1–6 provide screenshots of one particular student's mapping of his topic and the stakeholders involved, as he understands them. For the purposes of this project, I am reproducing the student's words as he originally wrote them, including errors. This particular student has chosen "Premature Births in United States Citizens" as his potential topic. Brueggemann argues throughout her essay for the idea of "disability as insight," a way of incorporating disability into a classroom space in which discussions are opened and research and writing projects can lead to new ways of understanding the world. She argues that incorporating disability into a classroom enables insight—"critical, experiential, cognitive, sensory, and pedagogical insight"—even if disability is not the sole focus or subject of the course (795). Imagine the possibilities for investigating and analyzing a topic like this student's, "Premature Births in United States Citizens," in a composition course in which the instructor has integrated DS into the curriculum via Brueggemann's "disability as insight." I will explore some of these possibilities momentarily.

If he chooses to do so, this student will focus on this topic throughout the entire semester, exploring it in different ways as he works his way through all three projects. He will research scholarly and popular sources on the topic, he will explore the visual communication strategies that stakeholders in this topic have utilized, and he will try to convince an audience that this is an issue about which they should care and act, even if they do not initially believe it requires their participation. At this point in the semester at USF, however, the student is in the process of conceptualizing his topic and deciding how to narrow it down so that he can begin his research. USF FYC instructors have introduced "stakeholder theory" to students with the goal of helping students understand the complexity of the social issues and topics they wish to research. Too often, students rely on oversimplified binaries in order to understand controversial issues: pro-life versus pro-choice; the 99% versus the 1%; illegal immigrant versus U.S. citizen; able-bodied versus disabled; and so on. In asking students to think about stakeholders and the wide variety of individuals, organizations, businesses, and other groups who care about controversial issues, the hope is that students will learn to avoid such binary thinking. This is a common theme in composition studies. Indeed, it is because we so often challenge such binaries in our composition classrooms that "we should be well equipped—even eager—to embrace he critique of the (false) abled/disabled binary system" (Brueggemann, White, Dunn, Heifferon, Cheu).

For his stakeholder visualization exercise, this student was asked to map out the various stakeholders he sees as being involved with his chosen issue, and, ultimately, to choose one stakeholder to analyze for Project 1. In this particular curriculum, in order to facilitate such complex thinking, students are encouraged to use visualization tactics to map out the stakeholders involved in their chosen issues. This student has chosen to use Prezi.com in order to map stakeholders and demonstrate his focus for Project 1, but there are many other programs that can facilitate similar mapping strategies.[6] Figure 1 shows the main entry screen for this student's Prezi-based stakeholder visualization exercise, and I have provided written explanations of each figure so that audiences of this paper will have multiple methods of reading this student's project.

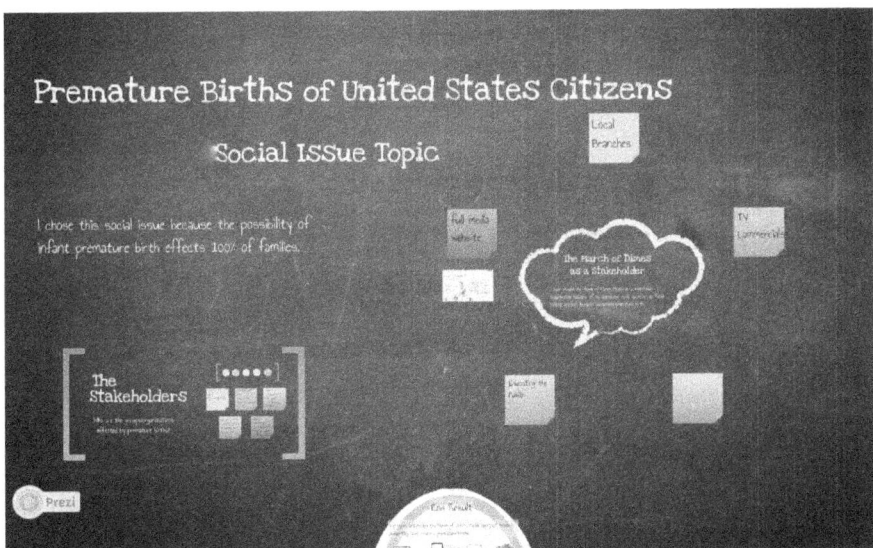

Figure 1.

In Figure 1, the student uses a Prezi template that is made to look like a chalkboard, with text written in white "chalk" at various points on the board. The title reads, "Premature Births of United States Citizens." Below this the student originally included his name, but it and other identifying information has been removed for the purposes of this paper so that this student may remain anonymous. The student has written, "I chose this social issue because the possibility of infant premature birth effects 100% of families." When one clicks to the next "slide" of the presentation, the view zooms into a small, bracketed section of the chalkboard in which the student has laid out the stakeholders he understands to be involved in the issue of premature births in the United States (see Figure 2).

Beneath the title of this bracketed section ("The Stakeholders") the student has written a question: "Who are the groups/organizations effected by premature births?" He has answered this question by identifying five stakeholders he sees as being impacted by or having a stake in the issue of "Premature Births in United States Citizens:" doctors, families, the infant, government, and charities (see Figure 3).

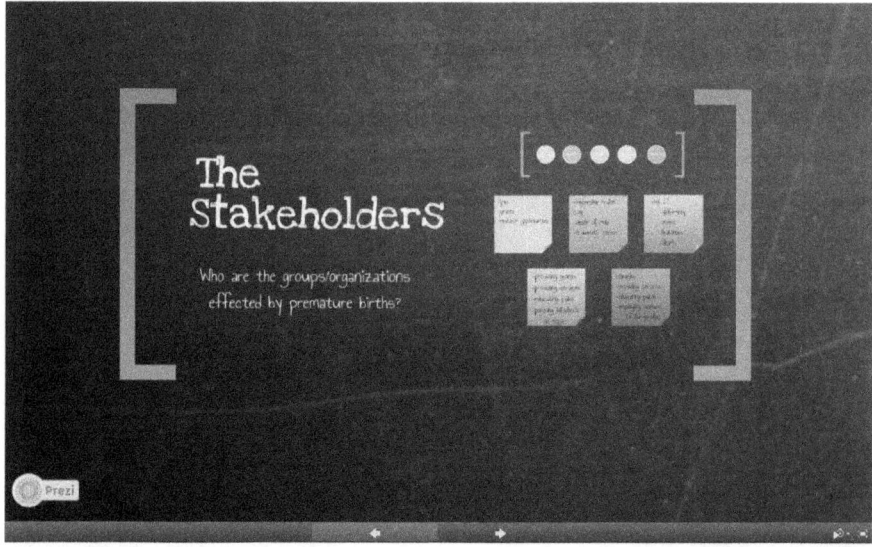

Figure 2.

I will focus here exclusively on the stakeholder this student has labeled as "The Infant." Before exploring this student's understanding of "The Infant," however, I'd like to first turn to Margaret Price's articulation of disability as critical modality. Like Brueggemann, Price considers the ways that DS might be more fully incorporated into a composition classroom. In "Accessing Disability: A Nondisabled Student Works the Hyphen," the task, she says, "is not simply to include disability; it is to include disability studies" (54). This is key. Simply including disability can come dangerously close to the charge of "add-then-stir." Including DS, on the other hand, means thinking critically about the ways that language, space, action, and inaction construct and sustain the dis/ability system.

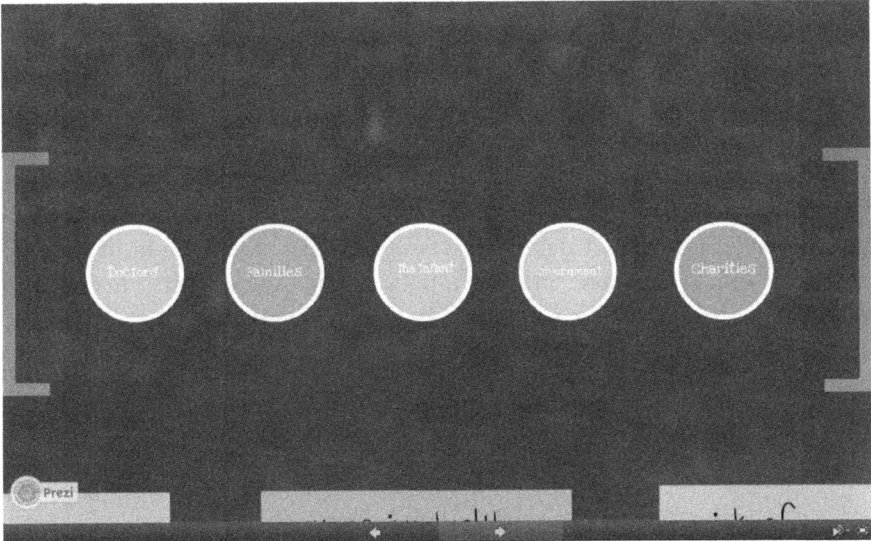

Figure 3.

For Price, this means incorporating disability as critical modality, a social construction, and a community issue. Quoting her past collaborative work with Cynthia Lewiecki-Wilson, Price recalls that one key aspect of disability as critical modality is the recognition that "students' critical thinking cannot be adequately assessed in the context of a single piece of writing . . . instead, we must accept that progress—as DS itself reminds us—means something more complicated than a singular coming-to-consciousness, or than linear movement toward a fixed goal" (57). She calls for instructors to question "the common assumption that students' critical thinking can be adequately represented through written artifacts" (57). This means more than simply asking students to complete a "what have you learned" reflection at the end of a semester. Rather, it means being open to the ways that students may develop critical thinking in a nonlinear, nonwritten way. As instructors, we should be open to and keenly aware of the various artifacts that can help us see this kind of development.

Price's focus here is on in-person conversations she had with her student, Tara, which Price argues can help represent Tara's critical thinking processes and development. I would extend Price's claim and argue that in addition to in-person conversations, student-created visual artifacts can also be a means of demonstrating the evolution of their critical thinking processes. In the example here, the student's combination of visual and written artifact in the form of his stakeholder visualization assignment gives us a glimpse into his starting point for this semester. Similarly, this example gives us an idea of the (potential) evolution of his critical thinking about disability and how it might progress if we were to integrate a DS perspective into this curriculum. Figure 4 shows the student's understanding of how an infant might be affected by the risk of premature birth. He has written, "risk of . . ." followed by the words "deformity," "me[n]tal disabilities," and "death." His assessment of the reasons why infants have a stake in the issue of premature birth can thus be summarized as follows: infants have a stake in the issue of premature birth in the United States because if born prematurely, infants risk being born with mental and physical disabilities, or they risk not being born alive at all.

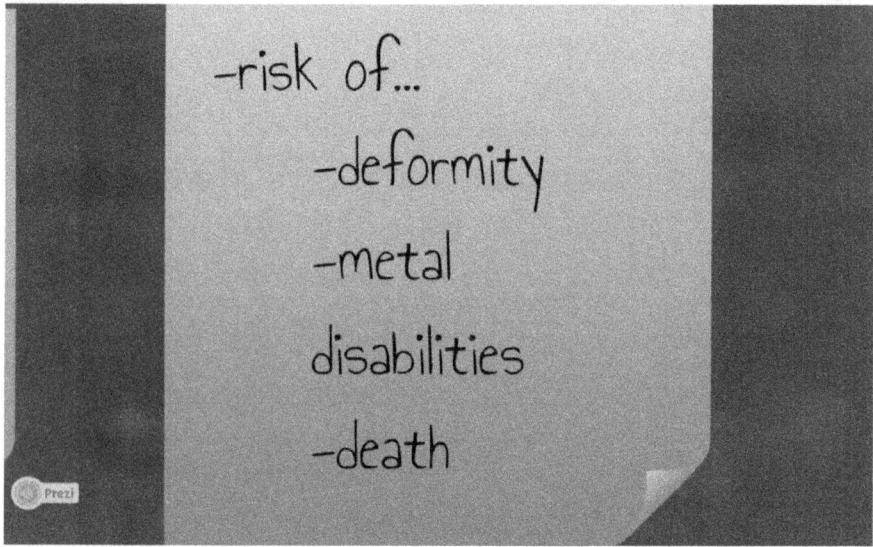

Figure 4.

In their 2013 article "Liminal Spaces and Research Identity: The Construction of Introductory Composition Students as Researchers," James P. Purdy and Joyce R. Walker note that in theorizing the composition classroom as a liminal space, it is important to recognize the skills and knowledge that students already possess when they enter our classrooms. If instructors ignore these things and assume that students come into our classrooms having no experience with the skills or ideas about which we try to teach them, we lose the opportunity to take advantage of the composition classroom as potentially transformative because we fail to meet students "where they are" when they enter our classrooms. In Figure 4, it is clear that this student has some knowledge of disability prior to entering this particular composition classroom. It is important to note, too, that this composition instructor did not knowingly emphasize disability in teaching this project or in teaching stakeholder theory. Regardless, it is clear that this student knows that there are different types of disabilities, which he identifies as mental disabilities and physical disabilities. Similar to how western civilization has historically viewed nonnormative bodies, however, he refers to these bodily variations as "deformities." As well, he identifies mental and physical disabilities as "risks," as potentially negative outcomes for babies who are born prematurely, in line with the ways our society typically reads disability: something tragic a person must overcome, rather than an alternative way of living in the world that can result in a fulfilling life. This student even goes so far as to associate disability explicitly with death.

In a composition classroom in which the instructor is utilizing a DS perspective, the stakeholder visualization exercise shown in Figures 1–4 provides an opportunity for discussions about the concept of disability and the place disability has in our culture. Brueggemann's notion of disability as insight and Price's call for disability as critical modality could both be utilized within this classroom context. Stakeholder theory itself provides an opportunity for productive discussion about complex ideas, and the different ways those complex issues may affect different individuals. Furthermore, the pedagogical techniques outlined above could result in an even more productive and prolonged (re)consideration of disability. Instructors might ask individual students or the class as a whole about the ways that people with disabilities are portrayed in our society, and raise questions about why this student (and perhaps others) believe(s) that mental and physical disabilities should be aligned with death. These are important questions to ask.

Depending on how much freedom an instructor has within his or her particular standardized curriculum, instructors may also wish to assign readings written by authors with disabilities. The goal in assigning such readings would be to avoid "overcoming narratives" and instead choose texts demonstrating the ways that such individuals can and do live fulfilling, happy lives even if they live with one of the "risks" the student has listed here.[7] It would also be worth having a discussion about how individuals with disabilities might respond to this student's portrayal of mental and physical disabilities, or how a person with a family member who has a disability might respond.[8] Depending on the class, instructors could even introduce Rosemarie Garland-Thomson's explanation of disability as a flexible identity, "a concept that pervades all aspects of culture: its structuring institutions, social identities, cultural practices, political positions, historical communities, and the shared human experience of embodiment" (16). Incorporating a DS perspective into a composition curriculum like the one explored here means beginning with the belief that disability is something worth exploring. Furthermore, in this particular case, it means utilizing stakeholder theory and taking advantage of the other structures of this standardized curriculum in order to have these kinds of challenging but important discussions about stakeholders, dis/ability, bodies, environments, medicine, society, and individuals when presented with opportunities to do so.

In his stakeholder visualization assignment, once the student has provided an overview of the stakeholders he sees as being involved with "Premature Births in United States Citizens," he chooses one particular stakeholder to research and analyze. The ultimate goal of Project 1 in the ENC 1102 project sequence is for students to analyze two images created by the stakeholder, and construct an argument about how those images reflect the overall mission or goals of the stakeholder. As students learn stakeholder theory, then, they are also learning about visual arguments and visual analysis. This student chose to focus on the March of Dimes nonprofit organization as the stakeholder for his project. He explains, "I have chosen the March of Dimes (MOD) as a stakeholder organization because of its aggressive media approach to fundraising research towards preventing premature birth" (see Figure 5).

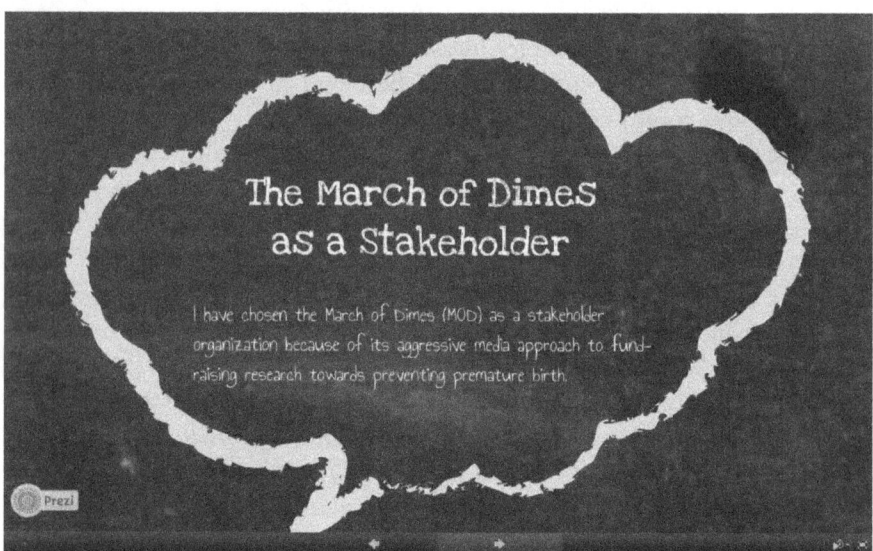

Figure 5.

The student notes that in order to raise funds to research ways to prevent premature birth, the March of Dimes utilizes a variety of media strategies. He explains that he will produce a project analyzing the ways that this nonprofit organization utilizes media in order to prevent the premature births of what he refers to as "United States citizens." In particular, he highlights the March of Dimes' website as a specific example of this (see Figure 6).

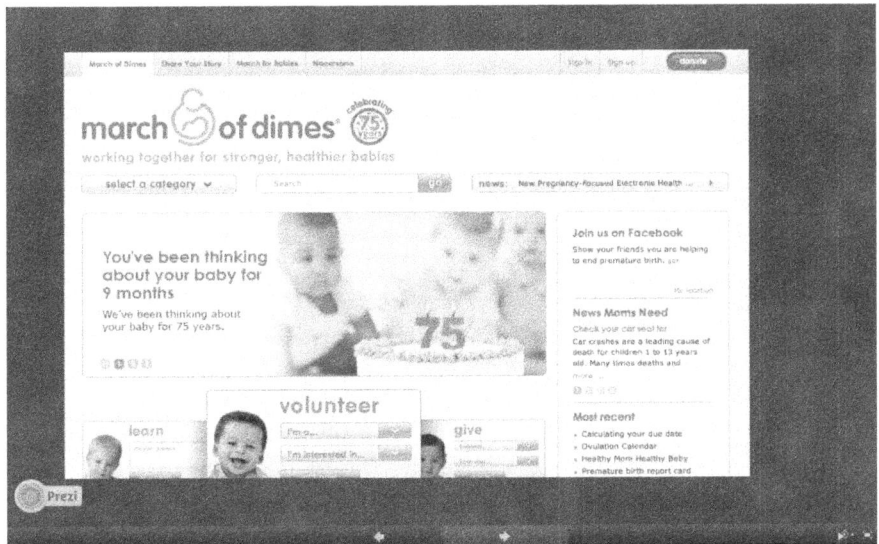

Figure 6.

Figure 6 shows the March of Dimes' slogan, "working together for stronger, healthier babies," in the upper left-hand corner of the website's home screen. If this student's instructor had chosen to approach this curriculum with a DS perspective, perhaps one aspect of the March of Dimes' campaign this student would be focusing on would be the use of the notion of a "strong, healthy baby." How might we use disability as a critical modality to problematize the notion of a "strong, healthy baby"? How does the language used in this slogan represent certain constructions of what it means to be a valued member of the community? What assumptions do we see here about what kinds of bodies are valuable? What about assumptions about what kinds of bodies need to be worked for or against? This discussion could then turn to the ways that this kind of rhetoric perpetuates not only ableist ideology, but also creates what could be considered to be a hierarchy of bodies within our society, in which some are considered more valuable than others. Again, the first step for instructors wishing to incorporate a DS perspective into their classroom is to identify these kinds of opportunities for discussion and take advantage of them.

It is particularly interesting that this student chose to focus on the March of Dimes organization as a stakeholder in light of Rosemarie Garland-Thomson's essay, "Integrating Disability, Transforming Feminist Theory." One of the images Garland-Thomson uses as an example of the ways that disability has been historically portrayed as being intolerable, curable, and, often, as requiring the assistance of able-bodied allies in order to overcome its supposed tragedy, is the 1949 March of Dimes poster (see Figure 7).

Figure 7.

The text in this poster (Figure 7) reads, at the top, "Look! I can walk again!" Positioned next to an image of a white, curly-haired little girl stepping tentatively out of a wheelchair, additional corresponding text asks viewers to join the March of Dimes and fight infantile paralysis. As Garland-Thomson writes, "Nowhere do we find posters suggesting that life as a wheelchair user might be full and satisfying, as many people who actually use them find their lives to be. This ideology of cure is not isolated in medical texts or charity campaigns, but in fact permeates the entire cultural conversation about disability and illness" (15). The project for which this student is preparing does not stipulate from what time period images should come. Considering the rich historical material we have available for analysis thanks to basic online search tools like Google Image, an instructor utilizing a DS perspective within this curriculum might encourage this student to analyze the March of Dimes' historical media representation and strategies. The student could explore the ways that the images this organization has created over time reflect particular messages about which bodies are "broken" and which are "whole." This exploration could be especially fruitful in light of in-class discussions about the constructed dis/ability system in our society and the ways disability has historically been and continues to currently be portrayed.

There has been quite a bit written on the ways that organizations like the March of Dimes have historically promoted an ultimately damaging medical model of disability. Instructors interested in complicating students' understandings of these kinds of nationally known fundraising organizations could incorporate a number of these pieces into their curriculums. Before her death in 2008, disability activist Harriett McBryde Johnson was one of the most outspoken protestors against Jerry Lewis' muscular dystrophy telethon, which has often been referred to as the "Jerry's Kids" campaign (McBryde Johnson). Johnson's writings and public appearances focusing on the rights of people with disabilities and the ways that the "Jerry's Kids" campaign demeans people with disabilities are accessible and powerful statements on the importance of discussions about how and where the medical model of disability can be seen amongst organizations meant to "raise awareness." Another useful text for critically re/considering the ways that public service campaigns engage with the concept of disability is Joseph Kras' analysis of the New York University Child Study Center's 2007 public service campaign through the use of "ransom notes." One example he cites is the ransom note the campaign designed to be understood by readers as "to parents" and "from Autism." It reads, "We have your son. We will make sure he will not be able to care for himself or interact socially as long as he lives. This is only the beginning." Elizabeth Scherman's analysis of Christopher Reeve's speech to the 1996 Democratic National Convention is an additional example of the often damaging and dangerous implications of such campaigns and organizations. There are also plenty of current-day activists utilizing the Internet to get their responses to these kinds of campaigns out to the public. While not always the most reliable source, Wikipedia can be a helpful starting place in asking undergraduate students to explore the world of disability rights activism while also teaching students how to use popular sources in an appropriate manner, a skill many composition instructors already teach in their courses.

Conclusion

Below are a number of questions instructors might ask themselves in order to more consciously avoid ableist ideologies in aspects of their teaching, curricula, and classroom setup. These are adapted from suggestions by DS scholars across the field, notably those included in *Disability and the Teaching of Writing: A Critical Sourcebook* and others. Considering these questions may help instructors begin to incorporate a DS perspective into their teaching without necessarily changing the curricula being taught.

- Is my classroom space physically accessible? Who is excluded? How might it be made more physically accessible for more students?
- Do the technologies I ask students to use exclude any students? Do these technologies make assumptions about students' abilities? How might these be improved?
- When I conceptualize the openness of my course and my awareness of important issues of identity, are there identities I leave out? How might I change this?
- Does my language inadvertently further ableist ideology? What about the language of my course materials?
- How heavily do I rely on culturally accepted "rules of normalcy" in the ways I interact with my students, in person and online?
- Do my classroom activities and pedagogical strategies privilege able-bodiedness? Do I allow for various modes of embodiment, various ways of learning, various ways of composing, various ways of making meaning? How might my pedagogy be more inclusive?
- How might I incorporate Brueggemann's practice of "disability as insight" in order to further complicate and problematize the ideas my students are exploring, researching, analyzing, and composing?
- Keeping in mind the way that DS approaches the notion of "progress"—that is, as not necessarily linear—how might I incorporate Price's call for "disability as critical modality" in order to trace my students' critical thinking processes and evolution throughout the semester? How might I do so while also being open to individual ways of composing, learning, and developing?

Ideally, a composition classroom that fully incorporates a DS perspective would be one in which an instructor is able to design a themed course and fully integrate the suggestions made by the scholars I have referenced here as well as the myriad other DS scholars writing and researching these issues. It would also be one in which students would register for the course willingly, interested in and excited about entering into these kinds of discussions with a focus on disability. The composition classroom, however, is not always such a place. It can be challenging for composition instructors to incorporate these suggestions to the extent that we might like to due to lack of time, lack of freedom, lack of resources, or any combination thereof. That does not mean, however, that we cannot find opportunities in our own classrooms to take advantage of disability as a means of insight, as a way of generating and developing critical thinking. There are ways to incorporate disability in meaningful, productive ways, avoiding the "add-and-stir" condemnation. As composition instructors, we not only have the opportunities to do so (should we take advantage of them), but we also have the ethical obligation to have these kinds of challenging discussions in our classrooms. It is only by asking our students to think critically about the world around them, and to think creatively and productively about ways to change it, that we have any hope of transforming our future and working against assumptions that constrain the possibilities of what bodies and minds can and should accomplish.

Acknowledgments

The author wishes to acknowledge the support of her colleagues at the University of South Florida, especially Dr. Diane Price-Herndl, Kristen Gay (now at Clemson University), and Julie Gerdes (now at Texas Tech University), with whom the author had valuable conversations while working through the ideas discussed here. An earlier version of this paper was presented at the 2013 Feminisms and Rhetorics Conference at Stanford University.

Notes

1. These kinds of discussions often include reference to or use of Universal Design principles, developed at North Carolina State University. Although too complex to address meaningfully here, it is worth noting that a number of scholars within rhetoric and composition have explored ways of incorporating Universal Design principles into the writing classroom. See, for example, Jay Dolmage's "Mapping Composition: Inviting Disability in the Front Door" from Cynthia Lewiecki-Wilson and Brenda Brueggeman's *Disability and the Teaching of Writing: A Critical Sourcebook*. Dolmage explains, "I choose to write about Universal Design mainly because of the verb, *design*. This suggests that UD is a way to plan, to foresee, to imagine the future. The *universal* of UD also suggests that disability is something that is *always* a part of our worldview. Thus, when UD is successful, it is hopeful *and* realistic, allowing teachers to structure space in the broadest possible manner" (24). See also Patricia A. Dunn and Kathleen Dunn De Mers' "Reversing Notions of Disability and Accommodation: Embracing Universal Design in Writing Pedagogy and WebSpace" and

Shannon Walters' "Toward an Accessible Pedagogy: Dis/ability, Multimodality, and Universal Design in the Technical Communication Classroom."

2. It should be noted that these two models of disability have been contested by some DS scholars as being overly simplistic. See, for example, Tom Shakespeare's excellent history and critique of the social model of disability and his call for more sophisticated and complex approaches to disability in his essay, "The Social Model of Disability," which can be found in Lennard Davis' fourth edition of the *Disability Studies Reader*, a useful resource for anyone interested in learning more about the field of DS.

3. Although beyond the scope of this project, there has been extensive scholarship done on the neurodiversity movement, some specifically within the field of rhetoric and composition. For a brief introduction, see, for example, Ann Jurecic's "Neurodiversity," "Two Comments On 'Neurodiversity'" by Cynthia Lewiecki-Wilson, Jay Dolmage, and Paul Heilker, and Joseph F. Kras' "The 'Ransom Notes' Affair: When the Neurodiversity Movement Came of Age."

4. Brueggemann references this particular course further in "Performing (Everyday) Exceptionalities: A Web-Text on Disability in Drama and Performance Art," part of *Kairos*' Spring 2002 special issue devoted to "Disability—Demonstrated By and Mediated Through Technology."

5. The curriculum explored in this project relies on the notion of "stakeholder theory." The texts instructors teaching this curriculum typically utilize to help students understand stakeholder theory include the following: "Whither Stakeholder Theory? A Guide for the Perplexed Revisited" by John Hasnas, "Toward a Theory of Stakeholder Identification and Salience: Defining the Principle of Who and What Really Counts" by Ronald K. Mitchell, Bradley R. Agle and Donna J. Wood, "Writers Emphasize Complexity" by Ella Bieze, and "Who Has a 'Stake' in the Argument? An Introduction to Primary and Potential Stakeholders" by Alex Watkins and Julie Gerdes. The concept of stakeholder theory is generally attributed to R. Edward Freeman, and most scholars interested in stakeholder theory cite his 1984 book, *Strategic Management: A Stakeholder Approach*, as the origin of the concept. Freeman and many scholars following him have generally utilized stakeholder theory in terms of business management strategies as it elucidates the complexity of business and business models. This usefulness in exploring complex relationships means that such a theory can also help scholars in the humanities consider or reconsider the complexities of our own research and scholarship, and can also help us teach students to recognize and explore such complexities in their own writing and research.

6. A few of these resources include http://www.mindmeister.com, http://www.xmind.net, http://mind42.com, and http://popplet.com, in addition to www.prezi.com.

7. See, for example, Kenny Fries' edited collection *Staring Back: The Disability Experience from the Inside Out* and *Disability Study Quarterly*'s 2008 special issue on "Disability Studies in the Undergraduate Classroom" (Brueggemann and Danforth) in which a few essays written by students with disabilities appear. It would be worth selecting one or two of these readings and asking students to map out the stakeholders they see present or referenced, or to ask students to trace how an author's disability

is framed within the various scenes or moments of a particular narrative, especially in the context of a high school, college, or other familiar, taken-for-granted space.

8. It should be noted that instructors should avoid asking if any students in the classroom themselves have disabilities, assuming that all disabilities are visible, or asking students with known or visible disabilities to "speak to" this perspective. Students should share this information voluntarily and instructors should receive students' permission to use this information as a part of class discussion prior to doing so.

9. See, for example, http://en.wikipedia.org/wiki/List_of_disability_rights_activists and http://en.wikipedia.org/wiki/Disability_rights_movement.

Works Cited

Bieze, Ella R. "Writers Emphasize Complexity." *Rhetoric Matters: Language and Argument in Context*. Ed. Jason Carabelli and Brogan Sullivan. Tampa, FL: U of South Florida, 2013. N. pag. PDF file.

Brueggemann, Brenda Jo. "An Enabling Pedagogy: Meditations on Writing and Disability." *JAC* 21.4 (2001): 791-820. Print.

---. "Performing (Everyday) Exceptionalities: A Web-Text on Disability in Drama and Performance Art." *Kairos: A Journal of Rhetoric, Technology, and Pedagogy* 7.1 (2002): n. pag. Web. 1 Mar. 2014. <http://kairos.technorhetoric.net/7.1/binder2.html?coverweb/brueggemann/index.html>.

Brueggemann, Brenda Jo, and Scot Danforth, eds. *Disability Studies in the Undergraduate Classroom*. Spec. issue of *Disability Studies Quarterly* 28.4 (2008): n. pag. Web. 4 Sept. 2014. <http://dsq-sds.org/issue/view/7>.

Brueggemann, Brenda Jo, Linda Feldmeier White, Patricia A. Dunn, Barbara Heifferon, and Johnson Cheu. "Becoming Visible: Lessons in Disability." *CCC* 52.3 (2001): 368-98. Print.

"Disability Rights Movement." *Wikipedia*. Wikimedia Foundation, 25 June 2014. Web. 1 July 2014. <http://en.wikipedia.org/wiki/Disability_rights_movement>.

Dolmage, Jay. "Mapping Composition: Inviting Disability in the Front Door." Lewiecki-Wilson and Brueggemann 14-27.

Dunn, Patricia A., and Kathleen Dunn De Mers. "Reversing Notions of Disability and Accommodation: Embracing Universal Design in Writing Pedagogy and WebSpace." *Kairos: A Journal of Rhetoric, Technology, and Pedagogy* 7.1 (2002): n. pag. Web. 28 Feb. 2014. <http://english.ttu.edu/kairos/7.1/coverweb/dunn_de-mers/index.html>.

Erevelles, Nirmala. "The Color of Violence: Reflecting on Gender, Race, and Disability in Wartime." *Feminist Disability Studies*. Ed. Kim Q. Hall. Bloomington: Indiana UP, 2011. 117-33. Print.

---. "Rewriting Critical Pedagogy from the Periphery: Materiality, Disability, and the Politics of Schooling." *Disability Studies in Education: Readings in Theory and Method*. Ed. Susan L. Gabel. New York: P. Lang, 2005. 65-84. Print.

First Year Composition at USF. *Composition II (ENC 1102)*. University of South Florida, n.d. Web. 4 Sept. 2014.

Freeman, R. Edward. *Strategic Management: A Stakeholder Approach*. Boston: Pitman, 1984. Print.

Fries, Kenny, ed. *Staring Back: The Disability Experience From the Inside Out*. New York: Plume, 1997. Print.
Garland-Thomson, Rosemarie. "Integrating Disability, Transforming Feminist Theory." *Feminist Disability Studies*. Ed. Kim Q. Hall. Bloomington: Indiana UP, 2011. 13-47. Print.
Hasnas, John. "Whither Stakeholder Theory? A Guide for the Perplexed Revisited." *Journal of Business Ethics* 112 (2013): 47-57. Print.
Jurecic, Ann. "Neurodiversity." *College English* 69.5 (2007): 421-42. Print.
Kras, Joseph F. "The 'Ransom Notes' Affair: When the Neurodiversity Movement Came of Age." *DSQ* 30.1 (2010): n. pag. Web. 28 Feb. 2014. <http://dsq-sds.org/article/view/1065/1254>.
Lewiecki-Wilson, Cynthia, and Brenda Jo Brueggemann, eds. *Disability and The Teaching of Writing: A Critical Sourcebook*. Boston: Bedford/St. Martin's, 2008. Print.
Lewiecki-Wilson, Cynthia, Jay Dolmage, Paul Heilker, and Ann Jurecic "Two Comments On 'Neurodiversity'." *College English* 70.3 (2008): 314-25. Print.
"List of Disability Rights Activists." *Wikipedia*. Wikimedia Foundation, 25 June 2014. Web. 01 July 2014. <http://en.wikipedia.org/wiki/List_of_disability_rights_activists>.
Martin, Deb. "Add Disability and Stir: The New Ingredient in Composition Textbooks." Lewiecki-Wilson and Brueggemann 74-91.
McBryde Johnson, Harriet. "Worth Living." *DSQ* 22.1 (2002): n. pag. Web. 28 Feb. 2014. <http://dsq-sds.org/article/view/338/424>.
Mitchell, Ronald K., Bradley R. Agle, and Donna J. Wood. "Toward a Theory of Stakeholder Identification and Salience: Defining the Principle of Who and What Really Counts." *The Academy of Management Review* 22.4 (1997): 853-86. Print.
Price, Margaret. "Accessing Disability: A Nondisabled Student Works the Hyphen." *CCC* 59.1 (2007): 53-76. Web.
Price, Margaret. "Access Imagined: The Construction of Disability in Conference Policy Documents." *DSQ* 29.1 (2009): n. pag. Web. <http://dsqsds.org/article/view/174>.
Purdy, James P., and Joyce R. Walker. "Liminal Spaces and Research Identity: The Construction of Introductory Composition Students as Researchers." *Pedagogy* 13.1 (2013): 9-41. Print.
Scherman, Elizabeth. "The Speech That Didn't Fly: Polysemic Readings of Christopher Reeve's Speech to the 1996 Democratic National Convention." *DSQ* 29.2 (2009): n. pag. Web. 28 Feb. 2014. <http://dsqsds.org/article/view/918/1093>.
Shakespeare, Tom. "The Social Model of Disability." *The Disability Studies Reader*. Ed. Lennard J. Davis. New York: Routledge, 2006. 214-21. Print.
Walters, Shannon. "Toward an Accessible Pedagogy: Dis/ability, Multimodality, and Universal Design in the Technical Communication Classroom." *TCQ* 19.4 (2010): 427-54. Print.
Watkins, Alex, and Julie Gerdes. "Who Has a 'Stake' in the Argument? An Introduction to Primary and Potential Stakeholders." *Rhetoric Matters: Language and*

Argument in Context. Eds. Jason Carabelli and Brogan Sullivan. Tampa, FL: U of South Florida, 2013. N. pag. PDF file.

Wilson, James C., and Cynthia Lewiecki-Wilson. *Embodied Rhetorics: Disability in Language and Culture.* Carbondale: SIUP, 2001. Print.

Course Design

Engaging Writing about Writing Theory and Multimodal Praxis: Remediating WaW for English 106: First Year Composition

Fernando Sánchez, Liz Lane, Tyler Carter

"Literacy alone is no longer our business. Literacy and technology are. Or so they must become."

—*Cynthia Selfe, Technology and Literacy in the 21st Century*

Course Description

English 106: Introductory Composition is a mandatory four credit hour course offered at Purdue University, a large, public land-grant institution located in northwestern Indiana. English 106 is offered by the English department through the Introductory Composition at Purdue program (ICaP), supervised by the Writing Program Administrator (WPA) of first-year composition (FYC). According to the university catalog, students enrolled in English 106 gain "extensive practice in writing clear and effective prose and instruction in organization, audience, style, and research-based writing" ("Introductory Composition"). All English 106 students are required to purchase a copy of ICaP's *Composing Yourself* handbook, a university-specific guide to institutional resources, ICaP policies, the eight topic-specific sections of English 106 (detailed in the Institutional Context section), and library research tips. The majority of students enrolled in English 106 are first-year students from a variety of majors, though a small number of students come to the ICaP program in their sophomore, junior, or senior year.

Institutional Context

Of the approximately 39,000 students who attend Purdue University, 30,000 are undergraduates. Currently, all freshmen enrolled at Purdue are required to take English 106. Because there is no placement examination at Purdue, incoming students are allowed to satisfy their introductory composition requirement by self-enrolling in English 106, 106i (a course that is focused on teaching English as a second language),[1] or English 108 (an accelerated composition course with an emphasis on service learning). All of these courses make up ICaP.

Sections of 106 (by far the most numerous of the composition courses, with roughly 150 sections per semester) are divided into eight different "syllabus approaches," as they are called within ICaP, which have been approved by the WPA at Purdue. These approaches are:

- Academic Writing and Research
- Composing Through Literature
- Composing with Pop Culture
- Digital Rhetorics
- Documenting Realities
- UR@
- Writing Your Way Into Purdue
- Writing about Writing.[2]

ICAP incorporated Writing about Writing (WaW) as its latest syllabus approach in 2011. Although students have some say in which type of composition course they would like to enroll (whether 106, 106i, or 108), if they take the standard English 106 course, they have no control over the syllabus approach that their instructor selects. They may, for instance, be asked to analyze popular media and their place within it, or to compose in academic genres throughout the semester. Despite this variety in 106, all syllabus approaches emphasize rhetorical knowledge, critical thinking, writing processes, knowledge of conventions, and literacy for composing in electronic environments (see the Council of Writing Program Administrators' "WPA Outcomes Statement" for more detail on each outcome). No matter which approach they choose, instructors are encouraged to develop assignments that will help students reach these outcomes.

All English 106 courses meet five days a week: twice a week in a traditional classroom, once a week in a computer lab, and twice a week in the 106 conferencing room (half of the students meet with the instructor on one day, the other half on the other day). That said, there is no standard schedule across 106 sections for these types of meetings—one section of 106 may have classroom days, a computer lab day, and conference days that fall on similar or different days of the week as another section depending on a number of factors.

In this course design, we discuss the ways in which we incorporate social media and multimodal assignments in order to help students better understand the concepts in a FYC course centered on the WaW pedagogical approach. Although WaW helps to build a meta-awareness of the writing process and the rhetorical constituents of a situation, as some in the field of writing and composition have noted, using scholarly composition articles to teach first-year students how to write can be somewhat problematic. Hence, we articulate the theoretical rationale behind our WaW approach to readings, activities, and assignments; we also provide the same level of theoretical justification for the incorporation of digital rhetorics in our class, detailing how the latter helped us achieve the aims of the former.

Theoretical Background

In "Teaching about Writing: Righting Misconceptions," Douglas Downs and Elizabeth Wardle argue that teaching students to write by introducing them to a "set of basic, fundamental skills" they can use across all academic contexts creates the false impression that all academic writing looks the same, when in fact similar features in writing "are realized differently within different academic disciplines, courses, and even assignments" (556). A non-differentiated approach to teaching writing, as the authors note, assumes that, for example, lessons in writing reports will not only correlate from one discipline to another, but will also be generic enough to apply across contexts (557). Downs and Wardle propose that writing instructors prepare students to write across disciplines not by teaching various genres, but by teaching what we, as composition scholars and researchers, understand and accept about writing itself. The goal is to have students develop a meta-awareness of the contextual elements that shape writing so that they can become familiar with how they write on a regular basis and what type of writing specific communities value (559).[3]

Although we could see WaW's capacity to teach for transfer, as instructors of writing, we were also cognizant of the fact that students might feel daunted by the material and by the lack of a user-friendly textbook to access this information pertaining to the knowledge and practice of writing.[4] However, by incorporating hands-on invention exercises involving technology and social media platforms with which many students are already familiar, we hoped to cushion the learning curve for students. Additionally, we hoped that by bringing in these technologies students would be better able to make the necessary connections between the texts we read and their own daily writing practices. In effect, we saw our activities—drawing from Jason Palmeri—as powerful tools that aided in forming connections across assignments, applying course theory, and streamlining invention processes. He argues that "if we limit students to only alphabetic means of invention and revision, we may unnecessarily constrain their ability to think intensively and complexly about their work" (44). Given the scholarly nature of WaW texts, we designed assignments that bridged course readings with composing elements that emphasized multimodality and rhetorical skills in an effort to encourage students to work with different composing spaces and creative processes.

In our syllabi, we aimed to maintain technological inclusion in the composition classroom by offering a stream of assignments and activities that complement our students' growing literacies in technology and composition theory. We worked to reinvigorate the broad FYC goals of inventing, composing, and arranging with timely foci such as web design and social media audiences. Our initial goal was to encourage a focus that experimented with the changing *locations* of writing, geared toward a general audience that students were more familiar writing to in their day-to-day literacy practices such as peers and blog readers. "Compositionists," Stephanie Vie asserts, "should focus on incorporating into their pedagogy technologies that students are familiar with but do not think critically about: online social networking sites, podcasts, audio mash-ups, blogs, and wikis" (10). It is this inclusion of technologies that many students use every day and that can be used to deploy metacognitive rhetorical skills relevant to FYC.

Palmeri advocates for technological literacy when he asserts that "even when we are composing a solely alphabetic product, we often are thinking with multiple symbol systems (visual, auditory, gestural). As a result, multimodal composing activities can be a powerful way to help students invent ideas for and consider revisions of their alphabetic texts" (44). We see our task as FYC instructors as offering students new perspectives on what counts as "writing" and how WaW, and other syllabus approaches for that matter, might benefit from assignments created with new technologies and literacies in mind.

In the following sections we provide a rationale for the major projects that we assigned in our English 106 sections, focusing on the units that asked students to apply the theoretical concepts of WaW in digital spaces. We used the selections in Wardle and Downs' textbook, *Writing about Writing*, for many of these assignments but also included various readings that lent themselves to each of the particular assignments. We should note that these sections are written in the past tense as they discuss our pedagogical and theoretical work during the two semesters that we taught this syllabus approach (though we occasionally deviate into the present when appropriate).[5]

Assignment 1: Literacy Self-Study

We began by having students interrogate their writing practices through a self-study for two reasons: first, the self-study allowed students to immediately begin developing metaknowledge regarding their own writing practices, and second, it challenged and expanded traditional notions of literacy. To accomplish these goals, students kept a running log of everything they read and wrote over the course of two to four days. Our intention was to break students from their mindset that reading and writing are acts merely confined to academic practices or the English classroom. During this self-study, students noted how often they were texting, checking their cell phones or browsing the internet during the day, reading billboards or fliers, or engaging in other nontraditional habits of reading and writing.[6] Although many of our students initially claimed not to be readers or writers, those who engaged with the assignment were typically surprised by how long their lists became after one day.

Simultaneously, we asked students to read articles from newspaper sources about contemporary literacy trends and technology so that they could gain a better understanding of what some writers think of their literacy practices. For instance, David Mehegan's 2007 *Boston Globe* article, "Young People Reading a Lot Less," portrays young people as worse readers and writers than students from previous generations, placing the blame squarely on technology. And a quick Google search uncovers numerous other articles and blog posts about the "dangers" of new media and their ill effects on reading and writing. We paired these readings with Dennis Baron's "From Pencils to Pixels: The Stages of Literacy Technologies" in *Writing about Writing* to help present students with a more balanced historical overview of the fears typically associated with new technologies in writing. Taking all of these readings together gave students plenty of resources for framing their own self-studies within the present day context.

For their first assignment, students had the option of agreeing with, disagreeing with, or expanding on either the academic or newspaper articles. Typically students took an argumentative approach against the popular (mis)conceptions of how technology affects literacy, using the data they collected from their self-studies. Thus at the completion of this project, when transitioning to the literacy narratives project, students thoroughly expanded their definitions of literacy to include not just traditional alphabetic reading and writing, but digital and other literacies as well. This framing of literacy as a fluid concept prepared students to think broadly in terms of types of literacy, literacy sponsors, and literacy stories.

Assignment 2: Literacy Narrative with Tumblr Blogs

Once students had a broader understanding of literacy, we introduced them to the literacy narrative assignment with the hope that they would be better able to expand their understanding of the different agents that have played a role in their literacy—whether they be people, corporations, software programs, or a combination thereof. We relied heavily on Deborah Brandt's "Sponsors of Literacy" for this unit, as her essay centers on how sponsors help individuals acquire literacy.

We augmented the literacy narrative assignment by asking students to assemble a visual collection of digital artifacts on the blogging site Tumblr. We chose this blogging platform for several reasons: it is popular among students for personal blogging, the interface is simple, and creating an account and building a blog are fairly straightforward.[7] Additionally, we approached the literacy narrative assignment as a chance for students to experiment with a variety of media—personal photographs, favorite books, audio recordings of foreign language lessons, and videos of pivotal movies that sparked interests, to name a few examples. Tumblr allowed for easy integration of such media and a moderate level of visual customization.

As they completed this assignment, we encouraged students to see themselves as curators of their own history, building online collections of literacy moments and blog entries that would form an aesthetically cohesive composition that resembled a digital scrapbook or living digital timeline. We approached curation as both the selecting and building of a collection of media artifacts—processes which require students to develop their critical thinking skills for both creating literacy stories and comprehending how arrangement affects audience perceptions of these stories (Castro-Lewandowski 1). Additionally, because an increasing amount of personal and professional research is conducted online, it behooves students to get a sense of how organization becomes even more vital to the digital composing process. As the Pew Research Center's 2013 report on internet users as creators shows, 47% of adult internet users engage in some form of "curation" while viewing, sharing, or reposting online media (Duggan).

Given its multidisciplinary reach, curation borrows skills from new media composing, filmmaking, journalism, art creation, and a number of other fields. Palmeri, for example, attests that "both filmmakers and writers often rely on crafting narratives, setting up contrasting oppositions, or grouping material by topical categories" (134). The work of composing online then relies not only on collecting pieces but also on knowing how to connect them. In our case, we required students to curate on several levels: collecting important literacy artifacts and events in a variety of media, organizing these items and moments to reflect on or respond to a chosen literacy theme, and tagging Tumblr posts with categorical identifiers that placed each student's post in Tumblr's larger tag database. Further, this overarching emphasis on curation urges students to "come to a dynamic rhetorical understanding of how patterns of arrangement can be adapted to audience and purpose" (Palmeri 134). Students were able to consider how each arrangement of their literacy moments told particular stories and presented information to readers in different manners.

As students collected and connected their literacy moments and sponsors, we discussed other literacy narratives like Sherman Alexie's "Superman and Me" and Malcolm X's "Learning to Read," as well as the less traditional stories, videos, and podcasts that can be found in Ohio State's excellent and easily accessible Digital Archive of Literacy Narratives (DALN). Typically, we assigned students the task of identifying two or three literacy narratives on the DALN and asked them to analyze what was most effective or memorable about the presentation of the narrative. This mixture of theoretical articles, personal (alphabetic) literacy narratives, and multimodal narratives created a wide repository for class discussion about media, memory, and arrangement.

Because students were asked to compose a narrative based on the themes that began to slowly emerge from their posts, we also discussed approaches to constructing narratives and supporting themes. To help introduce notions of narrative arrangement and invention, Liz distributed a "Timeline of Literacy Moments," an activity that asked students to storyboard important experiences of literacy in their lives centered on a theme or a series of connected themes. Liz presented students with a digital Microsoft Word flowchart template with fillable text boxes and image placeholders, enabling students to map a literacy trajectory through personal artifacts and memories of sponsors (see Figure 1).[8] The students' timelines ultimately enabled them to populate their Tumblrs with posts centered on this outlining activity.

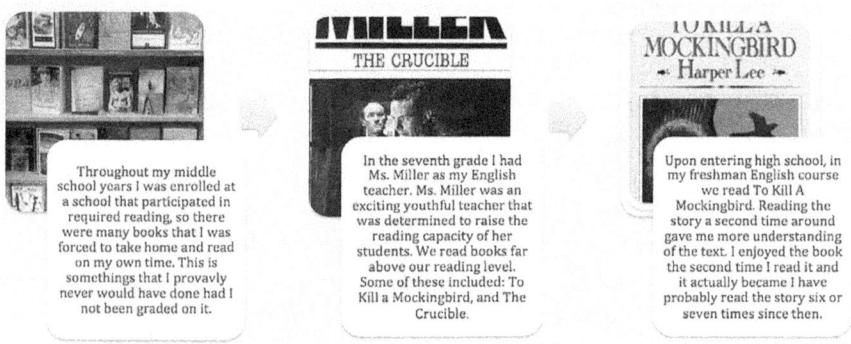

Figure 1. Timeline of Literacy Moments. 2013. Liz Lane.

Tyler, on the other hand, covered traditional narrative structure in class (exposition, conflict, rising action, transformation, etc.) in addition to presenting Karen Schriver's ideas of how text and images interact (taken from her book *Dynamics of Document Design: Creating Texts for Readers*). Together, the use of visuals along with traditional narrative elements worked to develop multiliteracies by encouraging students to augment description in their stories with images as they often do in their social media-infused lives. Both Tyler and Liz incorporated these smaller activities and discussions to explore the questions our respective students presented; we also incorporated these elements to further explore and bridge the digital literacies that students draw on regularly.

By the unit's end, we saw students making connections between writing theory and multimodal practice while using technology to create digital literacy narratives. The narratives that our students consume today are not strictly textual—they are movies, songs, brochures, social media messages, and more. As multimodal learners and writers, our students live in a complex environment of social media, tangible texts, and traditional composition. Wardle and Downs write that our classrooms are populated with "experienced student writers, and they're engaged in many other discourses as well—blogging, texting, instant messaging, posting to social networking sites . . . and otherwise using language and writing on a daily basis" (*Writing About Writing* v). Our multimodal assignment made this particularly salient to us.[9]

Assignments 3 and 4: Discourse Community and Writing for the Public

For the third assignment, students engaged in primary and secondary research in order to write an ethnographic essay in which they analyzed the practices of a discourse community of their choosing. We tied this directly to the fourth project as well, wherein students remediated their essay into a blog form, focusing on audience considerations.

At the center of the concept of discourse communities is the idea of a "common means of communication." By expanding the idea of literacy during the first two projects, students were prepared to see literacy, writing, and discourse as fluid and socially constructed categories. James Gee's "Literacy, Discourse, and Linguistics: Introduction" reframes the terms "literacy" and "discourse," and, along with Tony Mirabelli's "Learning to Serve: The Language of Literacy of Food Service Workers," expands the definition of literacy to include implicit, socially constructed power dynamics. Interestingly, we found that students were quick to embrace the idea of groups of people coming together for common goals and/or engaging in shared literacies; their difficulty, rather, lied in differentiating communities with common goals and practices from any assembled group of people. Although it is difficult to give students a specific heuristic for identifying each type of group clearly, we had—and continue to have—very good discussions with our students about what separates one from the other and how thin the line between the two actually is.

In their ethnographic study, students conducted observations and interviews to uncover how their chosen discourse communities function. Because of the accessibility of on-campus clubs and organizations, the majority of our students tended to research the practices of local communities like the management major learning communities and residence life floor communities. Part of the assignment also required students to conduct secondary research on their discourse community, meaning that students came to familiarize themselves with the library and its services.

Once students had created a final draft of their essays, we segued into the final project of the course, in which students created a custom WordPress site and presence for the community they had researched in depth. Students remediated their written research projects into a readable, concise blogging platform with the goal of informing and engaging an outside audience—those students in our other WaW sections who were also working on their own WordPress sites. These online spaces were inherently public in that students often approached the assignment as if they were creating informative spaces for other students seeking information about communities at Purdue and in the West Lafayette, Indiana area. We had students compose a website in hopes of introducing an alternative place for typical FYC writing assignments grounded in theory. This unit would equip students with general knowledge of web design and blogging practices. As the academy increasingly focuses on multimodality, we felt that a toolkit of digital skills would be important and transferable to most any pursuit a student chooses after their introductory composition course (Figure 2 displays a final student website for the Purdue Cooperative Housing discourse community).

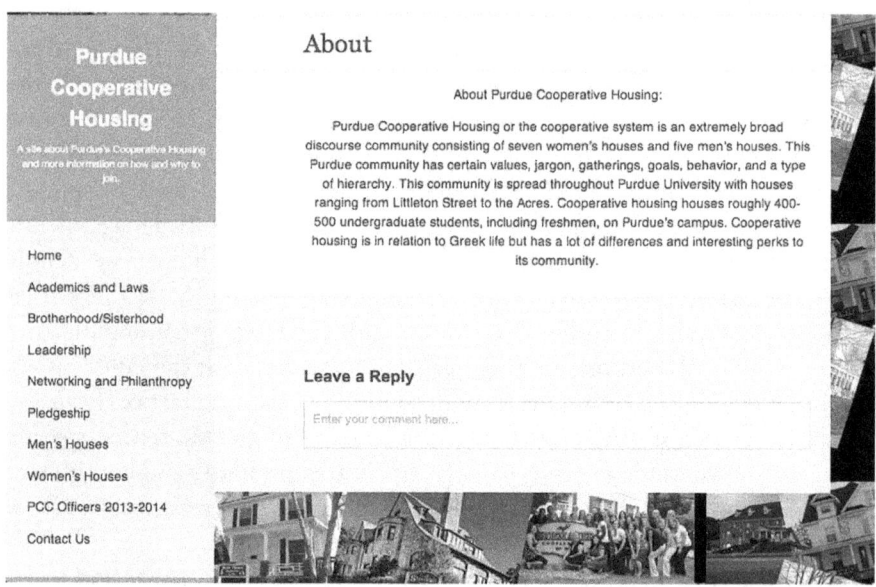

Figure 2. Purdue Cooperative Housing Student Website. 2013. Heather Mink and Liz Lane. WordPress, 26 Apr. 2013. Web. 19 June 2014. <http://hmink12.wordpress.com/>.

Students created ten posts that could be spread across multiple pages and menus on their sites. They determined the layout of their pages, using the variety of customizable options offered by WordPress; they could add menu links, pages, widgets, and a great deal of multimedia to help promote their discourse community. We then evaluated these products in terms of audience expectations, logical arrangement of information, and links and other typical web site structures.

From the beginning of the project, students set their blogs with the public comment features enabled so as to conduct asynchronous peer review and feedback sessions between our three class sections. Doing so opened up an atypical dialogue about readership and audience as students could get a sense of the variety of organizational tactics and remediation choices their larger peer group (among all three sections) was making. Peer reviews were scheduled near the latter three weeks of the assignment and required each student to post at least five separate feedback comments on various peer WordPress sites outside of their own class section.

Although we had used peer review in our other assignments, we were especially pleased with students' ability to provide specific feedback to one another on web design, usability, readability, and other higher-order concerns that related to the assignment criteria. For example, one of Fernando's students had focused her blog on the local choir group at Purdue to which she belonged; in a post describing the community's expectations for dress, she wrote that members of the choir "are required to color coordinate and wear similar clothing so that they look together and like a group." In her response, one of Liz's students not only offers suggestions on the content of the post and how it needs more description, but also notes that Fernando's student is not following the guidelines of the assignment, as she could use more multimodal aspects "to draw in the reader" (see Figure 3).

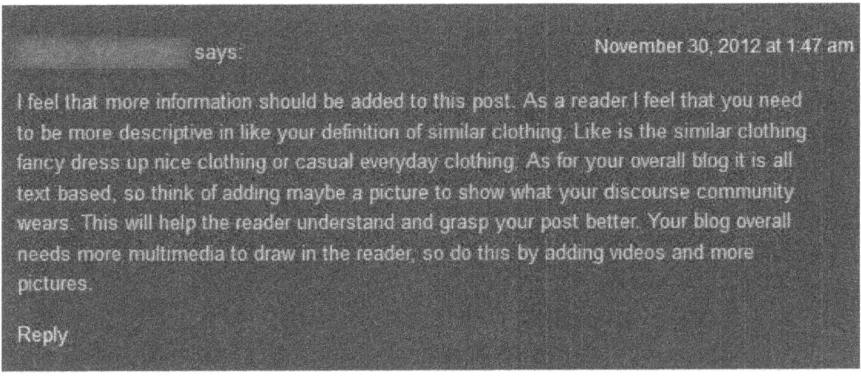

Figure 3. WordPress Comment on Student Blog. 2013. Liz Lane.

Critical Reflection

We recognize that this is not a syllabus that can be incorporated into any course at any institution. However, given the emphasis on technology at Purdue and the requirement for composition classes to meet in a computer lab at least once per week, we developed these assignments for our particular student audience. As we reflected upon the semesters in which we implemented this assignment sequence, we noticed several pros and cons to our approaches. In particular, Liz noticed that she started developing carefully scaffolded materials that led up to major assignments such as handouts, checklists, and in-class activities in an effort to help students organize and manage the required number of blog posts, meet the larger assignment requirements, and submit the materials required for successful assignment completion.

For example, Liz created the "Timeline of Literacy Moments" for the literacy narrative assignment in the hopes that it would turn student focus to the collection, arrangement, and presentation of literacy artifacts on a blog. Students were asked to fill in a timeline template with influential literary moments and memories alongside images or links to potential media they could then post to Tumblr (see Figure 1). Our initial concern with using Tumblr as both the invention mechanism and final product for assignment two was a concern about *how* the students' individual sites would look. Once we scaffolded the assignment and discussed how we would present narrative structure and visual rhetoric, Liz saw student enthusiasm increase with the direction this assignment was taking.

Not surprisingly, students struggled with the academic language and unfamiliar conventions of the scholarly articles we assigned. However, we saw these struggles as an opportunity to discuss audience and genre, in turn helping students to develop a language for the difficulties they were experiencing. And while our students did not express any more enthusiasm for reading the actual composition articles than did Todd Ruecker's students, our students did remember the important aspects of each unit and connect them to what we had covered in the readings. We believe that using Tumblr helped students to see that their literacies came from many sources, and provided fertile ground for meta knowledge. For example, in one of Fernando's classes, when anonymously surveyed at mid-semester, students stated that the Tumblr assignment was helpful in writing their papers (see Table 1). Students responded that such an activity allowed them to have a more visual understanding of what was meant by sponsorship. In the sample of responses included in Table 1, students' answers vary from one who stated that s/he thought the assignment "helped spark ideas" for his/her paper to another who saw the point of the Tumblr exercise as helpful in articulating "who/what influenced us—beyond the obvious choices" in terms of literacy.

What do you think the goal of Assignment 2 was?	What did you think of posting images and captions on Tumblr for this project?
To make us think about our history of reading and writing.	[It was helpful because it] helped us see who/what influenced us—beyond the obvious choices."
[To discuss] different forms of our literacies and who had an impact in helping us learn them.	[Without the Tumblr activity] I wouldn't have known how far I would go in finding sponsors.
[To see] how literacy is a group effort between the number of people and objects in your [sic] life.	[It] helped spark ideas [for the main assignment].
[To understand] who our most important sponsors are and how they helped shape the way we read, write, talk etc.	[It was] interesting to see what others posted because it gave me some ideas and different perspectives about my sponsors.

Table 1. Student reactions to Assignment 2.

To make sure that students were not simply stating that they enjoyed blogging on Tumblr, they were also asked to describe what they had perceived the point of assignment two to have been. In other words, Fernando wanted to ensure that the students who thought that the Tumblr activity had been helpful could actually articulate why. Many students were able to fully convey the connections that we had hoped they would make. What is immediately evident in these responses is not only how students are comfortable using the metacognitive language of writing (as evidenced by how frequently terms such as "sponsor," "literacy," etc. appear) but their grasp on what these terms mean. For example, one student wrote that the purpose of assignment two was to help students identify their sponsors and "how they helped shape the way we read, write, talk" (the broad definition we give students).

Admittedly, these are only a few responses, and they are, of course, not representative of every class that we have taught, but they do highlight some general student reactions to our curricular design. We do not mean to imply that all students automatically develop a meta-awareness of their writing practices by incorporating technological aspects into a WaW curriculum. Students certainly express having difficulty in keeping up with posting, and if they neglect reading the assigned articles for class, the point of the Tumblr assignment does become altogether unclear for them, often resulting in captions that do not address the importance of literacy. As some students communicated in the survey, the captions and postings are particularly important to the final product.

Similarly, most students were able to understand the difficulties that can arise when trying to communicate to public audiences as they remediated their discourse community assignments into blog form for assignment four. Some students enjoyed the blogs because they "let us be original while still including our thoughts in writing. It was the best of both worlds between English and technology." However, we were excited by the number of students who mentioned the constraint of audience for the project. For instance, one wrote "[I feel that I gained] an understanding for different audiences. I used to only have to write primarily for my teachers, so this class has opened my writing to many different audiences." This is particularly important as WaW sees the point of FYC as extending beyond the classroom and teaching students skills that they can carry into other coursework and workplace settings. In effect, this approach teaches students to anticipate the responses of varied yet specific audiences. As one student noted, "My biggest challenge was to make people from Indiana, where [the discourse community of] lacrosse basically doesn't exist, want to engage in my posts and understand the topic. I had to try to relate the posts to them and I tried to do so by relating things in lacrosse to similar things in other sports."

In future iterations of this course, we would like to create an even more integrated relationship between our readings and networked spaces. For example, instead of blogging with each other, we could have students attempt to blog or tweet through a nationally recognized organization's social media channel (Twitter, Facebook, YouTube, etc.) in order to discuss expertise. This would merge the writing for the public section of the course with our discussions of rhetorical situations. As students are already considering the constraints, this seems particularly relevant.

Acknowledgments

We would like to thank Kendall Leon for encouraging the three of us to work together on this syllabus approach, and for pointing out that this work might be of interest and benefit to other instructors. We are also grateful for Laura Micciche's feedback throughout the course of the last year, which helped refine our discussion in this piece.

Notes

1. Just over 8,500 (21%) of our students are from other countries, making it necessary to provide sections of the introduction to composition course that are aimed specifically at nonnative learners (Institute of International Education).

2. Incoming TAs are assigned to a specific syllabus approach for their courses (chosen by their teaching mentor) so as to encourage collaboration on assignment creation and course troubleshooting. Beginning with their second year of teaching, TAs have the option of selecting whichever syllabus approach they would prefer.

3. We are aware that there remain several challenges to teaching composition from a WaW approach. Libby Miles et al. worry that teaching through WaW removes students' exposure to various rhetorical situations and contexts (504), and Joshua Kutney also critiques WaW for lack of evidence of effectiveness. See Wardle's "Continuing the Dialogue," Downs' "Response to Miles et al.," and Barbara Bird for responses to these particular critiques.

4. For example, in his course design, Todd Ruecker reports that one of the main student complaints regarding his WaW curriculum deal with the difficulty of getting through dense composition articles. Although their main frustration centered on length, the fact that most of the articles that Ruecker assigned were ten pages or shorter suggests that students might object more to the style and content of academic articles than necessarily to their individual length (95).

5. Fernando and Tyler continue to teach using this approach and make iterative changes with each semester. As her interests lie primarily with digital rhetorics, Liz finds her pedagogy aligning more with the digital rhetorics syllabus approach.

6. We found that assigning articles like Sondra's Perl's "The Composing Processes of Unskilled College Writers," Christina Haas and Linda Flower's "Rhetorical Reading Strategies and the Construction of Meaning," or Dale Cohen, Sheida White, and Staffaney B. Cohen's "A Time Use Diary Study of Adult Everyday Writing Behavior" helped us discuss the benefits of documenting and interrogating our daily writing practices with our students.

7. Recently, we have experienced difficulty having students set up accounts when they attempt to do so in class through the same IP address. Having students do this for homework or using other platforms would be more efficient.

8. Instructions for this activity directed students to "[s]tart considering how your collection of literacy moments becomes a narrative on your Tumblr blog. There are a variety of ways to structure a narrative or story: chronologically, from beginning to end; non-traditional, beginning in the middle; or reverse chronological, beginning at the end; and many more. Use the boxes of the flow chart to determine a starting point for your narrative. Choose a structure and begin working with placement, arrangement, and storytelling through your various literacy artifacts (you can attach images, links, videos, and captions to explain or think through each artifact). You'll revisit this timeline as you continue to draft your literacy narrative." For readers interested in having students create their own "Timeline of Literacy Moments" for invention purposes, these graphical charts can be inserted into a Microsoft Word document using the "Smart Art" feature (there are a variety of shapes available). Liz chose "Picture Accent Process" under the "Process" menu. Once students select a type of chart, they can edit or add to the number of textboxes and image placeholders.

9. A video showcasing our collective student literacy narrative projects can be viewed on Vimeo at http://vimeo.com/user9295980/remediatingwaw.

Works Cited

Alexie, Sherman. "The Joy of Reading and Writing: Superman and Me." *The Most Wonderful Books: Writers on Discovering the Pleasures of Reading*. Minneapolis: Milkweed, 1997: 3-6. Rpt. in Wardle and Downs 362-6. Print.

Baron, Dennis. "From Pencils to Pixels: The Stages of Literacy Technologies." *Passions, Pedagogies, and 21st Century Technologies*. Ed. Gail Hawisher and Cynthia Selfe. Logan: Utah State UP, 1999. 15-33. Rpt. in Wardle and Downs 422-41. Print.

Bird, Barbara. "Writing about Writing as the Heart of a Writing Studies Approach to FYC: Response to Douglas Downs and Elizabeth Wardle, 'Teaching about Writing, Righting Misconceptions' and to Libby Miles et al., 'Thinking Vertically.'" *CCC* 60.1 (2008): 165-71. Print.

Brandt, Deborah. "Sponsors of Literacy." *CCC* 49.2 (1998): 165-85. Rpt. in Wardle and Downs 331-352. Print.

Castro-Lewandowski, Athena. "Pinterest in the Writing Classroom: How Digital Curation and Collaboration Promotes Critical Thinking." *The Common Good: A SUNY Plattsburgh Journal on Teaching and Learning* 1 (2013): 1-9. Web. 8 Dec. 2013. <http://digitalcommons.plattsburgh.edu/cgi/viewcontent.cgi?article=1001&context=commongood>

Cohen, Dale J., Sheida White, and Staffaney B. Cohen. "A Time Use Diary Study of Adult Everyday Writing Behavior." *Written Communication* 28.1 (2011): 3-33. Print.

Council of Writing Program Administrators. "WPA Outcomes Statement." Council of Writing Program Administrators, 17 July 2014. Web. 11 Aug. 2014. <http://wpacouncil.org/positions/outcomes.html>.

Downs, Douglas. "Response to Miles et al." *CCC* 60.1 (2008): 171-75. Print.

Downs, Douglas, and Elizabeth Wardle. "Teaching about Writing, Righting Misconceptions: (Re)Envisioning 'First-Year Composition' as 'Introduction to Writing Studies.'" *CCC* 58.4 (2007): 552-84. Print.

Duggan, Maeve. "Photo and Video Sharing Grow Online." *Creators, Curators, Instagram, and Snapchat. Pew Internet and American Life Project*, 28 Oct. 2013. Web. 8 Dec. 2013. <http://www.pewinternet.org/2013/10/28/photo-and-video-sharing-grow-online/>.

Gee, James. "Literacy, Discourse, and Linguistics: Introduction." *Journal of Education* 17.1 (1989): 5-17. Rpt. in Wardle and Downs 481-97. Print.

Haas, Christina, and Linda Flower. "Rhetorical Reading Strategies and the Construction of Meaning." *CCC* 39.2 (1988): 167-83. Print.

Institute of International Education. "Top 25 Institutions Hosting International Students, 2010/11." *Open Doors Report on International Educational Exchange*. N.d. Web. 29 May 2012. <http://www.iie.org/Research-and-Publications/Open-Doors/Data/International-Students/Leading-Institutions/2010-11>.

"Introductory Composition." *Purdue University Online Catalog*. MyPurdue.edu. N.d. Web. 11 Aug. 2007.

Kutney, Joshua, P. "Will Writing Awareness Transfer to Writing Performance? Response to Douglas Downs and Elizabeth Wardle, 'Teaching about Writing, Righting Misconceptions.'" *CCC* 59.2 (2007): 276-79. Print.

Malcolm X. "Learning to Read." *The Autobiography of Malcolm X*. Ed. Alex Haley. New York: Ballantine, 1965. *Rpt.* in Wardle and Downs 353-61. Print.

Mehegan, David. "Young People Reading a lot Less." *Boston Globe*. 19 Nov. 2007. Web. 11 Aug. 2014. <http://www.boston.com/news/nation/articles/2007/11/19/young_people_reading_a_lot_less/?page=full>.

Miles, Libby, et al. "Interchanges: Commenting on Douglas Downs and Elizabeth Wardle's 'Teaching about Writing, Righting Misconceptions.'" *CCC* 59.3 (2008): 503-11. Print.

Mirabelli, Tony. "Learning to Serve: The Language and Literacy of Food Service Workers." *What They Don't Learn in School*. Ed. Jabari Mahiri. New York: Peter Lang, 2004: 143-62. Rpt. in Wardle and Downs 538-56. Print.

Palmeri, Jason. *Remixing Composition: A History of Multimodal Writing Pedagogy*. Carbondale: SIUP, 2012. Print.

Perl, Sondra. "The Composing Processes of Unskilled College Writers." *Research in the Teaching of English* 13.4 (1979): 317-36. *Rpt.* in Wardle and Downs 191-215. Print.

Ruecker, Todd. "Reimagining 'English 1311: Expository English Composition' as 'Introduction to Rhetoric and Writing Studies.'" *Composition Studies* 39.1 (2011): 87-111. Print.

Schriver, Karen. *Dynamics of Document Design: Creating Texts for Readers*. New York: John Wiley & Sons, 1997. Print.

Selfe, Cynthia L. *Technology and Literacy in the Twenty-First Century: The Importance of Paying Attention*. Carbondale: SIUP, 1999. Print.

Vie, Stephanie. "Digital Divide 2.0: 'Generation M' and Online Social Networking Sites in the Composition Classroom." *Computers and Composition* 25 (2008): 9-23. Print.

Wardle. Elizabeth. "Continuing the Dialogue: Follow-up Comments on 'Teaching about Writing, Righting Misconceptions.'" *CCC* 60.1 (2008): 175-81. Print.

Wardle, Elizabeth, and Douglas Downs. *Writing about Writing: A College Reader*. Boston: Bedford/St. Martin's, 2011. Print.

English 106: First-Year Composition

Writing about Writing

Instructor: Fernando Sánchez

Schedule:
Monday: Classroom
Tuesday: Conference
Wednesday: Computer Lab
Thursday: Classroom
Friday: Conference

Course Description

Welcome to English 106: First Year Composition. In this class you will learn about practices in the research and analysis of writing. We will begin by investigating our own reading and writing habits and work our way to examining what it means to be a reader and writer in a community. In our course, we will emphasize the use and production of multimodal composition as a means and outcome of inquiry.

This course explores the social practice of writing; we are going to do a lot of writing and work collaboratively to understand what exactly constitutes "writing." Ultimately, this class is designed to serve you, to help you become more effective and appealing writers for your current and future academic, civic and personal endeavors.

Goals

By the end of the course, you will have a broader understanding of what it means to write; you will learn how to collaborate with others in order to strengthen your writing; you will be able to revise and edit your writing efficiently; and you will gain experience using multiple composing technologies to produce a variety of genres of texts. Introductory Composition at Purdue sees English 106 as helping you obtain greater awareness of the context in which writing happens, as well as the form that it takes.

Course Texts

Wardle, Elizabeth, and Doug Downs. *Writing About Writing: A College Reader.* New York: Bedford/St. Martin's. 2011. Print.
Other readings, as necessary, on Blackboard.

Grading

Assignment—Value

Project 1: Literacy Self Study—20%
Project 2: Literacy History—20%
Project 3: Discourse Community—20%
Project 4: Writing in the Public—20%
Daily Writing—20%

Major Projects: See Assignment Descriptions, Goals, and Evaluation Criteria Below

Course Calendar:

Week One—Introductions | Policies | Diagnostic Essay

Week Two—David Mehegan, "College Students Reading Less" and Ben Yagoda, "Seven Deadly Sins | Literacy logs introduction

Week Three—Grant-Davie, "Rhetorical Situations and Their Constituents" | MLA style

Week Four—Presentations of rhetorical situations| Peer review of Project 1

Week Five—Deborah Brandt, "Sponsors of Literacy" | Set up Tumblr accounts

Week Six—Literacy narrative structure and examples | Visual rhetoric

Week Seven—Transitioning from Tumblr to narrative | Drafting

Week Eight—John Swales, "Concept of a Discourse Community" | Brainstorm for Project 3

Week Nine—Peer Review of Project 2 | Analyses of fictional discourse communities

Week Ten—Ann Johns, "Discourse Communities and Communities of Practice" | Research Methods

Week Eleven—James Porter, "Intertextuality and Discourse Community" | Intertextuality of memes

Week Twelve—Library and secondary source scavenger hunt | Peer Review of Project 3

Week Thirteen—Set up WordPress | Kimball and Hawkins, "Principles of Design"

Week Fourteen—Ethos online | Workshop blog design choices

Week Fifteen—Booth, "Rhetorical Stance" | Reflect on all the writing we have done

Week Sixteen—Discuss the feedback on your blogs | Applying feedback

English 106: First-Year Composition

Writing About Writing

Instructor: Liz Lane

Schedule:
Monday: Classroom
Tuesday: Conference
Wednesday: Classroom
Thursday: Classroom
Friday: Computer Lab

Course Description

The goal of English 106, First Year Composition, is to help you learn strategies and practices of research, analysis, and rhetorical composition. Over the course of the fall semester, our class will focus on investigating writing and research broadly as a topic of study. To do this, we will begin by investigating our own reading and writing practices. Then we'll embark on an investigation of what it means to be a reader and writer in communities and public issues surrounding literacy. In our course, we'll explore various tools for creating unique composition arguments, such as images, videos and digital stories, web-based platforms, and more.

Goals, Means, and Outcomes

As the semester unfolds, we'll consider the various definitions of writing, composing, and reading and will discuss how those definitions change over time. This class is designed to serve you, to help you become more effective and appealing writers for your current and future academic, civic, and personal endeavors. At the end of this semester, you will have learned to:

- Recognize and evaluate the rhetorical situation of writing.
- Effectively employ primary and secondary research to develop, articulate, and support a purpose or topic.
- Understand what it means to write in different contexts and for different audiences—and know why this matters.
- Utilize writing as an integral part of inquiry about the material, social, and cultural contexts you share with others.

- Develop effective and efficient processes for writing through practice planning, drafting, revising, and editing in multiple genres using a variety of media.
- Understand, evaluate, and organize your ideas.
- Evaluate others' commentary on early drafts and incorporate these suggestions into subsequent drafts.
- Edit and proofread writing to maximize credibility and authority.

Required Texts
- Wardle, Elizabeth, and Doug Downs. *Writing About Writing: A College Reader*. Boston: Bedford/St. Martin's, 2011. Print.
- *Composing Yourself* (ICaP guide for students)

Grading

Assignment	Value
Assignment 1: Literacy Self Study	20%
Assignment 2: Collecting Literacy Stories	20%
Assignment 3: Community Discourse	20%
Assignment 4: Writing in the Public	20%
Reading Journals and In-class Writings (graded credit/half credit/no credit)	10%
Participation and Attendance	10%
Total	100%

Assignment Sequence: See Assignment Descriptions, Goals, and Evaluation Criteria Below

Course Calendar

Week 1	Course introduction/ *Composing Yourself* policies/ professional email diagnostic

Week 2	Assignment 1 introduction/ Yagoda, "Seven Deadly Sins"/ Perl, "The Composing Process of Unskilled College Writers"/ Collect literacy logs
Week 3	Bitzer, "The Rhetorical Situation"/ Grant-Davie, "Rhetorical Situations and Their Constituents"/ Baron, "From Pencils to Pixels"
Week 4	MLA presentations/Review literacy logs/Attribution and Citations/ Reflection memos
Week 5	Revision tactics/ Peer Review/ "Who is a Writer?" video
Week 6	Assignment 1 submission/ Assignment 2 introduction/ Brandt, "Sponsors of Literacy"
Week 7	"In Defense of Rhetoric"/ DALN introduction and assignment/ Malcolm X, "Learning to Read"/ Tumblr account sign-up and initial posts
Week 8	Narrative structure/ Alexie, "Joy of Reading and Writing"/ Timeline of Literacy moments/ Tumblr posts/ DeVoss et al., "The Future of Literacy"/ Kimball and Hawkins, "Principles of Design"/ Outline of literacy narrative/
Week 9	Visual rhetoric/ Tumblr posts/ Peer Review/ St. Martin's Handbook, "Narrative Structure"/Reflection memos/ Editing and Polishing (extra lab days)/ Assignment 2 submission/ Assignment 3 introduction
Week 10	Branick, "Coaches Can Read Too"/ Fictional Discourse Communities presentations/ Swales, "Concept of a Discourse Community"/ Johns, "Discourse Communities"/ Discourse Community proposal
Week 11	Gee, "Literacy, Discourse, and Linguistics"/ Research writing and interview questions/ *Fieldworking* readings and ethnography (external)
Week 12	Wardle, "Identity, Authority, and Learning to Write in New Workplaces"/ Peer Review of Rough Draft/ Cultural artifacts and image integration
Week 13	Assignment 3 submission/ Assignment 4 introduction/ Remediation plan/ Extending research and new research considerations
Week 14	Usability and writing for the web/ Booth, "Rhetorical Stance"/ Remediation/ WordPress account sign-ups/ Initial WordPress discourse community posts

Week 15	WordPress posts/ Multimedia and remediation/ Peer response comments/ Attribution, fair use, and citations online/ Awareness of online public
Week 16	WordPress posts/ Peer response comments/ Visual rhetoric and design critique/ Using peer feedback effectively/ Assignment 4 submission

Assignment Descriptions, Goals, and Evaluation Criteria

Fernando

Project One: Literacy Self-Study

For Project One, you will collect data regarding your reading and writing practices. You will keep a record of everything you read and write (Facebook posts, books, text messages, etc.) on a weekday and on a Sat or Sun. You will then interpret this data through the lens of what we learn about rhetorical situations. Essentially, you will figure out the meaning behind your acts of reading and writing. You will then draft a 750-word essay in which you respond to the readings we have done in the class. You can agree with writers we have read regarding what they think of your generation's literacy practices, or you can disagree with them.

Liz

Assignment 1: Literacy Self-Study

For Assignment 1, you will keep a record of everything that you read and write for two days (i.e. class assignments, your daily online reading habits, social media posts, text messages, food labels, etc.). You'll reflect and comment on each of your experiences while answering these questions: What thoughts occurred to you? How do you choose your words in this rhetorical situation? What were the overall aims of this practice? Then, using the data you collected on your reading and writing practices, you will create a profile of yourself as a reader and writer that responds to one of the author's we've read (Perl, Baron, Bitzer, and/or Yagoda). You might choose to agree with the author's findings, disagree with his/her claims, or update the research about literacy. The point is for you to use your data as research and support for your profile and stance. Write 750-1,000 words that create a portrait of yourself as a reader and writer. Consider how your findings can contribute to a larger conversation about contemporary literacy and rhetorical situations.

Goals:

- To record and reflect on your own reading and writing practices.
- To learn to collect, use and integrate primary research to support your purpose.
- To develop your understanding of the rhetorical situation of writing.
- To improve your use of MLA citation style.

Assignment Goals:

- Reflect upon your reading and writing practices.
- Learn about collecting primary research and crafting a well-supported argument using this evidence.
- Encourage an understanding of the rhetorical situation of writing.

Evaluation Criteria:

This project will be evaluated based on how successfully you:
- Look back on your recorded data and make a consistent argument about your particular reading and writing practices.
- Use your literacy log as detailed evidence in your paper. You should quote it when necessary.
- Address issues of speaker, audience, message, and constraints in your paper AND connect your reading and writing practices to the readings we have done in class.
- Format your paper and cite your sources in MLA style.

Evaluation Criteria:

- This project will be evaluated based on the following elements:
- Thorough and well-supported discussion of your literacy self-study and evidence (this means full citations from your literacy log).
- Clear and carefully structured literacy narrative (drawn from self-study) that considers the argument(s) of at least one scholarly article we've read (Perl, Baron, Bitzer, and Yagoda).
- Discussion of the rhetorical situation(s) of various literacy practices, including audience, mode, and constraints.
- Inclusion of a minimum of three images that reflect your literacy habits and self-study findings.
- Correct MLA citation of self-study findings, images, and scholarly articles.

Project Two: Literacy History

For Project Two, you will look back and reconstruct your literacy history through a literacy narrative. The purpose of this assignment is to uncover those agents who have helped shape you as a reader and writer. Some of these agents may come to mind quickly, others will only be made clear to you after weeks of introspection. As part of this Project, you will create a Tumblr account. You will be responsible for posting three images every weekday on Tumblr that represent your literacy sponsorship—remember to keep Deborah Brandt's definition of sponsorship in mind as you post. Each entry should also include a forty word caption. After you have accumulated around fifteen images, we will begin finding patterns and themes in order to create a 750-word rough draft of your literacy history. This rough draft should begin to identify a consistent pattern or theme in the images and use rich description throughout the narrative to SHOW not just tell your audience about your reading and writing history.

Goals:

- To reflect on your own reading and writing practices.
- To connect our reading and writing practices to a social context.
- To learn to use visual media in support of an argument.
- To become familiar with interviewing as a form of primary research.

Assignment 2: Collecting Literacy Stories

For Assignment 2, we will draw upon our readings of literacy sponsorship and literacy history to plot key moments in your literacy history. Your resulting narrative of connected moments, memories, and artifacts will take shape on the blogging platform of Tumblr. This space is ideal for this assignment as it allows you to incorporate a variety of media: text, images, audio, video, hypertext, etc. We'll spend ample class time exploring and using the site. Aim to think of your narrative as a collage of your personal literacy made visible through a digital space. This goal will urge us to consider arrangement, visual rhetoric, audience, access, and much more. You'll complete outlines and a storyboard-style timeline to help plan posts. Each post will have a 200-300 word caption and you will also create one larger post that culminates in a 750-word literacy narrative. Thus, the length of this assignment is equal to that of a five-page paper in content.

Assignment Goals:

- Connect personal literacy with larger theories of literacy acquisition.
- Help validate and further explore individual literacy practices.
- Practice writing in a familiar genre.
- Gain experience in using multiple composing technologies to produce various genres of texts.

- To begin incorporating MLA citation and research into your work.

Evaluation Criteria:

This project will be evaluated based on how successfully you:
- Identify a consistent pattern or theme in the images from Phase One in your literacy narrative AND use rich description throughout the narrative to SHOW not just tell your audience about your reading and writing history.
- Discuss your literacy history in conversation with the readings we covered in class, including Brandt, Devoss et al., Alexie and others (use your journals and annotations to help you here).
- Incorporate images from Phase One in the literacy narrative document as evidence.
- Conduct a brief interview with someone familiar with your literacy history and use it as evidence to support your pattern.
- Cite everything (interviews, images, articles from WaW) in MLA style.

Project Three: Discourse Community Analysis

Project Three will ask us to collect data on the practices of discourse communities that we would like to join in the future. The final deliverable for this project will take the form of a 1,000 word rough draft. We will employ primary and second-

- Explore proper web/blogging citation and attribution conventions.

Evaluation Criteria:

This project will be evaluated based on the following elements:
- A final blog that includes a minimum of eleven literacy artifact posts using a variety of multimedia the Tumblr platform supports (image, video, audio, link, text, or quote).
- Proper tagging and attribution conventions included in each post (including links, captions, and any re-blogging information).
- A clear and well-constructed literacy narrative theme that connects each of your posts to your final narrative blog entry (minimum of 750 words). Turn back to our Timeline of Literacy Moments activity to consider how arrangement of moments and artifacts might change on your blog.
- Evidence and employment of visual design conventions including Kimball and Hawkins' principles of design, usability, and audience awareness (i.e. "web audience expectations").

Assignment 3: Community Discourse

Assignment 3 asks you to explore the discursive practices of a certain community. You will choose a community, either local or global, and examine the goals and characteristics of the discourse community. Our readings by Swales, Johns, Gee, and

ary research methods to investigate the discourse practices of a discourse community that you are hoping to join or that you are curious about. You will report your findings in an ethnographic essay that incorporates text and images. We will also be drawing from readings and excerpts by Tony Mirabelli, John Swales, and Anne Johns to deepen our understanding of how discourse communities function. After we read James Porter's "Intertextuality and the Discourse Community" we will revise the rough draft to include information about intertextual practices and elements within our communities.

Wardle will deepen our understanding of how discourse communities function. You will also be conducting research and interviews, and visiting your community, if possible. You will use Swales' "6 Characteristics of a Discourse Community" to guide your research. The final project will be in the form of a 1,000 word research essay with at least two images that supplement your text.

Goals:

- To use primary research methods that we learned in Projects One and Two.
- To properly identify the characteristics of a discourse community.
- To prompt our thinking about the practices of discourse communities.
- To continue to integrate visual media to support our writing.
- To continue to master the citation of sources.
- To inquire about the material, social and cultural contexts you share with others.
- To integrate secondary research methods into our writing.

Evaluation Criteria

This project will be evaluated based on how successfully you:

Assignment Goals:

- Prompt our thinking about the discourse practices that exist in our communities.
- Provide opportunities for interviewing, sharing, and observing communal agents and their practices.
- Continue to integrate media into our writing.
- Give us practice at conducting and integrating ethnographic research in our writing.
- Inquire about the material, social, and cultural contexts you share with others

Evaluation Criteria

This project will be evaluated based on the following elements:
- A comprehensive record of interviews, meetings, and observational

- Conduct interviews and take notes on your observations of a scene or a "text" related to the community.
- Discuss the community's discourse and how it relates (or does not relate) to its goals.
- Tie the discourse community's practices and its goals to the ideas of Swales, Johns, etc. How do you see what our writers talk about in the practices of actual communities—what doesn't fit?
- Include three relevant pictures with captions in your paper that help elaborate on your discussion.
- Cite your primary and secondary sources in MLA style.
- Investigate some practice or aspect of your discourse community that is intertextual. Integrate James Porter's discussion of intertextuality to determine how texts and practices are "borrowed" from previously accepted sources.
- Use the library database to find relevant secondary sources (we will discuss this in class) that will help you support your discussion.

Project Four: Writing in the Public

For Project Three, we selected and studied discourse communities specific to our interests, and saw how the goals and values of these communities are reinforced and realized through their means and ways of communication. For the last project, we will extend our work on discourse communities into the public, while both exploring current issues and remediating our work into the form

notes you conducted/attended/gathered during research of your community.
- Clear thesis and argument of how the discourse community accomplishes and relates to its overall goals (turn back to Swales for examples).
- Inclusion of at least one scholarly article's theoretical definition of "discourse community" to help support or refute your findings (Swales, Johns, Wardle, Gee, etc.).
- Inclusion of a minimum of three images that illustrate artifacts, documents, communication mechanisms, or membership in this community (include captions and MLA citations).
- Employment of this unit's discourse community jargon: intertextuality, hierarchy, mushfaking, discourse, ecology, and more.
- Proper MLA citation of your primary and secondary sources, images, and scholarly articles.

Assignment 4: Writing for the Public

Assignment 4 asks you to consider writing outside of the classroom. Specifically, you will remediate your essay and research from Assignment 3 into a public blog. Essentially, you will be writing for the public and informing them about your discourse community. We will use WordPress as a platform for this assignment and will share our blogs-in-progress of a blog. We will therefore become familiar with the conventions of blogging. To become more familiar with the consequences of writing for a public, we will also share our blogs with students in two other sections of ENGL 106 who are also blogging about their discourse communities. We will post responses to their blogs (they will respond to our blogs too). Our aim is to discuss not only how we write for an audience "out there," but also how we respond to the public's messages. We will read work by Wayne C. Booth and by Kimball and Hawkins to aid us in this project.

with students in two other sections of ENG 106. Opening our writing process to other peer groups will generate unique feedback and encourage you to consider how to approach online readers and larger audiences. Our aim is to discuss not only how we write for an audience, but also how we respond to the public's messages. We will read supplementary texts focused on blogging conventions, visual rhetoric, and usability to help inform our experience writing for the public. To jump start this remediation of a pre-existing assignment, consider the following questions:
- What are people saying about your discourse community?
- How and where are these conversations taking place?
- How can you remediate what you've already written to fit the rhetorical situation of blogging?
- What kinds of subjects generate responses within this community? Why?
- What are the current issues or problems this community faces?

Goals:

- Prompt our thinking about how remediation affects and is affected by the rhetorical situation.
- Provide opportunities to write for an audience outside of our classroom.
- Further our work on multimedia composition.

Assignment Goals:

- Prompt our thinking about remediation and the rhetorical situation.
- Provide opportunities to write for an active audience outside of the classroom.
- Further our work in multimedia composition and multiliteracy studies.

Engaging Writing about Writing Theory and Multimodal Praxis 145

- Use the conventions of discourse communities and blogging.
- Demonstrate coherent structure, effective style, and grammatical and mechanical correctness.
- Use secondary and primary research to explore current issues in a given discourse.

Evaluation Criteria:

This project will be evaluated based on how successfully you:
- Demonstrate a rigorous effort in remediating your third written project into an online space.
- Address issues of audience explicitly in your reflections and implicitly in your actual product.
- Include multimodal aspects in your final product, such as videos, images, and sounds.
- Integrate what you have learned about how to effectively communicate in your discourse community (content) and how to effectively present that information in blog form (design).
- Apply grammatical and mechanical rules properly in your product.
- Provide citations to all of your multimodal sources so that your readers can locate them.

- Use secondary and primary research to explore current issues in a given discourse.

Evaluation Criteria:

This project will be evaluated based on the following elements:
- Evidence and employment of visual design conventions including Kimball and Hawkins' principles of design, usability, and audience awareness.
- Completion of five (5) full-length (150-200 word) comments on peer blogs that speak to the assignment goals and questions.
- Proper citation and attribution of secondary and primary sources (including links, images, and other multimedia).
- Grammatically correct blog entries and successfully remediated research content made to fit the constraints of the blogging platform (i.e., page breaks, length, and editing considerations).

Where We Are: Disability and Accessibility

Moving Beyond Disability 2.0 in Composition Studies

Tara Wood, Rockford University
Jay Dolmage, University of Waterloo
Margaret Price, Spelman College
Cynthia Lewiecki-Wilson, Miami University

Our perception, as specialists at the intersection of disability studies and composition studies is that disability has arrived in the sense that it is now on most peoples' radar. We seldom hear questions anymore such as, "Aren't there special colleges for those students?" or "How would a disabled student even get into college?" We have come to what we might think of as "Disability 2.0": now that disabled students and teachers are accepted as belonging in our classrooms, and we affirm that their presence is an asset rather than a deficit, what should we be doing?

When we give workshops or presentations on disability and the writing classroom, we are often asked whether there is a checklist of things that writing teachers can do to make their classrooms more accessible. Spoken truthfully, our answer would closely resemble that time-honored teacher response: "Welllll . . . yes and no."

Checklists are useful in some circumstances because they offer a place to start. When one's head is swimming with the question, "How do I even approach this?", a checklist gives a sense of grounding, of crystallizing a vague lack of knowledge into recognizable themes: how to check in, language to avoid, perhaps some individual accommodations. But that crystallization process is also, inevitably, a reductive process. Even teachers experienced in working with disabled students, including teachers who are disabled themselves, may find themselves gravitating without realizing it toward reductive assumptions about students based upon diagnoses or symptoms. Disability has all too often been seen as something that must be fixed or accommodated minimally. So checklists get yoked to diagnoses in ways that discipline disabled bodies and minds.

A checklist approach locates disability over there, isolates disability within the body or mind of one student in one class, freezes disability as a set of symptoms rather than as a social process—or demands that disability be overcome—and allows us to perpetuate the fiction that disability is not me or not now. Instead, composition teachers should be prepared for and actively working within the times and spaces of disability.

Disability's presence, like the presence of students with race, class, or gender differences, is not a "problem" but rather an opportunity to rethink our practices in teaching writing. So the truth is, while we could offer a checklist, and it would cover many important topics, it would be contrary to the direction in which we want to push writing teachers, which is a more holistic, recursive approach, one in which disability becomes a central, critical and creative lens for students as well as teachers.

In what ways should and could disability actually be central and centered in all classrooms? How does disability better help us to understand the learning process and the writing process? Disability sharpens our focus on important concepts including adaptation, creativity, community, interdependency, technological ingenuity and modal fluency. Could such a focus replace traditional pedagogical ideals like correctness, the autonomous writer, bootstrapping, and reverence for final drafts?

Instead of rules or norms flowing from teachers to students, we see classrooms as spaces where teachers, along with students, explore and discuss and write to audiences with the knowledge that disability is *us*. This kind of classroom discussion could be as minute as what pronouns include or exclude implied audiences, or as far ranging as what do I need to do as a writer to make this particular project accessible to people with a range of disabilities, and why should I make it accessible? This last point requires teachers to inject some history, art, and writing by and about disability, and so we realize that moving beyond Disability 2.0 requires us to start with teacher training.

Teacher workshops should stress accessible course design and emphasize a dynamic, recursive, and continual approach to inclusion rather than mere troubleshooting. This focus can relieve some of the pressure instructors might feel to design the Perfectly Accessible course prior to the onset of a given semester. Ironically, the most common objection we hear to anticipating disabled students invokes the infinite diversity of human minds and bodies; or, "How can I accommodate everyone?" This is a good question, but a misdirected one. A better question might be, "How can a classroom community be productively and continually transformed by an orientation of inclusion?" Understanding access and accommodation as recursive projects that exist before, throughout, and even after a course allows for deliberate and proactive course design while also inviting and drawing on the diversity that each roster provides.

Yes, legal requirements for accommodations under the Americans with Disabilities Act (including the 2008 amendments and Section 504 of the Rehabilitation Act, both of which apply to colleges) should be introduced in teacher training and faculty development workshops.[1] These laws are easily available online and can be searched for and read together during workshops. But we ought to go further, making instructors aware of disability's deep connection to rhetoric, especially to the rhetorical concepts of *metis* (Dolmage;

Walters) and *kairos* (Price)—adaptive and alternate ways of moving in time and space. In addition to introducing disability law and rhetoric, teaching workshops can suggest ways to build a shared responsibility between instructors and students, especially since many students with impairments do not disclose. Some examples:

- Have teachers in small groups brainstorm ways of including disability topics as part of larger discussions and as options for research (when a course is not disability themed). Have groups present their ideas, followed by short reflective writing on teacher moves that work. If time permits, allow one group to demonstrate a teacherly move to the whole class.
- In a writing class, invite students to create audience profiles suggested by particular compositions (their own or others'). Whether a short reflection or a preliminary assignment before essay drafting begins, this activity encourages awareness of the type of body-mind a piece may privilege as well as critical reading and thinking, with attention to inclusivity and access.
- Ask students to choose and design an adaptation to an assignment that foregrounds their strengths as learners and writers. For example, students asked to write a research memo could choose to create that memo instead as a visual map. Ask them to accompany this assignment with a short written reflection on why they created the adaptation, how it meets the goals of the assignment, and what they learned from carrying out this adaptation. A kairotic teaching move at the end of this sequence might be to spur a class discussion of accommodations in general, charting students' ideas on the board or on a computer screen and digitally saving the chart on a class website for future reference, as a text to later write back to, or as brainstorming for future research topics.
- Many rhetorical choices include some audiences and exclude others. Ask students working in small groups to brainstorm ways to include and address people with a range of sensory disabilities, and then ask the group to collaboratively create guidelines for inclusive writing and publishing, suitable for college writers. End with a reflection on the difficulties of this task. Was there a tendency to revert to universal rules? Norms?
- Another modification of this exercise is to ask students to focus on a particular text, such as a website, analyzing not only its accessibility to those with sensory but also physical and mental disabilities. Have students expand their list of possible accommodations or adaptations for such audiences. This can then serve as a precursor to the "create your own accessible text" assignment.

- Ask students to create a composition (for example, a video essay, podcast, infographic, or traditional written essay) that is widely accessible to a range of learning styles and abilities. This will involve discussions about audience—what assumptions does a text normatively make about its readers/viewers—and how to broaden accessibility using multiple modalities, such as accessible web design, or accompanying an image with descriptions, captioning a video, including transcripts with sound files, and so on.
- Assign writing projects that use disability as a point of inquiry. For example, assign a writing project that asks students to perform some sort of critical university study. Students could examine the geography of campus to assess its accessibility, examine specific colleges or majors for inclusivity, or write about the culture of disability on campus.

We composition teachers no longer consider giving students a list of do's and don'ts as the best practice for the teaching of writing. We want students to engage in inquiry, research, conversation, and critical thinking and to experiment and write as they make rhetorical decisions about what to say, what forms their writing should take, how to reach broad or selected audiences. Our approach to disability should likewise move beyond mere lists and individual accommodations. There's room for those, but we want to engage our students in researching and thinking about disability in relation to writing, audiences, purposes, and access via various modes of dissemination.

Notes

1. "Students with disabilities attending post-secondary schools are protected from discrimination by both the ADA and Section 504 of the Rehabilitation Act of 1973. In accordance with these laws, a school must make its programs, including its extra-curricular activities, accessible to students with disabilities in an integrated setting. This includes providing accessible architecture, such as classrooms and housing, accessible transportation and auxiliary aids and services, if requested" ("Disability Connection Newsletter – July 2014").

Works Cited

"Americans with Disabilities Act of 1990, as Amended." *ADA*. 25 March 2009. Web. 10 Aug. 2014. < http://www.ada.gov/pubs/ada.htm>.
"Disability Connection Newsletter – July 2014." *Disability.gov*. Web. 10 Aug. 2014. < https://www.disability.gov/disability-connection-newsletter-july-2014/>.
Dolmage, Jay Timothy. *Disability Rhetoric*. Syracuse: Syracuse UP, 2013. Print.
Price, Margaret. *Mad at School: Rhetorics of Mental Disability and Academic Life*. Ann Arbor: U of Michigan P, 2011. Print.
Walters, Shannon. *Rhetorical Touch: Disability, Identification, Haptics*. Columbia: U of South Carolina P, 2014. Print.

Creating a Culture of Access in Composition Studies

Elizabeth Brewer, Central Connecticut State University
Cynthia L. Selfe, The Ohio State University
Melanie Yergeau, University of Michigan

Although our profession has long been committed to the goal of accessibility, our movement toward that goal has proved dismally slow and frustratingly uneven. Consider, for instance, the printed articles and books that so many of us publish. We have not, as yet, taken on the professional responsibility of making sure that all such texts—both those aimed at students and those aimed at fellow teachers and scholars—are easily readable: by ensuring that they are in a digital form accessible by screen readers (and not simply a PDF with a single image unrecognizable to optical character scanners), by offering aural forms of such texts, or by providing large-print versions of such texts. This is also true, of course, of many digital texts, especially those that rely on multimedia elements, contain uncaptioned video, neglect to describe visual elements within the text itself, or mix sound and image but fail to provide plain-text transcripts. We could extend these critiques to the in-person aspects of our profession as well, our conferences and classrooms that are too often designed for nondisabled users. Inaccessible texts and spaces are deeply sedimented in our academic culture and structurally aligned along the axes of existing cultural formations—efficiency, capitalism, ableism, among other factors—all of which resist efforts affecting increased accessibility (Yergeau et al.).

Also complicating accessibility efforts is a shifting understanding of access itself. As a term, access is a moving target, a concept that sounds promising on its surface yet frequently offers little more than empty gestures. Critiques of the field's failure to engage the who, how, and what of access have been many, emerging from disability studies, critical race theory, and gender and sexuality studies (Banks; Dolmage; Mingus). Such critiques ask us to examine complex and intersecting politics around identity and participation. When access is only a question of texts—products divorced from labor/ers—those individuals seeking access are positioned as consumers, as bodies in need of help from those more able and privileged. A culture of access, then, is a culture of transformation, as opposed to a culture that "flattens" access as rehabilitation, or as inclusion for the sake of increased consumption (Alexander and Rhodes 431). Transformation, as Kristie Fleckenstein describes, is a "change radical enough to rewrite the rules supporting a particular arrangement of culture," a move that disables the very design of cultural and institutional spaces (761).

The challenges we have identified are many. They are barriers to creating a culture of access, or what we might otherwise describe as an expectation that accessibility is a defining feature of our composing processes and our professional practices. How might transformative access live in practice? We briefly highlight examples of two significant efforts—by no means exhaustive of the access initiatives taking place—while also highlighting obstacles toward realizing a culture of access. We encourage compositionists to see these efforts and obstacles as shaping the values in our field, rather than representing "special" (read: marginal) exigencies.

Accessibility and the CCDP

Such complex challenges as those described above have inspired the efforts of the Computers and Composition Digital Press (CCDP) to make accessibility efforts both a pragmatic and political feature of its born digital book-weight projects. At the simplest level, the CCDP has adopted an accessibility policy that articulates our goal of making projects available to users who have a wide range of needs and preferences for accessing communicative modalities (visual, aural, alphabetic). In addition, over the past five years, the CCDP has attempted to build accessibility into the composition of all projects, so that such efforts are designed into the fabric of projects from the very start rather than added, reluctantly, at the end. The CCDP lets authoring and editing teams know—even at the earliest stages of proposing a project—that projects must include captioning and/or transcription for all audio, video, and multimedia content and authors should be prepared to "provide alternate formats for readers who request them." As our awareness of accessibility issues has grown, the Press has also worked with authors to create web texts that can work well with screen readers, to include descriptive text for all images in published projects, to enable keyboard navigation of web pages, and to support browser settings for enlarging text. As a way of encouraging the profession's larger recognition of accessibility as a social and cultural goal, in 2014 the CCDP inaugurated an annual award for Accessibility in Digital Composition, given to projects that further our understanding of accessibility in design and/or content. The truth is, however, that these first steps in publishing accessible multimodal projects are small, tentative, and insufficient. Ultimately, we aim to broaden our own and the profession's understanding of accessibility practices in ways that extend beyond simple standards to embrace, instead, the spirit and practices of both universal and participatory design. To put it simply, the aim is to transform texts as much as it is to transform readers, audiences, expectations, and composing practices.

Composing Access

The Composing Access Project (composingaccess.net), co-sponsored by the Committee on Disability Issues in College Composition and the CCDP, is a collection of resources for creating more accessible conferences. Disability scholars have long advocated for more equitable conditions at conferences in the field. 2001 saw the publication of Brenda Jo Brueggemann et al.'s "Becoming Visible: Lessons in Disability" in *CCC*, a groundbreaking article that detailed the ways in which composition studies has systematically engaged in ableist and exclusionary practices. Composing Access, arriving some years later, emerged from this longer tradition of activism within the profession. In particular, this resource site grew out of the need for accessible presentations, of which there were (and still are) few. The site has since expanded beyond tips for individual presentations to advice for conference organizers on creating accessible conferences. Composing Access rhetorically positions access as woven into all aspects of a conference, from captioning videos, posting copies of presentations prior to the conference, and providing note cards as a non-verbal channel for audience members to pose questions to presenters. Furthermore, the resources address the creation of user-friendly social spaces that can be made more accessible with interaction badges and quiet rooms. Composing Access is expansive in its view of access, envisioning conference organizers, presenters, and attendees—the entire conference and professional community—as responsible for creating a culture of access that transforms the work of those in the profession.

Conclusion

While we do not believe that composition studies has established a culture of access, there are significant efforts beyond CCDP and Composing Access that indicate a culture shift is underway. For the past several years, the Computers & Writing conference, for example, has hosted web infrastructures that enable presenters to share work, across modality, before and after the conference has occurred. So too can we locate cultural shifts in the work of scholars such as Elizabeth Grace, who tirelessly advocate for the use of plain language, across academic and professional contexts, so that the work of our field might be transformed by those who have been historically characterized as intellectually incapable.

And yet, despite these efforts, our field too often remains attached to a vision of access that has more in common with helping the Other consume inaccessible texts than it does with radical transformation of the profession. A culture of access is a culture of participation and redesign. To put it simply: There is a profound difference between consumptive access and transformative access. The former involves allowing people to enter a space or access a text. The latter questions and re-thinks the very construct of allowing. We encourage all colleagues to join in this project of questioning and re-thinking—for the future of the profession.

Works Cited

Alexander, Jonathan, and Jacqueline Rhodes. "Flattening Effects: Composition's Multicultural Imperative and the Problem of Narrative Coherence." *CCC* 65.3 (2014): 430-54. Print.

Banks, Adam J. *Race, Rhetoric, and Technology: Searching for Higher Ground*. Mahwah, NJ and Urbana, IL: Lawrence Erlbaum-NCTE, 2005. Print.

Brueggemann, Brenda Jo, Linda Feldmeier White, Patricia A. Dunn, Barbara A. Heifferon and Johnson Cheu. "Becoming Visible: Lessons in Disability." *CCC* 52.3 (2001): 368-98. Print.

Dolmage, Jay. "Disability, Usability, Universal Design." *Rhetorically Rethinking Usability*. Eds. Susan Miller Cochran and Rochelle L. Rodrigo. Cresskill, NJ: Hampton P, 2009. 167-90. Print.

Fleckenstein, Kristie S. "Bodysigns: A Biorhetoric for Change." *JAC* 21.4 (2001): 761-90. Print.

Grace, Elizabeth J. "Cognitively Accessible Language (Why We Should Care)." *The Feminist Wire*. 22 Nov. 2013. Web. 31 July 2014. <http://thefeministwire.com/2013/11/cognitively-accessible-language-why-we-should-care/>.

Mingus, Mia. "Some Questions on Disability Justice." *Criptiques*. Ed. Caitlin Wood. May Day Publishing, 2014. 107-13. Print.

Yergeau, Melanie, Elizabeth Brewer, Stephanie Kerschbaum, Sushil Oswal, Margaret Price, Michael Salvo, Cynthia Selfe, and Franny Howes. "Multimodality in Motion: Disability and Kairotic Spaces." *Kairos* 18.1 (2013): n.pag. Web. 13 Aug. 2014. <kairos.technorhetoric.net/18.1/coverweb/yergeau-et-al/index.html>.

Book Reviews

Reading Diverse Rhetors and Rhetorics: Rewriting History, Reimagining Scholarship

Women and Rhetoric Between the Wars, edited by Ann George, M. Elizabeth Weiser, and Janet Zepernick. Carbondale: SIUP, 2013. 302 pp.

The Rhetoric of Rebel Women: Civil War Diaries and Confederate Persuasion, by Kimberly Harrison. Carbondale: SIUP, 2013. 241 pp.

Educating the New Southern Woman: Speech, Writing, and Race at the Public Women's Colleges, 1884-1945, by David Gold and Catherine L. Hobbs. Carbondale: SIUP, 2014. 188 pp.

Reviewed by Virginia Crisco, California State University

Feminist historiography in rhetoric and composition has its roots in studying the gendered nature of texts and writing instruction, but it has also served to interrogate methodological approaches that value dominant rhetorical purposes, goals, genres, and teaching practices. Indeed, scholars in women's rhetoric have been calling for a revision of this dominant rhetorical tradition and our collective values as researchers for over 20 years. For example, Andrea Lunsford's edited collection *Reclaiming Rhetorica* argues that the rhetorical tradition has not recognized the "forms, strategies, and goals" of women rhetoricians (6). Joy Ritchie and Kate Ronald offer a similar sentiment in their book's title, *Available Means: An Anthology of Women's Rhetoric*, which alludes both to Aristotle's famous reference to rhetors' "available means of persuasion" (xvii) and to the historical reality that, even while inhabiting marginalized social roles, women have used their available means to achieve rhetorical agency. The scholars and rhetors assembled in both Lunsford's and Ritchie and Ronald's volumes point to important questions feminist historiographers ask: Who are women rhetors? What counts as rhetoric? How do feminist practices inform our knowledge of the research, study, and canon of rhetoric? How will our scholarship change rhetorical practice and theory? The three books under review make compelling contributions to broadening and modeling where we seek out, how we interpret, and what it means to research women's rhetorical practices and women's rhetorical education.

The authors of *Women and Rhetoric Between the Wars*, *The Rhetoric of Rebel Women*, and *Educating the New Southern Woman* contribute to current scholarship that opens up what counts as women's rhetoric, including who counts as a woman worthy of study, what histories and geographies are available for research, and what it means to practice rhetoric as a woman. In this regard, *Between the Wars, Rebel Women,* and *New Southern Woman* go beyond what Elizabeth Tasker and Frances B. Holt-Underwood identify as the recovery and revision method, which while dominant over the last forty years does not do enough to revise the rhetorical tradition. In fact, as Jacqueline Jones Royster and Gesa Kirsch argue in *Feminist Rhetorical Practices,* research practices are in the process of "tectonic shifts" that move away from revision and recovery and toward at least four new methodological categories (279): "critical imagination, strategic contemplation, social circulation, and globalization" (306). While each of the works under review employ some element of recovery and revision, they also each engage in some of these emerging categories. Below I highlight the different contributions each text makes to feminist historiography and consider how these books can influence teaching and future research.

***

In *Women and Rhetoric Between the Wars,* editors Ann George, M. Elizabeth Weiser, and Janet Zepernick include a diverse range of subjects, rhetorical strategies, and research methods. The women researched across the collection include individuals and groups as well as white women, black women, an American Indian woman, a disabled woman, a Latina, poor women, wealthy women, and women who write about their global experiences or who are from nations outside the United States. While white, upper-class women's rhetoric still dominates, the editors clearly attended to diversity in the collection. Ultimately, their book is an attempt to create a "usable past" (5), a way to recognize how the past can inform current and future activist, feminist, and rhetorical contexts. This usable past highlights women rhetors during the 1920s and 1930s, while also attending to how the analysis of these rhetors can inform our current conversations in feminist historiography. In particular, many essays in this collection contribute to an understanding of "social circulation" (Royster and Kirsch 369), as chapters reimagine women's work, women's rhetoric, and the impact of both on cultural phenomena.

The book is broken into three sections that cover the public, popular, and professional spaces of women's rhetoric. The first section, "Voluntary Associations for the Civic Scene," includes five chapters that point to the successes and challenges women faced in traditional rhetorical contexts, including activist work in the community and contributions to political policy. Section two, "Popular Celebrity in the Epideictic Scene," includes six chapters that focus on women and media and how women used media to change challenging or inhumane circumstances. The four chapters in section three, "Academia and the Scene of Professionalism," delineate what possibilities women had for professionalization as well as what public expectations women faced when seeking professional opportunities. All three of these sections reread diverse texts in new ways as well as emphasize the importance of relationships between women to support their rhetorical development. Below I focus on one chapter from each section to demonstrate the way the collection rereads women's rhetoric and revises research methodologies.

In section one, Janet Zepernick's "A Rhetor's Apprenticeship: Reading Frances Perkins's Rhetorical Autobiography" develops important research and analysis: most significantly, it revisions the purposes of Perkins' political memoirs about her work with Franklin D. Roosevelt and Al Smith from personal memoir to rhetorical textbook. In that rereading, Zepernick highlights the strategies and values Perkins described for being successful as a woman in politics during a time when men dominated this sphere. Additionally, the chapter points to the importance of meetings and small group collaborations to understand how deliberative democracy works. While Zepernick focuses on a white woman with high status doing traditional rhetorical work, she is able to reimagine and reframe the value of that work through alternate readings and by highlighting heretofore invisible rhetorical spaces.

Coretta Pittman's "Bessie Smith's Blues as Rhetorical Advocacy" stands out in section two because of the ways it points to tensions and conversations among the African American elite. Pittman analyzes songs as rhetorical texts, and argues that Smith—one of the most popular women blues singers of the 1920s and 1930s—created an unapologetic ethos, one that allowed her to examine taboo topics and sell millions of records. Smith's songs called for respect for everyday African Americans in general and African American women in particular, a sentiment that went against the dominant thinking of many African American intellectuals at that time. For me as a reader, this chapter serves as a model for feminist historiography and rhetorical listening because it not only draws on a nontraditional text but also gives voice to the working-class African Americans who found resonance in Bessie Smith's music.

Another example of research on alternate texts is the chapter that ends the collection and outlines a proposal for a new research methodology called "sideshadowing" (241). This method seeks to uncover invisible relationships, connections, and conversations that frame and contextualize women's work. Kay Halasek's "'Long I Followed Happy Guides': Activism, Advocacy, and English Studies" uses sideshadowing to focus on the work of two English teachers, Adele Bildersee and Helen Gray Cone. Sideshadowing is both a method and a genre, and throughout her essay there are several sideshadows that provide additional information about Halasek's subjects. I highlight Halasek's work because she and several authors in this collection value women's rhetorical writing that is hard to find or altogether unpublished, yet represent significant historical relationships and moments of collaboration and community building.

While certainly this collection is meant to recover women's rhetoric between the wars—rhetoric that has been neglected despite its great contributions—it also represents new directions in researching and redefining women's rhetoric. As a whole, this collection highlights how women's rhetoric can be recovered and reinterpreted to give current readers and researchers new perspectives into what women rhetors and women's rhetoric look like; importantly, then, *Women and Rhetoric Between the Wars* provides insight into the larger cultural impact of women's rhetorical work.

***

In *The Rhetoric of Rebel Women: Civil War Diaries and Confederate Persuasion*, Kimberly Harrison's feminist methodology includes a homogenous group of women rhetors, but challenges scholars' notions about the kinds of texts we use for rhetorical knowledge. While *Rebel Women* doesn't have the racial and class diversity of *Between the Wars*, Harrison does point to diversity even in the homogenous group of women she researches. Pushing beyond the examination of traditional rhetorical genres, Harrison's archive also includes women's diaries, which she argues provide important information about how women prepared for and learned from rhetorical situations. Harrison's interpretive practices help readers to understand the culture of the South and the culture of the era, while also analyzing pivotal moments of activism, shifting gender identity, and race relations. Applying Royster and Kirsch's methodology of "strategic contemplation" (341), rather than passing judgment on the women under study, Harrison's research seeks to understand the culture and contexts that led to racial, gender, and class biases commonly displayed by Southern women during the Civil War period.

In the introduction and chapters one and two, Harrison makes a case for diaries as artifacts of women's rhetoric, and she highlights that while women were fairly limited in their gender roles, they used the diary genre to adjust to new gender identities thrust upon them by war. To explain, many privileged Southern white women used what Harrison calls "gendered rhetorical honor for self-protection" (27), which were the rhetorical strategies women used to adjust to their changing roles, particularly new responsibilities to protect their homes, farms, and families. These gendered rhetorics were negotiated between the spaces of community values and traditional gender norms, and give insight into the ways women used diaries to negotiate their identity.

Chapter three, "Guarded Tongues/Secure Communities: Rhetorical Responsibilities and 'Everyday' Audiences," is a particularly important contribution to feminist historiography, as in it Harrison argues for a redefinition of the space of the home. Focusing on audiences such as family, community, and slaves, Harrison asserts that women took up "domestic rhetorics" (85), which were choices in verbal and nonverbal communication used in everyday social practices. Challenging the public-private dichotomy, Harrison maintains that homes were places of work, power, and controlled labor. For example, one domestic context Harrison examines is how women managed slaves, including the use of "rhetorics of affection" (106) to persuade slaves to stay and continue to work postemancipation. This chapter demonstrates the breadth and depth of rhetorical knowledge Harrison acquired from women's diaries, and points to the home as a political space where gender roles and race privilege shaped the decisions women made in everyday interactions.

In chapters four and five and in the conclusion, Harrison shows how during and after the war the purpose of diary writing shifted, with public and civic conversations dominating throughout the Civil War, transforming into local, family-oriented topics—or no diary writing at all—after. Harrison describes, for example, "writing-to-believe" practices to consider questions about the morality of slavery (132). Harrison argues that this kind of writing provided a space for many women to assert their race and class privilege in regard to slavery, and in tandem to justify other traditional hierarchies of race, gender, and class. In all, Harrison shows that diary writing provided important insights into how local and civic culture shaped the rhetorical practices of women.

Harrison's work is valuable to readers and researchers of women's rhetoric because it analyzes antebellum Southern women in their historical context while also connecting the significance of their actions to the present. Her focus on gender identity and race privilege demonstrate the limits of women's rhetoric, but also hold the women under study accountable for their privileged and—by contemporary scholarly standards—often offensive perspectives. Harrison's book illuminates the challenges of working toward equality both in that historical period and in current contexts, and one of the most fascinating and informative elements of *The Rhetoric of Rebel Women* is how it describes the power of class and race privilege in Southern white women's social spheres. All told, the book highlights the challenges of addressing structures of power and shows one view of the limited motivations those in power can have to change their practices.

***

The last book in this review, David Gold and Catherine Hobbs' *Educating the New Southern Woman: Speech, Writing, and Race at the Public Women's Colleges, 1884-1945*, builds from the historical time period just after *Rebel Women* and encapsulates the time period of *Between the Wars* and beyond. Unlike the other two books under review, however, it focuses on how women were taught rhetoric in college, giving readers a new perspective of this era's educational landscape. The purpose of the work is to argue for key distinctions between Southern women's colleges and more commonly researched Northern women's colleges, but the authors also revise conversations about the histories of women's rhetorical education and women's purposes for going to college. Gold and Hobbs' research demonstrates what Royster and Kirsch call "critical imagination" (315), a process that uses traditional documentation and inquiry, but also applies a method of meaning making that reads between the lines, revises previous assumptions, and redefines key frameworks.

Overall the book provides insight into several key issues about women's education in the South, as well as contributes to conversations about conducting archival research. To begin, Gold and Hobbs explain their research methods, including their method of collaborative research. They describe their meaning making with concepts such as "rough consensus," which they define as a consensus on the interpretation of larger, important issues (rather than fixating on smaller, lesser important ones), and "running code," which refers to their practice of creating working theoretical frames and testing them rather than working from just one frame (13). Their purpose is to challenge notions that Southern women's colleges were simply finishing schools for the privileged, and while they underscore that these colleges were founded for white, often wealthy women, they emphasize that many women enrolled were of moderate means. The ultimate goal of the book is to redefine current frameworks for thinking about women's college education during this period, to show similarities and trends among institutions, and to demonstrate key differences between institutions that can change the narratives we currently have about the purposes, practices, and outcomes of Southern women's college education.

In particular, chapter two, "Effective Literacy: Writing Instruction and Student Writing," illuminates how the authors revised prominent frameworks about women's education through their methods. Gold and Hobbs build on previous historical arguments that current-traditional pedagogy dominated during this period, and they complicate popular scholarly conceptions of current-traditional pedagogy. While the authors don't try to remake pedagogical taxonomies, they argue that even those using tenants of current-traditionalism did not do so monolithically. According to Gold and Hobbs, teachers taught writing and rhetoric to address particular local and national circumstances, and each institution had its own approach to teaching writing, which was driven by the faculty who taught as well as students' extracurricular activities. The authors show that while there was a lot of formulaic writing being taught—with a strong emphasis on correctness, the rhetorical modes, and the ordering of ideas—some teachers placed a surprising emphasis on writing for social purposes and writing to make meaning.

Chapter five also reframes key conversations in regard to rhetorical education. The authors draw on student writing to show how students engaged with issues of race, pointing to both students' development of their ideas about African Americans as well as their racist complicity. Gold and Hobbs highlight the influence of particular faculty, administrators, and organizations that supported—or did not support—integration, understanding, and appreciation of the African American community. In part the authors show the limits of the public's willingness to consider integration and how that lack of willingness affected decisions by administrators and, in turn, students' interpretations and analyses. But the authors also point to how some teachers exposed students to African American literature, which allowed students to write about and thus better understand African American perspectives.

In all, *Educating the New Southern Woman* covers a lot of ground, which makes the book sometimes read like a list of important people, places, and social movements. Gold and Hobbs cover eight institutions and a timeframe that exceeds sixty years, focusing on the history of women's institutions; literacy, public speaking, and home economic emphases in college programs; work opportunities in relation to educational emphases; and gender identity construction and race relations. They include multiple kinds of documents in their research as well, such as course catalogues, meeting memos, syllabi, textbooks, and student writing, as well as faculty publications, newspaper reports, and other writing from that time period. This book offers a valuable record of rich topics and historical figures for future students and scholars to investigate. The authors use their critical imagination to reframe current knowledge about the purpose of women's education in the South, as they open up expansive territory for future scholars to navigate.

***

All three books in this review engage in some revision and recovery research, but all three also challenge traditional feminist historiography by pointing readers to a larger view of the landscape, redefining what it means to be a rhetor, reconsidering what rhetoric is, and reimaging how history informs our present and future. While these texts build on scholarship in new and important ways, they also represent innovative models for research possibilities in women's rhetoric. *Women and Rhetoric Between the Wars* not only models diverse choices for researching rhetoric and rhetors, it also ends with Kay Halasek's argument for a new research methodology, sideshadowing. *The Rhetoric of Rebel Women* ends by describing several possibilities for further research, such as focusing on the rhetoric used in post Civil War women's organizations. *Educating the New Southern Woman* points readers to many, many influential individuals who could be the focus of further study. What's more, its authors describe a collaborative writing and research methodology. All three texts illuminate new practices and purposes for ways to engage imaginatively with women's rhetorical history and future directions in feminist historiography.

Fresno, California

Works Cited

Lunsford, Andrea A., ed. *Reclaiming Rhetorica: Women in the Rhetorical Tradition.* Pittsburgh: U of Pittsburgh P, 1995. Print.

Ritchie, Joy, and Kate Ronald, eds. *Available Means: An Anthology of Women's Rhetoric(s).* Pittsburgh: U of Pittsburgh P, 2001. Print.

Royster, Jacqueline Jones, and Gesa Kirsch. *Feminist Rhetorical Practices: New Horizons for Rhetoric, Composition, and Literacy Studies.* Carbondale: SIUP, 2012. Print.

Tasker, Elizabeth, and Frances B. Holt-Underwood. "Feminist Research Methodologies in Historic Rhetoric and Composition: An Overview of Scholarship from the 1970s to the Present." *Rhetoric Review* 27.1 (2008): 54-71. Print.

Vernacular Eloquence: What Speech Can Bring to Writing, by Peter Elbow. Oxford and New York: Oxford UP, 2012. 442 pp.

Reviewed by Jacquelyn E. Hoermann and Richard Leo Enos, Texas Christian University

"I'M AN ENTHUSIAST. I think that everyone can write better and with less frustration and anxiety if they harness the enormous powers of their vernacular speech: speaking onto the page for the early stages of writing and reading aloud to revise during the late stages of writing." (*Vernacular Eloquence* 317)

Introduction: The Democratizing of Written Rhetoric

On December 8, 1975, a very disturbing essay appeared in *Newsweek* called "Why Johnny Can't Write." This essay was unsettling because it publicly exposed America's literacy problem. The title would lead any reader to believe that the problem lies with the child, but in the following decades of research we have seen that the problems associated with literacy lie not with the child but rather the system the child learns from and society's view of what constitutes good writing. For his entire career, Peter Elbow, recently retired from The University of Massachusetts-Amherst, sought to correct this perception of the student as the problem. As the capstone to a long and prolific career, *Vernacular Eloquence* (*VE*) amasses much of Elbow's research and experiences in teaching literacy through orality, contributing to the field a philosophy of writing that is timely, needed, and exceptionally eloquent in its own right. Elbow's views on writing first came to national attention with his 1973 volume *Writing Without Teachers*, a work that challenged many assumptions about how students learn and how the process of writing unfolds. Such a radical challenge to the conventional notions of literacy and the teaching of English has not been without political consequence in academia.

As early as the 1960s, competing methods for literacy instruction were critiqued just as quickly as they were presented. Edward P. J. Corbett's method used principles drawn from classical rhetoric to provide a humanistic method for writing, while Richard Young, Alton Becker, and Kenneth Pike introduced tagmemic rhetoric as an alternative way of teaching writing. Not long after, Linda Flower and John R. Hayes employed empirical research from cognitive psychology to introduce the field to problem-solving strategies of writing. These and countless other works contributed many valuable methods to the field of composition studies, but adopting these methods did not come without public debate and discussion. Elbow took to the task of defending his method throughout his career. Most notably, in 1995 Elbow and his colleague, David Bartholomae, engaged in a spirited dialogue over their opposing methods, demonstrating how such dialogue can stimulate great intellectual production. Over time, Elbow's views gained support by offering a sensitive understanding of writing, particularly highlighting its close relationship to speech.

Approximately forty years after *Writing Without Teachers*, Elbow provides a late statement, one that bookends his nascent efforts to challenge our notions of literacy and how to teach it. The fruits of his life's work, the wisdom drawn from his career-long experiences, are lucidly captured in *VE*. Rather than be a cynic who carps criticism on the deficiencies of present writing approaches, Elbow offers a framework to help learners draw upon speech abilities—or traits which come much more naturally to most of us—as a platform not only to create effective prose, but also to revise prose, a task central to effective writing. This is not a how-to-write "textbook," but *VE* offers an approach so elegant in its simplicity that its application appears to be an obvious extension of everyday language practices.

America has changed greatly since discovering Johnny's (and Janie's) literacy problem. Now, America is a more diverse country, no longer having one Standard English (if it ever did) but many competing, plural "Englishes" that give shape and expression to wide-ranging thoughts and sentiments. Elbow's *VE* recognizes that America is a country of diversity and provides a method that facilitates not only multiple expressions of diverse voices but also ways to help writers reach a larger body of English speakers. That is, while there may no longer be one Standard English, there is a larger shared common form of English, and *VE* helps writers move from their own dialects to those more common, shared conventions of English writing or grapholect. (A grapholect is a written language based upon a spoken dialect or, as Walter J. Ong explains in his 1982 work, *Orality and Literacy: The Technologizing of The Word*, the grapholect permits an oral dialect to be written out and become the literate standard). That the diversity of our literacies grows more pronounced—especially as a variety of non-standard "Englishes" compete for expression—only reveals further that this grapholect approach is anything but obvious to American educators. The close relationships among speech, reading and writing may seem apparent to non-experts, but many educators and scholars have done a masterful job of Balkanizing themselves so that the fluidity of these communication processes are all but lost in our teaching and research. In short, reading and writing, speaking and listening are often treated as distinct and autonomous communication activities. For many decades, these fiefdoms did an effective, if not ironic job of not "speaking" to each other . . . until recently. However, efforts to break down isolating walls have resulted in innovative approaches to learning effective communication, both oral and written. As illustrated throughout *VE,* Elbow's position endorses orality as our solution:

> When "illiterate" children learn to write by speaking onto the page, a principle of profound simplicity emerges: writing comes naturally before reading! Very young children can write before they can read, they can write more than they can read, and they can write more easily than they can read. For they can write any word or sentence they can say. (320)

The key to understanding why Johnny and Janie can't write lies in an understanding of the oral vernacular and the power of literacy. Issues involving writing and speech are not unique to us or to our time; in fact, knowing the history of rhetoric can help us identify cultures that faced similar issues and, in identifying their struggles, we might better identify and solve existing literacy challenges.

A Historical Perspective on a Current Problem

Scholars studying the history of rhetoric have recognized that many cultures have facilitated writing by drawing upon the heuristics of their oral vernaculars. Ong's previously mentioned final volume, *Orality and Literacy,* confirms this, as does Eric Havelock's *The Muse Learns to Write: Reflections on Orality and Literacy from Antiquity to the Present.* Elbow examines how Ong, Havelock and other distinguished scholars culminated their respective careers by realizing the historical patterns and relationships that exist between speech and writing. Elbow draws upon the insights gained from these historians of rhetoric to address current literacy problems in relation to the vernacular. That is, what seems natural in speaking can enhance the necessary, critical skill of effective writing. It is widely acknowledged that writing came into existence as an aid to speech and memory but, over time, writing became an art unto itself, one dictating the "proper" mode of written and then spoken address. In our email correspondence with him in the summer of 2014, Elbow argues that the opposite ought to be the case, pointing out that "after a while, the rules for writing began to dictate what is acceptable or correct in speech" (Elbow "Re"). The natural mode of addressing others in oral discourse, as Elbow argues, should be used as a basis for refining writing. In truth, this process does happen naturally when speech habits begin to modify writing rules, but the transformation is often met with great resistance from guardians of the English tongue, decrying our loss of "good" English.

As mentioned above, the rise of the vernacular and its competition with proper English is hardly unique. Rather, it represents the latest version of a phenomenon that has historical precedent, and recognizing historical antecedents can give us a valuable perspective on the present problem of a Standard English that is incompatible with the diverse literacies of our society. One of the benefits of *VE* is that it provides many historical illustrations, the most dramatic being the literacy crisis that Italy experienced in the 14th century. At the peak of the Renaissance, Latin was the standard language for written communication, even though classical Latin was far removed from the everyday vernacular of Renaissance Italians. Elbow uses Dante as a prime example of a luminary who broke with convention by writing in his vernacular instead of Latin. Many of Dante's contemporary Italian philologists were outraged with his departure from Latin despite the fact that he wrote just as eloquently in his native Tuscan dialect. Even today, Italy remains a country of many, many dialects. Yet, Dante, Boccaccio and, yes, Petrarch (whom Elbow treats as an opponent) wrote so well in their vernacular that their works eventually attained high literate status. This historical example illustrates the impact of transforming to the vernacular not only in the mundane practices of everyday life but in high art as well. Understandably, Latinists of the 14th century were shocked and some appalled when Dante and other writers elected to depart from Latin as the mode of high literature and poetry and write in his Italian vernacular, the Tuscan dialect of Florence. There was, as a consequence, great resistance to this movement, but his vernacular was so eloquent that writing in Italian dialect(s) soon became tolerated, then acceptable, then preferred. When Italy became a nation and selected one of its many dialects to be "Italian," the vernacular of Dante was selected. In Florence, where the dialect and grapholect are essentially one and the same, the Tuscans are regarded as speaking and writing the best and purest Italian. Several examples of well-known writers departing from the proper Latin are illustrated throughout *VE*. Similar to other educators who have faced vernacular challenges, Elbow's career has been devoted to teaching others to write better. For Elbow, however, "better" means writing more clearly and directly by drawing from vernacular speech. Does this mean we ought to forsake Standard English? Not exactly, because eventually (and inevitably) even our vernaculars become standardized, helping bind speaker/writer with auditor/reader in mutual understanding. Hence, we might be better off replacing the expression "Standard English" with "Common English."

The Layout of *Vernacular Eloquence*

VE is divided into four parts: "What's Best in Speaking and Writing?," "Speaking onto the Page," "Reading Aloud to Revise," and "Vernacular Literacy." Conversational in tone, *VE* is inviting to general readers, not exclusively academics. Technical, academic treatments appear in gray blocks scattered throughout the chapters for readers wanting more in-depth information or research-oriented discussions, but both popular and academic audiences will find value in the book.

The eighteen chapters of *VE* reveal how orality benefits both the invention and revision of writing. For example, chapter three, "Speaking as a Process: What Can It Offer Writing?," presents Elbow's view of speech as naturally acquired, albeit acquired through systematic processes. Elbow's discussion anticipates the parallel argument of writing as a process—a topic familiar to most rhetoric and composition specialists. Specifically, his treatment of coherence and complexity in these processes unpacks and establishes the dynamic interrelationship between speech and writing beyond historical appreciation, showing the importance of speech's relationship to effective writing.

To his credit, Elbow discusses aspects of speech, such as tone and voice, which reveal relationships with writing. In everyday speech we seem to have little trouble understanding a speaker's tone and voice. Elbow discusses the relationship of speech to writing through personal observations and research into how famous writers compose—including unplanned speech and dictation practices. These illustrations help readers see concrete examples of oral and literate composition. Overall, the speech-writing relationship is best practiced by fusing vernacular speech to freewriting activities (or what Elbow calls "ink-spilling") to facilitate invention. Likewise, speech facilitates the invention or creation of written texts. No one ought to claim that the first draft of any essay will be the last draft. In fact, at the point of the last draft is when Elbow asks his own students to revise for mechanics. By providing non-standard oral approaches to writing, Elbow shows readers that unfettered vernacular expression is a way to help ideas flow, principally because such a mode of natural expression does not suffer the constraints of trying to be perfect at the moment of utterance. As Elbow argues, this self-imposed compulsion to write the perfect sentence out of the box leads to writer's block.

There are times when freewriting "frees up" the author so that she or he can draw from the comfort zone of speech. There are, of course, times for rigorous editing, what some teachers call "polishing the diamond." Overall, Elbow's treatment of speech and writing stresses a pedagogical point: all levels of writing are best learned after we've convinced the student to care. Freewriting, as Elbow points out, does not mean careless writing. Rather, teachers are helping the student so that all he or she cares about is the idea and expressing it. Revision is another facet of care. Many of us would admit that, like our students, we do not write good first drafts. Elbow's approach allows students to freely express ideas, and in the process to more easily engage them in the act of writing, equipping them with common conventions for expressing their thoughts and sentiments to a wider audience.

Standard English, Englishes, and the Rise of the Vernacular

Readers of *VE* will find the beginning of part three fascinating, especially Elbow's discussion of Standard English, which he shows to be anything but stable and shared. In England, for example, where the Royal Family are the guardians of Standard English, about 25% of the population speak "BBC English" and only about 3% of the people speak the "Received Pronunciation" of Standard English that is associated with prestigious English boarding schools and the Queen (215). Yet readers will see the communal construction of Standard English (including the grapholect) has enormous social implications. In brief, Elbow argues that we can learn the standardized form without compromising our dialect, identity, or culture. Dialects can be used to increase proficiency in common English.

Whereas part two of *VE* emphasizes using speech for invention, part three emphasizes speech for the later stages of writing, especially revising. That is, the practice of reading one's writing aloud is an aid in revising and proofreading because speaking slows the writer down, letting her or him hear errors more readily than one might see them, while also giving papers a more acoustic quality. Elbow also discusses another controversial point: using orality as a guide to punctuation. Elbow lays out the controversy over punctuation by discussing two incompatible traditions. The first and older one is the rhetorical/elocutionary tradition that punctuates for an oral culture and is more interested in punctuation's service to cadence and symmetry. Looking at theatrical prompt books reveals that this form of punctuation was done for listeners, not silent readers. Reading Shakespearean plays silently does a great injustice to those pieces, for Shakespeare intended his vernacular dialogue to be performed orally, not read as the great (silent) literature it has come to be considered today. In short, the punctuation and stage directions are made for orality.

The second tradition of punctuation that Elbow examines is the grammatical tradition, made famous by H. W. Fowler's *A Dictionary of Modern English Usage*. Fowler and his lineage of grammarians advanced preferential (i.e, rhetorical) selections of what ought to be considered Standard English and, conversely, what ought not to be considered Standard. The point, as Elbow reveals, is that both the rhetorical/elocutionary and grammatical traditions are socially constructed. For those reactionary advocates of prescriptivist punctuation, Elbow cites when they themselves have broken what amount to arbitrary rules.

Perhaps one of the more striking ideas in *VE* is the concept of "good enough," a theme that grounds Elbow's rationale and approach to effective punctuation as well as rhetoric itself. At first it sounds as though Elbow advocates the least acceptable standard of effective expression, but really he is guarding against those perfectionists who so over-react to grammar and proper punctuation as to induce writer's block. Elbow is saying that trusting the process of reading aloud—along with a good knowledge of grammar—is the best possible heuristic for the writer. One can trust the ear, tongue, and eye while simultaneously understanding common conventions of grammar, especially in revision stages. In Elbow's view, particularly during early stages of the writing process, being content with "good enough" can eventually lead to a higher quality of writing.

For us, however, the most controversial idea in *VE* waits in chapter sixteen, "The Benefits of Speaking onto the Page and Reading Aloud," where Elbow discusses two engaging issues. First, he argues that children naturally write before they read and should be encouraged to do so as early as possible. While children may not master the rules of standard grammar, nor even fully understand the alphabet, they nonetheless use writing in many positive ways. Those unbridled ways, Elbow argues, should be encouraged and not dulled by rigid rules of correctness in the form of prescriptive grammar and syntax. As the very title of this chapter reveals, Elbow raises a second controversial issue when he advocates for speakers to use their own speaking languages as the basis for "speaking onto the page." Arguing against rival views, Elbow makes the case that the ease of speaking onto the page with one's primary language is inherently better than imposing an artificially spoken English that must be learned and then applied as an aid to writing. Eventually, people can learn the standard forms, Elbow argues, and move around in different genres. In this respect, Elbow claims that literacy is not just at war with those who do not perform proper English; literacy is at war with speech itself.

Concluding Observations

VE closes by arguing that English will never become Standard English, not with so many "Englishes" available to us; in fact, the pluralization of English has long taken place. Our task, Elbow argues, is to respond to this phenomenon. First, as with different periods in the history of rhetoric, vernacular should and will be recognized as an *acceptable* mode of expression. Second, and complementary to the first point, vernacular Englishes should be recognized as *appropriate* for written expression. This occurs, Elbow asserts, as a challenge to the "powerful ideology of prescriptivism," in favor of the democratization of writing (369). Over time, we must begin to pay more attention to our speech habits so that we can better convey and share meaning with others. Yet, in the formative stages of composing, more freedom of expression, less bridling from artificial constraints, will prove just as helpful as "speaking onto the page" practices.

Ultimately, how are we to use Elbow's *Vernacular Eloquence*? While continued exposure to varieties of good writing is obviously helpful and should therefore be encouraged, making a conscious effort to facilitate the transition to "vernacular eloquence" is becoming increasingly essential. Elbow offers a democratizing heuristic, one that allows individuals to write more effectively by speaking onto the page. The use of speech for the invention of written text is a powerful heuristic that facilitates expression and creativity. Eventually, in the art of revision we must work deliberately to share meaning with others by recognizing conventions of grammar and style that enable the co-creation of meaning between writer and reader (who now is an "auditor" of sorts). How valuable is this contribution to solving "Why Johnny [and Janie still] Can't Write"? We have no doubt that *Vernacular Eloquence* will be one of the 21st century's pivotal works. For its treatment of rhetoric and composition's history with speech and its thoughtful reflection and recommendations for modern writers, it will change the course of our discipline by empowering all writers to write more eloquently in vernacular expression.

Fort Worth, Texas

Acknowledgments

We wish to thank Professor Elbow for corresponding with us during the writing of this review, for answering our questions, and for providing his views on the topics we covered.

Works Cited

Bartholomae, David. "Writing with Teachers: A Conversation with Peter Elbow." *CCC* 46.1 (1995): 62-71. Print.

---, and Peter Elbow. "Responses to Bartholomae and Elbow." *CCC* 46.1 (1995): 84-92. Print.

Corbett, Edward P. J. *Classical Rhetoric for the Modern Student*. New York: Oxford UP, 1965. Print.

Elbow, Peter. "Re: A 'Good Enough' Draft (For Now)." Message to Authors. 7 July 2014. E-mail.

---. *Writing Without Teachers*. New York: Oxford UP, 1973. Print.

Flower, Linda, and John R. Hayes. "A Cognitive Process Theory of Writing." *CCC* 32.4 (1981): 365-87. Print.

Fowler, H. W. *A Dictionary of Modern English Usage*. Ed. Sir Ernest Gowers. 2nd ed. Oxford: Oxford UP, 1965. Print.

Havelock, Eric A. *The Muse Learns to Write: Reflections on Orality and Literacy from Antiquity to The Present*. New Haven and London: Yale UP, 1986. Print.

Ong, Walter J. *Orality and Literacy: The Technologizing of The Word*. London and New York: Methuen, 1982; Routledge P, 1993. Print.

Sheils, Merrill. "Why Johnny Can't Write." *Newsweek*. Newsweek, 8 Dec. 1975. Web. 24 July 2014.

Young, Richard E., Alton L. Becker, and Kenneth L. Pike. *Rhetoric: Discovery and Change*. New York: Harcourt, Brace & World, Inc., 1970. Print.

Reclaiming the Rural: Essays on Literacy, Rhetoric, and Pedagogy, edited by Kim Donehower, Charlotte Hogg, and Eileen E. Schell. Carbondale: SIUP, 2012. 280 pp.

Reviewed by Jeffrey G. Howard, Idaho State University

Over the last several decades, much emphasis has been placed on urban environments as focal points of education and composition studies, surfacing in works such as Mike Rose's *Lives on the Boundary* and Bruce McComiskey's and Cynthia Ryan's more recent *City Comp: Identities, Spaces, Practices*. The urban emphasis has even invaded popular culture through cinematic or made-for-TV narratives in *To Sir, with Love, Stand and Deliver, Lean on Me, The Ron Clark Story*, and *The Freedom Writers*. Even the 2010 documentary *Waiting for Superman* focuses on children from urban centers as it argues for a better educational system. But while urban literacy is rightfully garnering much disciplinary and cultural notice, discussions about rural education have attracted less critical scrutiny.

Bringing well-needed attention to an often neglected landscape, *Reclaiming the Rural: Essays on Literacy, Rhetoric, and Pedagogy* is valuable because it provides a series of passionate folkloric, sociological, historical, rhetorical, and educational perspectives on the significance of rural communities and economies. It brings balance to contemporary academic conversations on literacy without relying on nostalgic or disparaging depictions designed to solicit sentimental reactions or dismiss rural communities as obsolete or out of touch. The work is a continuation of the editors' 2007 SIUP collection *Rural Literacies,* and it expands that conversation in order to address several important issues. The book is successful primarily because of the thoughtful and thorough way it addresses the underrepresentation of rural communities in academic discussions of rhetoric, the manner in which rural communities are and have been represented politically and socially, and the attitudes and methods that educators, citizens, and organizations can use to promote a sustainable literacy beneficial to students and the rural areas they call home.

As contributors to the collection argue, rural areas have much to offer, but urban technological advancement and derogatory attitudes about the non-urban have convinced many that rural communities are dead end communities, a sentiment that has led to migration out of the pastures, fields, and farms and into what many perceive as an urban future with endless opportunities. As the title communicates, the mission of this volume is to "reclaim the rural," but before doing so, the editors first define what it means to be *rural*, a term traditionally conceived as opposite to the urban, the metropolitan, the cosmopolitan. Donehower, Hogg, and Schell move away from this conception, claiming that the traditional urban-rural binary is false and that the rural should not be defined in terms of what it lacks, but rather in terms of its diversity and resources. These collected essays identify the existing connections among the rural, the urban, and the global—connections that have historically been ignored, diminished, or dismissed—and push the metaphor of sustainability as a defining component of rural literacy.

To accomplish this task, the editors divide the collection into three sections, "Land Economies and Rhetorics," "Histories," and "Pedagogies." Together, these sections demonstrate the past, present, and future roles of the rural as a component in the global community. The purpose of section one is primarily to "describe the struggles rural residents and stakeholders face as they engage in debates over how to sustain themselves in a globalized world" (10). Marcia Kmetz discusses the concept of *ethos,* or as she calls it, "a habitual gathering place," in the context of the Wind River water disputes, the laws of water use in the West, and the perpetual tensions that stem from those often unofficial regulations, which reflect the significance that water has played and continues to play in the formation of identity and the relationship between people and the landscape in that region (20). Cori Brewster discusses agricultural literacy campaigns whose main purpose involves the study of agriculture and the promotion of improved production methods through the teaming of rural community members with educational and political organizations. He argues that students need to know where food comes from and how it is made, but that they should also become adept at understanding and responding to the rhetoric of politicians and advocates whose policies manage the production, distribution, and consumption of food. This section is especially strong because it ties historical attitudes to present discursive practices and global outlooks.

Section two offers a significant conversation on the history of rhetoric in agricultural groups such as the Grange and 4-H, particularly in chapters authored by Carolyn Ostrander and I. Moriah McCracken. An important theme in this section is the representation of the underrepresented, including Native American and Chicana/o minority groups, women, children, and the rural populace in general. Jane Greer's essay "Women's Words, Women's Work: Rural Literacy and Labor" is especially compelling because of her careful treatment of the words and insider perspectives of farm women, particularly those found in the autobiography of Myrtle Tenney Booth, who lived in Appalachia during the twentieth century. Greer highlights the manner in which these narratives challenge (mis)conceptions about the lives, literacies, and culturally constructed personas of the women represented in Booth's autobiography. The presence of a wide range of individuals and groups in this section helps to disprove stereotypes concerning the lack of diversity in rural communities, and also demonstrates the capacities of rural communities to meet the needs of diverse constituents.

The individuals and communities represented in this section find solidarity and representation in rhetorical activism intended to keep their communities from crumbling under external pressures and negative attitudes.

Section two serves as a good platform for section three, which moves from community to classroom settings. As this section suggests, developing rural pedagogies makes sense because rural community members are increasingly pursuing a university education and the opportunities it provides. The editors' approach in this section unites administrators, teachers, parents, and students—particularly Robert Brooke's chapter "The Voices of Young Citizens: Rural Citizenship, Schools, and Public Policy"—inviting the rural sphere into the university in order to help people understand that rural life does not belong to a deficient past. Victims of diaspora from their own rural communities, students in Brooke's and other chapters are intellectually redirected to understand that rural by no means signifies "lesser" or "lacking." Like the Grange and other rural civic organizations, the classroom becomes a space where activism can take place, where teachers and students can engage in campaigns to help their rural communities achieve sustainability in a changing world. As Brooke argues, the "young voices" are the ones who will make rural sustainability possible, and they need the support of organizations, teachers, and citizens to employ effective rhetorical strategies that will counter the negative, life-draining attitudes currently affecting rural life (172).

When reading *Reclaiming the Rural,* one hears the voices of advocates for agriculture and the local, voices prompting us to imagine a future that establishes a connection with the past in order to move forward. This book is vital in identifying solutions to problems facing rural economies and communities today. Indeed, a work like this is what agrarian author and advocate Wendell Berry might call "a good solution," because it identifies methods in which students and teachers can harmonize with "larger patterns," namely "the whole complex of problems whose proper solutions add up to [. . .] the health of the soil, of plants and animals, of farm and farmer, of farm family and farm community, all involved in the same interested, interlocking pattern" (269). Sustainability is not simply something that farmers ought to worry about while the rest of us remain aloof; sustainable living applies to the complex network of relationships that exist in all spheres of life, whether rural, urban, or somewhere in between. The collection's message is not that we should forsake the global in exchange for the local, but rather that both are connected historically and rhetorically. *Reclaiming the Rural* demonstrates in a profound way that the rural does not become irrelevant simply because of current attitudes or the migration of its younger generations. As Donehower, Hogg, Schell, and their contributors demonstrate, the health of rural economies is significant across time, space, and knowledge domains. Anything but inert or empty, rural communities are sources of life and spaces saturated with meaning.

Pocatello, Idaho

Works Cited

Berry, Wendell. "Solving for Pattern." *The Art of the Commonplace: The Agrarian Essays of Wendell Berry*. Ed. Norman Wirzba. Berkeley: Counterpoint, 2002. 267-75. Print.

The Freedom Writers. Dir. Richard LaGravanese. Perf. Hilary Swank, Patrick Dempsey, Scott Glenn, Margaret Campbell, and Eva Benitez. Paramount, 2007. Film.

Lean on Me. Dir. John G. Avildsen. Perf. Morgan Freeman, Beverly Todd, Robert Gillaume, Lynne Thigpen, and Robin Bartlett. Warner Bros., 1989. Film.

The Ron Clark Story. Dir. Randa Haines. Perf. Matthew Perry, and Ernie Hudson. Granada Entertainment, 2006. Film.

Rose, Mike. *Lives on the Boundary: A Moving Account of the Struggles and Achievements of America's Educationally Underprepared*. New York: Penguin, 1989. Print.

Ryan, Cynthia, and Bruce McComiskey, eds. *City Comp: Identities, Spaces, Practices*. New York: SUNY P, 2003. Print.

Stand and Deliver. Dir. Ramón Menéndez. Perf. Edward James Olmos, Andy Garcia, and Lou Diamond Phillips. Warner Bros., 1988. Film.

To Sir, with Love. Dir. James Clavell. Perf. Sidney Poitier, Christian Roberts, Judy Geeson, and Suzy Kendall. Columbia, 1967. Film.

Waiting for Superman. Dir. Davis Guggenheim. Electric Kinney, 2010. Film.

Writing as a Way of Being: Writing Instruction, Nonduality, and the Crisis of Sustainability, by Robert P. Yagelski. New York: Hampton, 2011. 192 pp.

Reviewed by Paula Mathieu, Boston College

The belief that all things are inextricably connected can be found in the work of Native American writers and spiritualists, Eastern philosophies of Zen and Taoism, and Albert Einstein, to name just a few examples. In Robert Yagelski's latest book, *Writing as a Way of Being,* this interconnection of all things is paramount, both as a problem and a solution. For Yagelski, contemporary schooling is deeply connected to the current environmental crisis because of an unshaking reliance on a Cartesian separation between self and world. Such a separation erases the connections we humans have with each other, other living beings, and the planet itself. Absent these connections, Western education teaches students to pursue notions of success that are antithetical to the common good and the health of the planet. Writing and writing instruction, argues Yagelski, foster this disconnection, not because writing itself is an alienating activity, but because our teaching of it, despite advances in theory, still prioritizes textual production over the experience of writing itself. Writing as gerund, not verb: we teach *writing* as a thing, texts to be produced and evaluated, rather than encouraging the act of writing, the experience of writers writing, together. *Writing as a Way of Being* argues that a focus on producing competent texts privileges form over content, genre over inquiry, textual revision over shared conversation. Yagelski's book skillfully yet radically challenges most of the accepted orthodoxy in composition studies today and does so with a welcomed sense of ethics and urgency.

Analyzing the scope and depth of each of Yagelski's chapters helps to illustrate the profound contributions made in this work. The opening chapter, "Writing and the Crisis of Sustainability" asks, "How can we teach writing so that we stop destroying ourselves" (32). This question recalls Mary Rose O'Reilley's desire in *The Peaceable Classroom* to teach English in a way that prevents violence. In this chapter Yagelski connects the growing global environmental crisis directly with education. He argues that most principles of Western education rest on a notion of the self as primary and separate from the world (Descartes' "I think therefore I am"), which causes notions of success to be defined individualistically, often in stark contrast to what is in the common good.

The next chapter, "The Cartesian View of Writing," seeks to prove that writing instruction in both secondary and post-secondary schools fails to live up to its progressive promises, despite advances in theorizing teaching. Yagelski argues that "conventional writing instruction and assessment continue to operate on the assumption that writing is a sometimes challenging but relatively straightforward conduit for meaning" (24). While he uses the SAT as an example of the problem, he also asserts that standardized tests are based on the assumption that college faculty value similar criteria in student writing (24). Even social and post-process theories, argues Yagelski, fall short of their radical potential because of a tacit embrace of Cartesian dualism, which posits the self as an autonomous being, the world as separate and knowable from the knower, and language as a relatively unproblematic conduit for thought (45). While the content here straddles composition theory and philosophy, Yagelski does a particularly nice job working through the debates within composition studies regarding its social turn, stopping to dwell especially on the work of Richard Miller, some of the neo-Sophists, and Thomas Kent's post-process ideas.

In "Writing, Being and Nonduality," Yagelski calls on the Zen philosophy of Eihei Dogen and the phenomenological rhetoric of Barbara Couture to posit a view of writing that seeks communal truth through a focus on the process of writers writing together as a way to transcend Cartesian duality. This view situates writing as necessary but insufficient to help humans seek connection and understanding of the world; language is both vital and deficient. Unlike a purely relativist position, Yagelski posits the material world as real and separate from language, knowable only through communal inquiries toward truth. His goal is to imagine writing as action (not a thing) that can help writers move from subjective knowing toward a shared inquiry and intersubjective truth.

Yagelski moves from the theoretical to the practical in "Writing as a Way of Being" as he meditates on his own experiences of writing this chapter. He describes how he is both deeply rooted in a place while writing and connected to other familiar places; he is alone but filled with the voices of other scholars, his graduate students, and the inmates he taught in a local prison years earlier. He interweaves his meditation with further discussion to show similarities and differences between his ideas and those of Linda Flower's cognitive studies and Donald Murray's process writing. He ultimately describes his ontological theory of writing—one that posits writing as part of how we learn to be in the world. This theory focuses on the *act* of writing as intensifying the writer's awareness while writing. Yagelski asserts that such awareness is qualitatively different from other senses of awareness because the nature of language is important but unreliable, the effects of writing experiences are cumulative, and the context of a writing act shapes that experience of writing.

In "A Thousand Writers Writing," Yagelski begins with a memory of a National Writing Project event where he sat in a room with one thousand other teachers writing. That experience—rather than the texts produced—were powerful and act as a metaphor for writing as a way of being. He teases out specific pedagogical practices that prioritize his ontological view of writing: giving more time for the act of writing, creating shared inquiries, and making content a serious and real concern. Surprisingly, the practices are less dramatically different from current practice than one might imagine, and in citing an analogy of Michael Pollan's advice about food, Yagelski suggests that shifting toward writing as a way of being means changing our fundamental views about ourselves and our roles in the world, rather than changing specific classroom practices (163).

When I first started reading composition theory—early in the 1990s—I was drawn to writers who wrote in big ways, those whose ideas, metaphorically, swung for the fences. In writers like James Berlin, Alan France, Elspeth Stuckey, Michael Blitz and Mark Hurlbert, James Sledd, and Mary Rose O'Reilly, to name a few, I encountered scholars who deeply questioned the foundations of composition studies and tied their arguments passionately to ethical and political goals. Even in the diatribe of Maxine Hairston against leftists like Berlin, John Trimbur, Patricia Bizzell, and in the scholarship of other leftists (which Yagelski unpacks nicely), one finds agonizing and earnest debates about the deep purposes and stakes of writing classes. Great scholarship, I believe, should question our basic assumptions and overwhelm us, a bit, with its implications. In this category, I would happily place *Writing as a Way of Being*. It creates a powerful response to Berlin's *Rhetorics, Poetics, and Cultures,* which argues that the purpose of writing should be to create active citizens. Yagelski shows that the Cartesian separation of self and world prevents meaningful citizenship unless we make fundamental changes to how and why we teach writing. As such, this book goes against the trend of most prevailing scholarship, which stresses the need to prove our success as writing teachers, to persuasively enter public debates and quantitatively assess the outcomes of our courses. It also convincingly answers why, given an embrace of social and post-process theories of writing, classroom practices have not fully reflected those shifts.

This is a radical book. It questions and seeks to shift the foundations of what we think of as writing and why we teach writing. For me as a reader, this book filled me with the excitement of possibility and intimidation I have not felt since graduate school. Scholarship in more recent years seems to have become more careful, more circumscribed, working within what Yagelski calls a "silent consensus" about why we teach writing (52). Yagelski questions these frameworks and their assumptions, yet reasserts the excitement and value of teaching writing.

This book may have a revolutionary effect on what and how we teach, or it may be largely ignored. Because of how fundamentally it questions what we do as scholars and teachers, I imagine that many readers may dismiss it as quixotic. Or because individual scholars may be wedded to research projects and pedagogies that rely on a dualistic view of education, many might reject or not even read this work. I hope this is not the case. But especially for those of us who are already drawn to nondualistic ways of thinking and being—and those who at semester's end wonder if we really served our students well—will find much that will teach and provoke in this ambitious work.

My quibbles with the book are minor, and not related to Yagelski's critique of dualism in writing. First, I would have liked to have seen writing placed alongside other practices of being—such as meditation, mindful breathing, storytelling, or walking in nature—that can help orient humans so that they deeply experience themselves as part of and connected to the world. Without placing writing in such relation, Yagelski risks reinscribing a view of literacy that is separate from—and superior to—other human experience. Second, his use of Couture's theory suggests an ethical framework, but exploring questions surrounding pedagogical ethics more fully would have been helpful. For example, will giving students more space to write in less dualistic ways directly help them want to save the planet? If so, how do we do that?

But even for readers who might not be persuaded to embrace Yagelski's philosophy for composition studies, this book offers a compelling and engaging history of writing theory over the past twenty years. He interweaves complex philosophical and rhetorical positions with relevant stories of writing and teaching, making this book both challenging and accessible. My hope is that the field is ready to have its foundations shaken, even just a bit, by this important and rich work.

Chestnut Hill, Massachusetts

Works Cited

Berlin, James A. *Rhetoric, Poetics, Cultures: Refiguring English Studies*. Urbana: NCTE, 1996. Print.

Hairston, Maxine. "Diversity, Ideology, and the Teaching of Writing." *CCC* 43.2 (1992): 179-93. Print.

O'Reilly, Mary Rose. *The Peaceable Classroom*. Portsmouth: Heinemann, 1993. Print.

Literacy, Economy, and Power: Writing and Research After *Literacy in American Lives*, edited by John Duffy, Julie Nelson Christoph, Eli Goldblatt, Nelson Graff, Rebecca S. Nowacek, and Bryan Trabold. Carbondale: Southern Illinois UP, 2014. 244 pp.

Review by Kristina Fennelly, Kutztown University

Featuring a range of works by eighteen noted scholars, *Literacy, Economy, and Power* continues the diverse inquiries within and surrounding literacy studies. This edited collection functions as both a reflection on Deborah Brandt's *Literacy in American Lives* (2001) and as a response to one of her research questions, namely: "How has literacy learning changed over the last century and how have rising expectations for literacy been experienced as part of felt life?" (4). *Literacy, Economy, and Power* not only seeks to pay homage to the salient contributions provided by Brandt's eighty interviews on the subject of literacy, but it also provides a democratic approach to understanding how literacy functions as privilege, how economic standing and sponsorship shape access, and how power informs reading and writing practices. This collection offers tools for expanding pedagogical practices and interrogating theoretical frameworks in chapters that successfully complement and challenge Brandt's work. Overall, the volume is a conscientious invitation to scholars to reexamine definitions in, approaches to, and uses of literacy studies.

The editors outline three specific purposes of the collection: (1) to examine the influence of Brandt's work on literacy by asking contributors to detail how their own scholarship has been shaped in historical, conceptual, methodological, and pedagogical ways; (2) to convene the most current and relevant research taking place in literacy studies; and (3) to mark the span of more than a decade since Brandt's work was published. The volume's three sections consider the historical impact of literacy studies; the present use, value, and estimation of literacy; and the future of literacy research, theory, and practice. Ultimately, each section offers an inquiry-driven text that seeks to respond to and model the generative nature of questions initiated by Brandt's work.

The first section of the collection, "Looking Back at Literacy: What It Did to Us; What We Did with It," features chapters by Ellen Cushman, Rhea Estelle Lathan, Carol Mattingly, and Morris Young, and embodies the historical perspective at the core of Brandt's book. The section provides a nuanced consideration of sponsorship and the cultural and economic forces surrounding it. Of particular interest is the way in which Cushman's chapter draws on five years of research to offer a portrait of regional histories of literacy, namely that of the Cherokee Nation. Her work challenges Brandt's definition of sponsorship by asserting that rather than only exhibiting power over those acquiring literacy, sponsors are also "often beholden to the very people who sponsored them in the first place" (15). To illustrate this distinction, Cushman meticulously details the complicated history of Elias Boudinot, the first editor of the *Cherokee Phoenix*, showing how he sought to mediate the demands of the newspaper's white and Cherokee audiences. Although he preserved the use of Sequoyan in the tribe and provided literacy access to the Cherokee by publishing their language in the newspaper, history has often represented him as a traitor due to his alignment with white sponsors. Although several scholars read Boudinot as embracing a hegemonic view of literacy that sought to undermine his own people, Cushman offers a fresh and objective perspective on Boudinot's legacy and the complications of literacy sponsorship.

The second section of the collection, "Looking at Literacy Now: A Tool For Change?" offers chapters by Julie Nelson Christof, Kim Donehower, Bruce Horner and Min-Zhan Lu, Beverly J. Moss and Robyn Lyons-Robinson, and Paul Prior, among others. Like Cushman's chapter in the opening section, Eli Goldblatt and David A. Jolliffe's contribution to section two, "The Unintended Consequences of Sponsorship," also pushes at the borders of Brandt's definitions, although their focus is on the economic rather than the cultural implications of literacy sponsorship. Goldblatt and Jolliffe take issue with what they see as Brandt's too-narrow conception of the power dynamics at play between sponsors and the communities they serve. While they do not negate the advantages sponsors gain through their activities, they nonetheless emphasize that literacy sponsors and literacy networks also take risks, and through those risks "can be harmed, altered, or even transformed by the population and pedagogy they contract to teach" (128). Drawing on Jolliffe's fieldwork from the Arkansas Delta Oral History Project—an educational initiative sponsored by the University of Arkansas at Fayetteville—and Goldblatt's association with Tree House Books—a Philadelphia neighborhood literacy center supported by Temple University—the chapter contends that institutional sponsors and sponsored populations can mutually benefit. Also of note in section two is Michael W. Smith's chapter, "Seeking Sponsors, Accumulating Literacies," which is based on personal and professional conversations with Brandt. Smith makes a case for a closer connection between English education and composition studies as a way to interrogate, extend, and challenge definitions of literacy. One way to achieve this improved partnership is by "accumulating literacies," which Smith—by way of Brandt—defines as "creating new and hybrid forms of literacy" (162). Smith argues for the import of "transfer," wherein pedagogical practices equip "students for the literacy learning in which they will engage both in and out of our classrooms" (163).

Readers can find examples of accumulating literacies and best practices in section three, "Looking Forward at Literacy: The Global and Multimodal

Future," which marks the shortest section of the collection and contains contributions from Cynthia L. Selfe and Gail E. Hawisher, Harvey J. Graff, and Anne Ruggles Gere. Each contribution examines Brandt's question, "Can mass writing claim a moral authority powerful enough to transform the social institutions that were organized to serve readers over writers?" (229). In "Beyond *Literate Lives*: Collaboration, Literacy Narratives, Transnational Connections, and Digital Media," Selfe and Hawisher argue that literacy narratives composed through a range of mediums help writers form and articulate identity. By observing ways in which individuals are "composing themselves into the fabric of an increasingly technological world," Selfe and Hawisher renew Brandt's purpose to locate meaning in our personal relationships and through evolving approaches to literacy (194). As Selfe and Hawisher's and Ruggles Gere's contributions both emphasize, writing now appears to trump reading given the growth of social media and the exchange of digital rhetoric. This shift, they contend, will have profound implications on not just scholarship in literacy studies, but on the nature of literacy itself. Indeed, this final section compels all readers to learn more about the rise of writing in the literate world, and revisiting Brandt's work through the lenses provided in *Literacy, Economy, and Power* offers a concrete approach to doing so. Because the contributors' research reflects Brandt's influence on their own work, these essays speak to each other in meaningful ways. Though the dominant thread in the volume focuses on the complexities of sponsorship—and thus places less emphasis on other fascinating issues in literacy studies—it is successful in its interrogation of how economic, political, and cultural forces come to bear on access to literacy. Overall, *Literacy, Economy, and Power* provides a rich variety of essays that readily invite readers to affirm the value, relevance, and ongoing evolution of literacy sponsorship and literacy studies today.

Kutztown, Pennsylvania

Works Cited

Brandt, Deborah. *Literacy in American Lives*. Cambridge: Cambridge UP, 2001. Print.

First Semester: Graduate Students, Teaching Writing, and the Challenge of Middle Ground, by Jessica Restaino. Carbondale: Southern Illinois UP, 2012. 141 pp.

Reviewed by Margaret Briggs-Dineen, Wendy Fall, Beth Godbee, Danielle Klein, Laura Linder-Scholer, Alyssa McGrath, Michael Stock, and Sarah Thompson, Marquette University

This review emerges from our collective reading of Jessica Restaino's *First Semester: Graduate Students, Teaching Writing, and the Challenge of Middle Ground* in our composition pedagogy course. As a group of seven new graduate teaching assistants (TAs) and their course instructor, we relate to the experiences of Restaino's participants (also first-time TAs and new graduate students) who faced grading woes, limited curriculum input, and challenging interpersonal dynamics with their students. Restaino's *First Semester* offers a glimpse into the often-overlooked complications that TAs face as they work to balance the responsibilities that first-year writing programs require of their student-teachers. By focusing on graduate TAs, Restaino honors the many beginnings of graduate students, grounding our experiences within the theoretical structure of Hannah Arendt's three ontological categories of the human condition: labor, work, and action. For Arendt, labor is the daily cycle of effort, work is the creation of tangible products, and action creates long-term change. Examining the participants' experiences through this theory, Restaino makes a strong argument for valuing TAs' contributions to composition pedagogy and for sharing the work of co-creating first-year composition. We believe this argument is a key contribution of *First Semester*. Further, we appreciate that Restaino's descriptive portraits of TAs do more than *tell*—instead, they truly *show*—many of the complex conditions, relations, and responsibilities facing graduate students early in their careers.

First Semester contributes new ethnographic research on first-year composition and teacher education, valuing TAs' voices while weaving them with theory and with considerations of composition pedagogy, writing program administration, and graduate education. In doing so, this work builds on previous collections that value TAs' narratives, such as Tina Lavonne Good and Leanne B. Warshauer's *In Our Own Voice: Graduate Students Teach Writing* (2000) and Wendy Bishop and Deborah Coxwell Teague's *Finding Our Way: A Writing Teacher's Sourcebook* (2004). At the same time, Restaino situates her study alongside research on graduate student preparation, pointing to Betty P. Pytlik's and Sarah Liggett's *Preparing College Teachers of Writing* (2001) and Sidney Dobrin's *Don't Call It That: The Composition Practicum* (2005) as two collections indicative of the need to theorize how graduate students learn to teach writing. *First Semester* responds to this need by attending to TAs' narratives and valuing graduate students' experiences, while simultaneously theorizing the work involved in graduate teacher preparation. And, as with other recent publications in the Studies in Writing and Rhetoric (SWR) series, *First Semester* does so empirically—in a methodologically rich and detailed way.

Chapter one, "Arendt, Writing Teachers, and Beginnings," introduces the book's focus of examining graduate TAs' first semesters, identifying their "survival skills," and understanding these new teachers as the "shaky foundation on which writing programs . . . rest" (1-2). Restaino describes TA preparation as consisting of a brief orientation and typically a corresponding practicum or seminar on composition pedagogy, which aligns with our experience and represents the experiences of many of our peers throughout the country. Willing to share their negotiation of that "shaky foundation," four participants (Tess, Shirley, Nancy, and Anjel) provide Restaino access to their first semesters through a series of emails, interviews, and observations. The participants represent a diverse group in terms of gender, race, age, teaching experience, area of study, and approach to teaching and, as such, most new graduate teaching assistants will easily relate to their experiences. The participant case studies—introduced in chapter one and followed throughout the next three chapters—help us situate our own experiences within an Arendtian framework and provide the means through which Restaino argues for the importance of graduate students as contributing members of the university.

Restaino begins chapter two, "Labor and Endlessness: Necessity and Consumption in the First Semester," by acknowledging that many TAs must begin teaching before engaging with composition scholarship or developing their own theories on teaching. This chapter focuses on Tess's and Shirley's labors in process pedagogy, grading, and classroom management. They often feel drained and look for immediate solutions, ignoring the possibility that their efforts yield long-term, meaningful output when unification of theory and practice occurs. Restaino suggests that these early struggles to survive can prompt graduate students to adopt practices that are not theoretically sound. This concern leads Restaino to consider the tensions between practical application and theory and to argue for Arendt's notion of labor as the motor that drives teachers toward a balance between work and action. Further, Restaino discusses the resistance that these TAs expressed toward the externally imposed structure of the class and toward the writing process itself. As reviewers, we had some difficulty aligning our experiences with Restaino's description of Arendtian labor. Despite the challenges we faced as new instructors, many of us felt that the characterization of our labor as an arduous, endless cycle was extreme. We were glad, therefore, to see Restaino's conclusion that Arendtian laboring is not inevitable and cannot stand alone as a lens for analyzing the first-year teaching experience. Instead, Restaino suggests that Arendt's ideas could serve as a launching pad for new analysis and research.

Chapter three, "Teachers-as-Students: Work and Action in the Middle Space," is Restaino's most extensive chapter, exploring the complex relationship between the experiences of TAs and Arendt's theories of work and action. Although Restaino acknowledges that applying the terms of work and action to TAs' experiences can be "messy," she argues that these connections work well in conversation with the pedagogical theories of Paolo Freire and bell hooks, among others (55). She suggests it is most useful to consider work and action in light of Christopher Higgins's writings on the importance of seeking a middle ground between these concepts in the classroom. Through the lens of the middle ground and in her descriptions of the participants' first semesters, Restaino connects TAs' experiences to the concepts of premature action (when individuals must take on a public role before they are ready), silence as a form of action (silence can provide an individual with a public presence), and the function of grading in Arendtian terms (different forms of grading can mean the difference between labor and work). Thereby, Restaino provides many possibilities TAs could consider helpful when deciding how to approach teaching. In our class discussions, this chapter appealed to each of us in different ways: some focused on Restaino's ideas on grading, while others were drawn to the concepts of premature action and silence as a form of action. We found that the range of responses highlighted the individualized and sometimes conflicting nature of first-semester graduate teaching experiences.

The final chapter, "Thinking What We Are Doing: Knowledge Making in the Trenches," provides a summary of Restaino's ideas and observations shared in *First Semester* and her motivation for writing this book. She asserts that the purpose of her research has been to encourage reflection across local contexts on the best practices of preparing and supporting TAs. Restaino mentions the work already being done by writing program administrators (WPAs) to promote better teaching in first-year writing programs, but this "exciting work happens amid the swirling sea that defines the still-conflicted positioning of composition in the university" (112). Hence, the book concludes with a call for action, prompting WPAs to reassess the role of TAs and to offer new instructors a "chance of real connection and real change agency" (116). Namely, while TAs should have space to experiment and develop as writing instructors, composition programs should also foster TAs' contributions to the field. While Restaino acknowledges that reform takes time, she reminds us that our actions as writing instructors matter.

Though perhaps primarily intended for WPAs, *First Semester* is valuable reading for writing instructors (faculty and TAs) as well. Many of us found it meaningful to read that the joys, struggles, and frustrations that we have experienced during our first semesters are not localized to our university. However, others among us see potential danger in prospective or new graduate students reading the book too early in their teaching careers. Because Restaino repeatedly emphasizes the struggles of instructors and only briefly discusses their moments of triumph, this book could give a false impression that teaching as a graduate student is primarily a negative experience. Additionally, a number of us felt that Restaino's case studies had merit independent of the Arendtian model of labor, work, and action. For some of us, the Arendtian theory felt at times imposed and therefore detracts from the impact of the case studies and the book as a whole. Ultimately, we recommend the book for graduate students as a supplement to their own pedagogical studies, but we also caution that readers should not become discouraged by Restaino's descriptions of the graduate student–teacher experience.

These criticisms acknowledged, Restaino's chapters, when taken together, effectively depict the struggles of new graduate TAs to balance the labor of grading and lesson planning with the desire to have a lasting impact on students and writing programs. Most significantly, we appreciate that Restaino defends TAs' needs to feel empowered while also feeling protected, supported, and encouraged by program directors and the institution itself. As readers, we especially enjoyed the case studies and Restaino's advocacy of praxis; we see aspects of ourselves in the case study participants, and their experiences remind us of the importance of grounding our own teaching practice in sound theory. We are honored by the priority Restaino places on graduate students and on their (and our) voices. Overall, *First Semester* shows that though graduate students often feel overwhelmed and underequipped to teach a writing course, we do, in fact, make significant contributions and leave a legacy.

Milwaukee, Wisconsin

Works Cited

Bishop, Wendy, and Deborah Coxwell Teague, eds. *Finding Our Way: A Writing Teacher's Sourcebook.* New York: Houghton Mifflin, 2004. Print.

Dobrin, Sidney, ed. *Don't Call it That: The Composition Practicum.* Urbana: NCTE, 2005. Print.

Good, Tina Lavonne, and Leanne B. Warshauer, eds. *In Our Own Voice: Graduate Students Teach Writing.* Boston: Allyn and Bacon, 2000. Print.

Pytlik, Betty P., and Sarah Liggett. *Preparing College Teachers of Writing: Histories, Theories, Programs, and Practices.* Oxford: Oxford UP, 2001. Print.

Contributors

Elizabeth Brewer is an Assistant Professor at Central Connecticut State University. She has co-authored the *Arts and Humanities* volume of *The SAGE Reference Series on Disability* and has published in *Kairos* and *Disability Studies Quarterly*. She is currently co-editing a collection titled *Cripping the Computer: A Critical Moment in Composition Studies.*

Margaret Briggs-Dineen is a graduate student and first-year writing instructor at Marquette University. Her research interests lie in twentieth-century American literature, folklore, and animal studies.

Ella R. Browning is a PhD candidate in rhetoric and composition in the English Department at the University of South Florida. Her current research interests include disability studies, feminist rhetorical theory, first year composition, professional and technical communication, and writing program administration.

Tyler Carter is a PhD student in rhetoric and composition at Purdue University, and holds an MFA in Literary Arts from Brown University. In addition to teaching composition, creative writing, and speech, he also writes and publishes poems and essays. This is his first academic publication.

Dr. Virginia (Ginny) Crisco teaches writing, teaches teachers to teach writing, and administers first-year writing at California State University, Fresno. Her current research bridges areas of literacy and rhetoric, explores connections between language, diversity, and activism, and extends conversations about democracy and pedagogy in school and community contexts.

Laura J. Davies is Director of Writing and Assistant Professor of English at SUNY Cortland where she teaches in the English education program. Her scholarly interests include writing program administration, writing teacher pedagogy, and information literacy. She and her partner John live in upstate New York with their five children.

Jay Dolmage is an Associate Professor of English at the University of Waterloo in Ontario, Canada. He is the editor of the *Canadian Journal of Disability Studies*. His book *Disability Rhetoric* was published in 2014 by Syracuse University Press. His essays on rhetoric, writing, and disability studies have appeared in several journals and edited collections, including *Cultural Critique* and *Rhetoric Review*. Jay grew up in the disability rights movement in

Canada and remains committed to promoting greater access within higher education and across society.

Russel K. Durst is Professor of English at the University of Cincinnati. A former English department chair and writing program director, he has published four books and over forty articles and book chapters on composition.

Richard Leo Enos is a Piper Professor (State of Texas) and Holder of the Lillian Radford Chair of Rhetoric and Composition at Texas Christian University. His research emphasis is classical rhetoric with a concentration on oral and written discourse.

Wendy Fall is a graduate student at Marquette University. Her research focuses on the conventionality of gothic literature before 1820, particularly as expressed in chapbook publications. She works on the Gothic Archive, an online collection of chapbooks and supplemental materials that can be accessed at epublications.marquette.edu/gothic.

Kristina Fennelly is an Assistant Professor of English at Kutztown University. Her research and teaching interests include argument writing, social media rhetoric, composition theory and pedagogy, and gender studies.

Lynée Lewis Gaillet is Professor of English at Georgia State University where she directs the Writing Studio and Lower Division Studies. She is author of numerous works addressing Scottish rhetoric, writing program administration, composition/rhetoric pedagogy, and archival research methods.

Chris W. Gallagher is Writing Program Director and Professor of English at Northeastern University in Boston. He is the author or co-author of four books, most recently *Our Better Judgment: Teacher Leadership for Writing Assessment* with Eric Turley (NCTE), as well as numerous articles in composition and education journals.

Beth Godbee is Assistant Professor at Marquette University, where she studies how collaborative writing talk (and the relationship-building, writing, revision, and rethinking involved in that talk) brings about social change, or more equitable relations, for individuals and members of their social networks.

Jennifer Habel is the author of *Good Reason*, winner of the Stevens Poetry Manuscript Competition, and *In the Little House*, winner of the Copperdome Chapbook Prize. She is the coordinator of creative writing at the University of Cincinnati.

Jacquelyn E. Hoermann is a Radford Fellow and doctoral student in composition and rhetoric studies at Texas Christian University. Her research interests focus on issues pertaining to critical literacies, new media research, and women and gender studies.

Jeffrey Howard earned his M.A. from Utah State University, and he is working on his PhD at Idaho State University. His specialties include eighteenth-century British literature and folklore, but he is also deeply interested in rural literature. Jeffrey worked for many years on his family's farms in Washington and Idaho.

Danielle Klein is a graduate student and first-year writing instructor at Marquette University.

Liz Lane is a rhetoric and composition PhD student at Purdue with research areas of digital rhetoric and writing, and gender and technology. Her specific interests focus on women's voices and online writing, teaching multimodal composing in the first-year writing classroom, and professional and technical writing.

Cynthia Lewicki-Wilson is Professor Emerita of English and Disability Studies, Miami University. She has co-edited three collections on disability, including *Disability and the Teaching of Writing*, with Brenda Jo Brueggemann and Jay Dolmage.

Laura Linder-Scholer is a graduate student and first-year writing instructor at Marquette University. Her research focuses on gender and sexuality. Visit her website on gender-inclusive language in the First-Year English classroom at genderinclusiveclassroom.wordpress.com.

Aja Y. Martinez is Assistant Professor of English at Binghamton University, SUNY. Her scholarship focuses on histories of rhetorics and rhetorics of contemporary racism and its effects on marginalized peoples in institutional spaces. Her efforts as teacher/scholar strive toward increasing access, retention and participation of diverse groups in higher education.

Paula Mathieu teaches writing, rhetoric and pedagogy courses at Boston College, where she also directs First-Year Writing and the Writing Fellows Program. Her publications include *Tactics of Hope: The Public Turn in English Composition* and *Circulating Communities: The Tactics and Strategies of Community Publishing* (with Steve Parks and Tiffany Rousculp).

Alyssa McGrath is a graduate student and first-year writing instructor at Marquette University. Her primary research interest is investigating ways to build writer confidence among first-year collegiate students.

Margaret Price is an associate professor of rhetoric/composition at Spelman College. She is the author of *Mad at School: Rhetorics of Mental Disability and Academic Life* (University of Michigan Press, 2011), which won the Outstanding Book Award from the Conference on College Composition and Communication. With Stephen Kerschbaum, she is at work on a mixed-methods study of disability disclosure in academic contexts.

Fernando Sánchez is a doctoral candidate at Purdue University. His research interests center on issues in professional and technical communication, as well as writing program administration. His work has been published in *Writing Program Administration* and *Trans-Scripts*.

Cynthia Selfe is Humanities Distinguished Professor in the Department of English at Ohio State University. She is Co-founder and Executive Editor of Computers and Composition Digital Press/Utah State University Press (with Gail Hawisher), and Co-Founder and Co-Director of the Digital Archive of Literacy Narratives (with H. Lewis Ulman).

Michael Stock is a Marquette University graduate student and a writing instructor in the First-Year English and Upward Bound Math Science programs.

Sarah Thompson is a graduate student and first-year English instructor at the University of South Carolina.

Tara Wood has published work in *Open Words: Access and English Studies*, *Kairos: A Journal of Rhetoric, Technology, and Pedagogy*, *Disability Studies Quarterly*, and is also co-author of the WPA/CompPile bibliography on Disability Studies. She is currently Assistant Professor of English at Rockford University.

Melanie Yergeau is an assistant professor of English at the University of Michigan. She has published in *College English*, *Disability Studies Quarterly*, *Computers and Composition Online*, and *Kairos*. She is currently working on a book project titled *Authoring Autism*.

Fifth Annual Dartmouth Summer Seminar for Writing Research
July 26 - August 7, 2015
Hanover, NH

"The Summer Seminar was one of the most rewarding professional experiences of my career." (previous participant)

The 2015 Dartmouth Summer Seminar for Writing Research is designed for writing faculty from all types of higher education venues who are beginning to work on data-driven research about writing in higher education contexts, and who would like an intensive, high-powered two weeks to work on that research, review the best approaches and methods, consult directly with experts, and network long-term with a cohort of other researchers. Guided interaction about participants' projects is offered in the months leading up to the Seminar. The Seminar itself offers a quiet, resource-rich environment, coursework, small-group discussion and exchange, individual consultation with Seminar leaders, time to work alone or in groups on research projects, and a concluding presentation to the group with feedback from team leaders.

We encourage both individuals and research groups or teams to apply.

The Seminar coursework covers a range of topics, including data segmenting and coding, statistics, statistical analysis, effective literature reviews, research ethics, and so on. Special-interest topics are presented based on participants' projects.

If you've been asking yourself questions like the following, this is the seminar for you:

- How do I turn an interest into a viable data-driven investigation?
- I am very familiar with my primary research approach but would like to develop data-driven research abilities; where might I go?
- What data do I collect for my research study? How do I collect it?
- What should I look for when I analyze the data? What is the deeper phenomenon I am looking for? What is a good site for investigating it?
- What methods are the best for the questions I would like to answer?
- Where can I learn more about how to select a sample, how to identify a control group, and how to calculate statistical significance?
- Should I conduct a pilot study first? What are the advantages and disadvantages of a pilot study (including funding)?
- Is institutional (IRB) approval needed for my project?
- Why does my research question keep changing?
- What's the best way to present and publish my research?

More information and the seminar application (**due December 15, 2014**) available at <http://writing-speech.dartmouth.edu/research>. Program fee is $1500; partial scholarships funded by CWPA and CCCC available to community college, HCBU, and TCU participants. Contact Christiane Donahue at Composition.Research.Seminar@Dartmouth.Edu with any questions.

Queen City Writers
a journal of undergraduate writing & composing

Do your students want a wider audience for their work? Encourage them to submit their writing to our journal!

Queen City Writers is a refereed journal that publishes essays and multimedia work by undergraduate students

WE'RE CURRENTLY ACCEPTING SUBMISSIONS FOR UPCOMING ISSUES

For more information, visit us online at **http://qc-writers.com**

PARLOR PRESS
EQUIPMENT FOR LIVING

Congratulations to These Award Winners!

GenAdmin: Theorizing WPA Identities in the Twenty-First Century
Colin Charlton, Jonikka Charlton, Tarez Samra Graban, Kathleen J. Ryan, & Amy Ferdinandt Stolley
Winner of the Best Book Award, Council of Writing Program Adminstrators (July, 2014)

Mics, Cameras, Symbolic Action: Audio-Visual Rhetoric for Writing Teachers
Bump Halbritter
Winner of the Distinguished Book Award from Computers and Composition (May, 2014)

New Releases

First-Year Composition: From Theory to Practice
Edited by Deborah Coxwell-Teague & Ronald F. Lunsford. 420 pages.
Twelve of the leading theorists in composition studies answer, in their own voices, the key question about what they hope to accomplish in a first-year composition course. Each chapter, and the accompanying syllabi, provides rich insights into the classroom practices of these theorists.

A Rhetoric for Writing Program Administrators
Edited by Rita Malenczyk. 471 pages.
Thirty-two contributors delineate the major issues and questions in the field of writing program administration and provide readers new to the field with theoretical lenses through which to view major issues and questions.

www.parlorpress.com

STUDY
COMPOSITION
AND RHETORIC

Joint PhD Program in English and Education

UNIVERSITY OF MICHIGAN

SCHOOL OF EDUCATION

DEPARTMENT *of* ENGLISH

Bringing together the best of research, scholarship, and pedagogy from both English and Education, this interdisciplinary program draws on top-flight resources to provide a satisfying and rich doctoral experience. Among our strengths, we offer a supportive and engaging community of scholars that includes both students and faculty, and we provide the flexibility for students to craft a program centered on their individual interests. These interests have included rhetorical theory, literacy studies, new media composition, applied linguistics, English language studies, teacher education, and writing assessment; our faculty are happy to work with you to craft a program centered on your research and teaching interests.

This PHD program is designed for students who hold master's degrees in English or education and who have teaching experience. We have an excellent record of placing graduates in tenure-track positions in education and English departments in colleges and universities.

Phone: 734.763.6643 • Email: ed.jpee@umich.edu

soe.umich.edu/jpee

Education Faculty
Chandra L. Alston: teacher education, English education, adolescent literacy, urban education
Barry Fishman: technology, video games as models for learning, reform involving technology, teacher learning, design-based implementation research
Elizabeth Birr Moje: adolescent and disciplinary literacy, literacy and cultural theory, research methods
Mary J. Schleppegrell: functional linguistics, second language learning, discourse analysis, language development

Co-Chairs
Anne Curzan: history of English, language and gender, corpus linguistics, lexicography, pedagogy
Anne Ruggles Gere: composition theory, gender and literacy, writing assessment, and pedagogy

English Faculty
David Gold: history of rhetoric, women's rhetorics, composition pedagogy
Scott Richard Lyons: Native American and global indigenous studies, settler colonialism, posthumanism
Alisse Portnoy: rhetoric and composition, rhetorical activism and civil rights movements
Megan Sweeney: African American literature and culture, ethnography, pedagogy, critical prison studies
Melanie R. Yergeau: composition and rhetoric, digital media studies, disability studies, autistic culture

STEVEN PINKER
THE SENSE OF STYLE
THE THINKING PERSON'S GUIDE TO WRITING IN THE 21ST CENTURY

"This book is a graceful and clear smackdown to the notion that English is going to the proverbial dogs. Pinker has written the Strunk & White for a new century."
—John McWhorter, author of *Our Magnificent Bastard Tongue* and *The Power of Babel*

"Only Steven Pinker could have written this marvelous book, and thank heaven he has….*The Sense of Style* will flip the way you think about good writing. Pinker's curiosity and delight illuminate every page, and when he says style can make the world a better place, we believe him."
—Patricia T. O'Conner, author of *Woe Is I*

Viking • 368 pp.
978-0-670-02585-5 • $27.95

The **Sense of Style**
the THINKING PERSON'S GUIDE
to WRITING in the 21st CENTURY
Steven Pinker
author of THE LANGUAGE INSTINCT
and THE BLANK SLATE

The bestselling linguist and cognitive scientist creates a usage guide for the twenty-first century, applying the sciences of language and mind to the challenge of crafting clear, coherent, and stylish prose. In this short, practical book, Pinker shows how writing depends on imagination, empathy, coherence, grammatical knowhow, and an ability to savor and reverse engineer the good prose of others. Using examples of effective and ineffective prose, Pinker replaces dogma about usage with reason and evidence, encouraging writers, editors, and students to apply guidelines judiciously rather than robotically.

PENGUIN GROUP (USA)
Academic Marketing Department | 375 Hudson Street | New York, NY 10014
www.penguin.com/academic

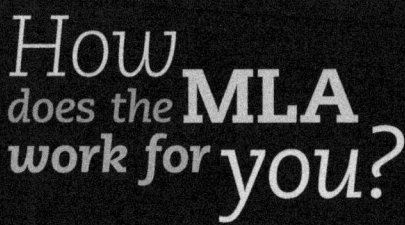

Promotes the study of language and literature

Publishes your scholarship

Hosts an annual convention where you can share your work

Compiles the *Job Information List*

Creates opportunities for scholarly interaction on *MLA Commons*

The MLA Annual Convention
8–11 January 2015
in Vancouver

featuring the presidential theme
Negotiating Sites of Memory

Join us at the largest gathering of teachers and scholars in the humanities for

- roundtables, workshops, and discussion
- special presentations featuring renowned thinkers, artists, and critics in conversation
- local excursions for registrants

2015 members receive reduced rates and special discounts for the 2015 convention in Vancouver. Visit www.mla.org/convention for more information.

www.mla.org

#mlanews
#mlaconvention

The Modern Language Association is a community of nearly 27,000 members dedicated to strengthening the study and teaching of language and literature. The MLA makes it possible for you to

- search the MLA *Job Information List* at no charge
- read reports and surveys issued by the MLA on the job market, enrollments, evaluating scholarship, and the state of scholarly publishing
- benefit from public outreach activities, including the popular MLA Language Map
- download the Academic Workforce Advocacy Kit, a tool for helping improve conditions for teachers and students
- access to the *MLA Handbook* Web site and FAQs about MLA style

Become an MLA member at **www.mla.org** and receive the following benefits:

- subscriptions to *PMLA* and the *MLA Newsletter*
- a 30% discount on all MLA titles, as well as the new, online edition of the *Literary Research Guide*
- access to directories of members and departmental administrators

Three easy ways to join:

▲ Visit www.mla.org.
▲ E-mail **membership@mla.org** to request a membership packet.
▲ Call 646 576-5151.

TCU Rhetoric & Composition PhD Program

PROGRAM
Pioneering program honoring the rhetorical tradition through scholarly innovation, excellent job placement record, well-endowed library, state-of-the-art New Media Writing Studio, and graduate certificates in new media and women's studies.

TEACHING
1-1 teaching loads, small classes, extensive pedagogy and technology training, and administrative fellowships in writing program administration and new media.

FACULTY
Nationally recognized teacher-scholars in history of rhetoric, modern rhetoric, women's rhetoric, digital rhetoric, composition studies, and writing program administration.

FUNDING
Generous four-year graduate instructorships, competitive stipends, travel support, and several prestigious fellowship opportunities.

EXPERIENCE
Mid-sized liberal arts university setting nestled in the vibrant, culturally-rich Dallas-Fort Worth metroplex.

English
DEPARTMENT

Contact Dr. Mona Narain
m.narain@tcu.edu
eng.tcu.edu

www.ingramcontent.com/pod-product-compliance
Lightning Source LLC
Chambersburg PA
CBHW031320160426
43196CB00007B/593

9 781602 356030